Nursing in Criminal Justice Services

Other books from M&K include

**Clinical Examination Skills for Healthcare Professionals**
ISBN: 9781905539710

**The Primary Care Guide to Mental Health**
ISBN: 9781905539109

# Nursing in Criminal Justice Services

Elizabeth Walsh and Ann Norman

# Nursing in Criminal Justice Services

Elizabeth Walsh and Ann Norman

ISBN: 9781905539-85-7

First published 2014

British Library Catalogue in Publication Data
A catalogue record for this book is available from the British Library

## Notice

Clinical practice and medical knowledge constantly evolve. Standard safety precautions must be followed, but, as knowledge is broadened by research, changes in practice, treatment and drug therapy may become necessary or appropriate. Readers must check the most current product information provided by the manufacturer of each drug to be administered and verify the dosages and correct administration, as well as contraindications. It is the responsibility of the practitioner, utilising the experience and knowledge of the patient, to determine dosages and the best treatment for each individual patient. Any brands mentioned in this book are as examples only and are not endorsed by the Publisher. Neither the publisher nor the authors assume any liability for any injury and/or damage to persons or property arising from this publication.

## Disclaimer

M&K Publishing cannot accept responsibility for the contents of any linked website or online resource. The existence of a link does not imply any endorsement or recommendation of the organisation or the information or views which may be expressed in any linked website or online resource. We cannot guarantee that these links will operate consistently and we have no control over the availability of linked pages.

## The Publisher

To contact M&K Publishing write to:
M&K Update Ltd · The Old Bakery · St. John's Street · Keswick · Cumbria CA12 5AS
Tel: 01768 773030 · Fax: 01768 781099
publishing@mkupdate.co.uk
www.mkupdate.co.uk

Designed and typeset by Mary Blood
Printed in Scotland by Bell & Bain, Glasgow

# Contents

# Foreword

The need for nursing to focus its attention on particularly vulnerable groups within our society is more urgent and vital than ever. A decent society should be measured by how well it cares for people who often do not have a voice. This is particularly true of people with health and nursing care needs who come into contact with our justice system.

This book identifies the challenges facing nurses in the criminal justice services. Importantly, it also pinpoints many of the practical solutions and opportunities that high-quality nursing care and delivery can offer.

In the past decade there have been extensive changes as well as progress in the way our health and justice systems work together. It is not at all unusual to see service innovation, new creative partnerships and stronger frontline practice delivered by nurses in prisons, in police custody, in our courts, probation services and immigration centres.

I am particularly pleased to recommend this book to you as an important reminder that nursing can and does operate well in many settings and services and provides a much-needed voice for people who otherwise remain unnoticed and whose citizenship is denied.

It is increasingly apparent that good health in the justice system also means good public health and I am delighted to see that, through nursing and partnerships, both can be achieved.

*Dr Peter Carter OBE, Chief Executive Officer, Royal College of Nursing*
*September 2014*

# Acknowledgements

We would like to thank all those who have contributed their time and talents to this book, especially the individual chapter authors, critical friends and peer reviewers. We owe particular thanks to our colleagues at the Royal College of Nursing, Nursing in Criminal Justice Services Forum, who have supported this book from conception to completion.

Thanks also to my nephew Andy Turpin, for assistance with the cover design concept.

Finally, we would like to acknowledge the tireless practice of all nursing staff working in criminal justice healthcare settings, who are providing high-quality, sensitive care for patients in a context that truly tests professional standards, ethics and resilience.

# List of contributors

**Dr Colin Dale, PhD, MA, RN, Dip (N) Lond, Cert Ed, RNT, DMS, Dip Couns**

Dr Colin Dale is the Chief Executive Officer of Caring Solutions (UK) Ltd, a mental health and learning disability consultancy company based in the north-west of England, which carries out national, regional and local healthcare projects throughout the UK. He is the Vice-Chairman of 5 Boroughs Partnership NHS Foundation Trust, a Senior Research Fellow at the University of Central Lancashire, and a member of the Mental Health Review Tribunal.

Dr Dale has a particular interest in the care and treatment of offenders with a learning disability and has edited three books on this topic. He runs an annual international conference in the UK that is now acclaimed as the foremost academic conference on the subject in Europe. In 2009 he was invited to become the editor of the *Journal of Intellectual Disabilities and Offending Behaviour*. Colin is leading the development of the Autism and Offending Partnership on behalf of the National Autistic Society, Northumberland Tyne and Wear NHS Foundation Trust, Calderstones Partnership NHS Foundation Trust, and St Andrews Healthcare. This national partnership focuses on people on the autistic spectrum who become involved with the criminal justice system.

**Dr Steve Dilworth, D. Prof, MSc, RN, Dip Hum Psych**

Steve is a freelance facilitator with expertise in reflective practice across a wide range of settings, including prison and police custody. Reflective practice is a central professional passion for Steve, who has spent a great deal of time helping people to reflect on their work, both as individuals and in groups. He comments, 'Others call me a supervisor (clinical/professional/managerial), executive developer and coach – I think of myself as a facilitator.' He is currently completing a book on the subject of facilitator presence, which combines his academic and practical professional experience.

**Emma Durmaz, RGN, DipN, MA Bioethics, PGCE, DFCASA**

Emma Durmaz is the Clinical Manager and Forensic Nurse Examiner at The Glade Sexual Assault Referral Centre (SARC), West Mercia. She is an experienced sexual offences examiner, and was the first nurse to be awarded the Diploma in Forensic and Clinical Aspects of Sexual Assault (DFCASA). Emma is dedicated to ensuring that all aspects of the forensic examination are victim-centred and that each victim experiences a holistic approach to their therapeutic care and ongoing support. Emma offers clinical supervision and peer review to nurses across the UK who are practising as Forensic Nurse Examiners in the field of Sexual Offences. She is also a part-time Advanced Nurse Practitioner and Nurse Prescriber at a GP Walk-in Centre. Emma is currently studying for a PhD and her thesis is entitled 'The Sexual Offence Examination – Coercive or therapeutic?'

### Richard Evans, BSc (Hons), RNMH

Richard is a registered Mental Health Nurse who began his career working in a medium-secure unit, before moving to a court diversion scheme. He currently manages a Mental Health Liaison and Diversion Service that operates in police custody suites and criminal courts across two counties in the south-west of England. He chairs the Bristol Criminal Justice and Mental Health Operation Group.

### Professor Dawn Freshwater, PhD BA (Hons), FRCN, RGN, RNT, Dip Psych

Dawn Freshwater is Professor of Mental Health at the University of Leeds and Senior Deputy Vice-Chancellor at the University of Western Australia. She is a Fellow of the Royal College of Nursing and a health professional and academic of some 30 years' experience. She has developed a portfolio of research that ranges from issues of workforce strategy and practice development to leadership in organisational effectiveness and change. Her mental health expertise has enabled her to undertake a number of research projects related to offender health and psychological therapies. She has also supervised 15 PhD students to completion, and written 15 textbooks and contributed to over 100 academic publications. She is the Co-Editor of the *Journal of Mixed Methods Research* and was Editor of the *Journal of Psychiatric and Mental Health Nursing* for 10 years, from 2004 to 2014. She has worked internationally for the British Council and the Worldwide Universities Network (WUN).

### Dr Pamela A. Inglis, DNSc, BA (Hons), RNLD, ENMH, PG Dip Ac Practice, PG Dip Psychology

Most of Dr Inglis's research has taken place in the forensic arena of the NHS, in particular with people who have a learning disability. Her doctoral thesis examined the ideologies that underpin nursing in forensic settings. Pamela sits on the Editorial Board for the *Journal of Learning Disability and Offending Behaviour*, and regularly presents at the International Conference for the Care and Treatment of Offenders with a Learning Disability. She is a member of the national steering group for academics involved in learning disability and has close links with the National Autistic Society and their National Autism Partnership, developing programmes that raise awareness in professionals working across the British criminal justice system.

### Ann Norman, RGN DipN

Ann is the Royal College of Nursing (RCN) Professional Nurse Adviser for Learning Disability Nursing and Nursing in Criminal Justice Services. Her career in nursing within the National Health Service and HM Prison Service has been varied. Ann joined the Prison Service in 1992 and received a Nursing Standard award in 1998 in recognition of her work on developing services for female prisoners. In 1999 she was awarded a further Prison Service award for her work at HMP Winchester. She has been a long-standing RCN activist and was chair of the RCN Prison Nurses' Forum between 1998 and 2000. Ann has contributed to several publications on nursing roles in prisons and vulnerable people in our society and she co-edited *Prison Nursing* (Wiley Blackwell 2002) and is an editorial board member of the *International Journal of Prisoner Health*. In 1999 Ann was seconded to the Department of Health (Prison Health Task Force) and in 2000 she took on the role of Assistant Director of Nursing in a national cross-government department. Ann has now worked for the Royal College of Nursing for ten years as the UK adviser on Nursing in Criminal Justice Services and Learning Disability Nursing. She supports nursing members, represents nursing to promote excellence in practice, and helps to shape health policy.

### Chrissy Reeves, PGDip Solution Focused Brief Therapy, PGC Leadership, Dip HE Nursing

Chrissy is the Deputy Head of Healthcare at HMP Young Offenders Institution Holloway (Central and North-West London NHS Foundation Trust). She is a Mental Health Nurse, who worked for the majority of her career in Acute Mental Health Services, both in-patient and home treatment teams, prior to coming into prison nursing more than five years ago. In her current role she oversees the Mental Health Services at Holloway (Mental Health Assessment Unit, Prison Mental Health Team, Acute Day Centre and Psychological Therapies), and supports the Head of Healthcare in managing other clinical services. Chrissy is a facilitator in the RCN Clinical Leadership Programme. She has worked with colleagues and published research on the mental health of women prisoners.

### Warren Stewart, MA, PG Dip, BSc (Hons), PG Cert, RN (M)

Warren currently works at the University of Brighton as a senior lecturer in the field of mental health. His practice experience includes working as a nurse, practice educator and healthcare manager within the Prison Service. He went on to work in a regional and national capacity on workforce-orientated projects for Offender Health Services, for example, developing mental health awareness training and student placement materials for the Prison and Probation Services. He also developed and led Foundation Degrees in Offender Care and Service User Involvement and led a small government-funded project to promote peer care among prisoners.

### Jennie Smith, RGN, University Certificate in Postgraduate Professional Development (UCPPD) Forensics, V300 Non-Medical Prescriber, ABPI IT Diploma

Jennie has been a qualified nurse for over 20 years. Her experience has been varied. She has worked in emergency care, as a sales representative in the pharmaceutical industry, as a nurse in a large chain of nightclubs and, more recently, in the National Health Service at a walk-in medical centre. In 2008 she set up the Forensic Nursing Team for Merseyside Police and managed this team until in 2011 it was passed to a private provider, for whom she now works. She has two part-time roles, as a Forensic Nurse Practitioner and as a Forensic Nurse Trainer, providing the only nursing input on a three-day induction course for Forensic Nurse Practitioners. She provides training for Forensic Nurses across the UK. She also manages and provides the Forensic Nursing Services for British Transport Police for the Merseyside area. She is very active in the UK Association of Forensic Nursing (UKAFN) and is very proud to have been elected their President in May 2013.

## Karen Swinson, RN

Karen's career in forensic healthcare began in 1999 when she was appointed to lead an inaugural Home Office pilot at Kent Police to introduce nurses into police custody suites. This created a unique healthcare service within a police setting, for which she received a Home Office Beacon Award in 2000. She was then appointed to manage the Forensic Medical Services Department, including the Forensic Medical Examiners. She moved to the Metropolitan Police Service in 2009, as a custody care consultant. She was appointed Director of Nursing at the commencement of the new healthcare service that introduced nurses into police custody suites across London. As the 2008 Nursing Standard's Nurse of the Year in Innovations in Criminal Justice Award winner, she was able to highlight the fantastic nursing provision work going on across many different police forces to Prime Minister Gordon Brown at 10 Downing Street. Karen has worked with the Home Office, the Medicines and Healthcare Products Regulatory Agency, Skills for Health, the Department of Health and other national bodies on numerous projects that seek to improve the quality and standards of care delivered within police settings.

## Paul Tarbuck, SRN, RMN, RNT, TCert, ForCert, DipMan, DipN, BATheol

Paul is Deputy Head of Health Inspection, for HM Inspectorate of Prisons. He has over 39 years' experience of nursing in the UK and abroad, working in both general and mental health settings for NHS, private and independent providers. He has significant clinical, managerial, education and research experience. Paul has 25 years, forensic experience, including as former Director of Adult, CAMHS and Deaf Forensic Services in low, medium and high-security health services in the Criminal Justice Service. He is a former Director of Nurse Education and a university lecturer. Paul has been part of several enquiries and panels investigating serious untoward incidents (SUIs), including homicide. He has occasionally published his work, including a textbook on forensic nursing and papers on behalf of the Royal College of Nursing. Paul is a member of several national and international specialist and advisory groups.

## Jane Littlewood, Associate Solicitor

Jane Littlewood is an Associate Solicitor in the Healthcare Team at Berrymans Lace Mawer LLP in London. She is one of the team leaders representing healthcare professionals at inquests and regularly carries out advocacy. Based on this experience, she has developed a particular interest in issues relating to the provision of effective healthcare in custody. Her practice also includes a broad range of clinical negligence claims in which she represents consultants, GPs and nurses. She has also represented healthcare professionals under investigation by their regulatory body.

### Elizabeth Tysoe, RGN, MA

Elizabeth held the post of Head of Health Inspection for HM Inspectorate of Prisons from 2006 until 2014, having previously been the Deputy Head for two and a half years. She was the first nurse to hold the position and managed a team of healthcare and substance use professionals who inspect custodial settings. She provided expert advice on health and social care to the Chief Inspector of Prisons and worked closely with health and social care regulatory bodies. Previous posts included Head of Healthcare in a high-security prison, as well as senior nursing and management posts in the NHS.

### John Walker

John is a volunteer at the Hope Outside Prison Environments (HOPE) Project in Manchester, which supports offenders with mental health issues who are at risk of being taken into custody. Using his experience, he mentors, supports, advises and helps others to take positive steps in terms of treatment, training, education and employment. John himself has travelled through the criminal justice system in the past, and provides an 'expert by experience' view of how best to support people. The results so far have been remarkable, with service users benefiting from his approach and finding it much easier to engage in peer support. John's work has been recognised by No Offence, a charity that champions and celebrates such services, and makes awards to individuals and services that strive to make a difference in people's lives. In 2013, John was invited to speak by the Royal College of Nursing at their annual congress in Liverpool about his experiences in the criminal justice system, focusing on inspirational nursing and the positive effect it has had on him. John is also contributing to a Pain in Prison programme in West Yorkshire, which aims to improve primary care in prisons (again using his own experience to benefit others).

### Dr Elizabeth Walsh, RN, BSc (Hons), MSc, PhD

Liz is an Associate Professor in Offender Health at the University of Leeds. She is a registered general nurse who has worked for HM Prison Service in clinical, educational and practice development roles since 1995. In 2007, she completed her PhD, in which she explored the emotional aspects of prison nursing. She has been involved in implementing clinical supervision and reflective practice in offender healthcare settings and developing prison healthcare as a learning environment for both staff and students. She has also worked closely with non-healthcare custodial colleagues to promote inter-professional working. Liz's work currently focuses on the care of older prisoners, pain management in prison, and the support and development of the offender healthcare workforce through reflective practice and clinical supervision. She is also the elected Chair of the Nursing in Criminal Justice Services

Forum at the Royal College of Nursing, a Visiting Professor at the University of Ottawa and a member of the Editorial Board of the *Journal of Forensic Nursing*.

### Mark Warren, RMN, PGDip Social Learning Theory, PGDip Nurs, Adv Cert Rehabilitation

Mark is a mental health nurse who has worked as a clinician, manager and educator for people with mental health difficulties within criminal justice settings since 1998. His experiences include running Court and Police Liaison Services, providing support and advice for probation officers and managing prison in-reach services for men and women. He has worked in criminal justice settings in Jersey, New Zealand, England and Wales.

He is currently involved in a team developing Criminal Justice Mental Health Liaison Services in partnership with Wales Probation Trust and South Wales Police and has a particular interest in developing new ways of working with specialist police public protection teams.

He is a member of the Royal College of Nursing Steering Committee on Nursing in Criminal Justice Settings and actively promotes the practice of mental health nursing in these settings. Mark understands the challenges faced by nurses working within the criminal justice system but is also aware of the opportunities these settings present for nurses to develop practice and provide care for a marginalised group of service users.

# Introduction

Ann Norman and Elizabeth Walsh

It is more than a decade since the first book on prison nursing in the 21$^{st}$ century was published (Norman & Parrish 2002). During this time there have been significant changes in the way healthcare services have been developed and delivered in the field of health and justice. Firstly, healthcare services for prisoners are now commissioned by the National Health Service (NHS), rather than HM Prison Service. In more recent years, the same commissioning arrangements have been put in place for healthcare services in police custody settings, thus shifting responsibility from individual police services to the NHS.

The Health and Social Care Act 2012 gave the Secretary of State the power to require NHS England to commission certain services directly, instead of via Clinical Commissioning Groups (CCG). This included 'services or facilities for persons who are detained in a prison or other accommodation of a prescribed description'. The NHS then assumed these powers from April 2013. NHS England is responsible for ensuring that services are commissioned to consistently high standards across the country. It also promotes the NHS Constitution (DH 2013) and delivers the requirements of the Secretary of State's Mandate and the section 7a agreement with NHS England. Commissioning intentions and structures were set out by the NHS in 'Securing Excellence for Offender Health', published in February 2013 (NHS Commissioning Board 2013).

Public Health England (PHE) works in partnership with health and social care commissioners, service providers, academic and third sector organisations to identify and meet the health and social care needs of people in prisons and other prescribed detention settings, as well as those in contact with the criminal justice system in the community. The principal aim of PHE is to reduce health inequalities, support people in living healthier lives and ensure continuity of care in the community.

Following these changes within the NHS, an NHS England Health and Justice Clinical Reference Group (CRG) was also established. This brings together specialist nursing and medical expertise with carer and service user input to support the direct commissioning function of NHS England. It promotes high standards of treatment, delivers a strong and consistent clinical voice, and promotes equivalence and information sharing. These policy changes should help to reduce the sense of isolation that some nursing and other professional staff have experienced when working in criminal justice services.

Another seminal publication that has influenced policy development is Lord Bradley's 2009 review of mental health and learning disability provision in the criminal justice system. This review set out clear recommendations for the evolution of liaison and diversion services (Bradley 2009). The NHS's new interest in offender health with regard to commissioning, combined with Lord Bradley's report, has changed the nursing landscape within prisons and the wider criminal justice pathway. These developments have in turn offered new opportunities for nurses working in this field – for example, in mental health liaison and diversion services. This is a real improvement on the way many services previously operated. We now have true collaboration and shared partnership working across policing, nursing, courts and related services. The very early data from initial liaison and diversion pilot sites is showing that shared ownership between health and justice is working well. We suggest that positive feedback from these sites illustrates the value of nursing care and intervention. Lord Bradley's review made over 80 recommendations. At the time of writing, some progress has been made on certain specific headline actions, whilst more time has been needed to progress other areas. These include the development of more robust services for offenders with a learning disability and this subject will be further explored in later chapters of this book.

Nursing is usually perceived as a profession in which nurses practise their 'art and science' within a traditional hospital setting, the community or a primary healthcare facility. People are often surprised to learn that many nursing staff work so closely with prison staff, police officers, court staff and probation officers, and there are many ethical and professional issues that arise, such as the need to find a balance between prisoner and patient, custody and care, security and therapy. Indeed, nurses working in criminal justice settings are continually balancing care and nursing needs, and focusing on contradictory elements, in order to achieve the best outcomes, with health and justice in strong partnership promoting health and well-being. Resources are starting to become more readily available for nurses working in these settings, and also for students wanting to gain experience in this area. For example, the RCN Nursing in Criminal Justice Services Forum has created a web resource where the RCN Principles of Nursing Practice have been contextualised for application in criminal justice settings (RCN 2014).

This book brings together experts from different stages in the criminal justice pathway to provide the reader with a greater understanding of the nurse's role in police custody, courts, prison and in the community with probation services, whilst also offering more academic reflection on caring in the custodial setting. The authors have highlighted both the challenges and the rewards of working with patients in all areas of justice and health. Whilst many other texts provide a criminological, medical and/or forensic perspective, this book offers a *nursing* viewpoint that encompasses both mental and physical nursing care, and also acknowledges the professional development and support needs of the nurse working in these settings.

Careful consideration has been given to the content and structure of this book. However, we need to make a few comments on terminology at the outset in order to provide some clarity and focus. The term 'forensic' is used freely and interchangeably in the world of criminal justice nursing. For instance, offenders with mental health problems are known as forensic patients (Byrt 2013); and nurses working with mentally disordered offenders in secure settings are known as forensic nurses (Martin *et al.* 2013), as are nurses working with the victims of sexual assault and violence (Trujillo *et al.* 2014), and nurses working in police custody (Loeb *et al.* 2013). We suggest that, whilst the use of the term 'forensic' is understandable in these contexts, it is a congested concept that can cause confusion. Therefore, in this book we refer to nurses working with offenders and victims of crime as 'working in criminal justice settings'.

We start with a reflection on experience of receiving care in criminal justice settings from Mr John Walker. John's honest and moving narrative reminds the reader that the patient is central to care in criminal justice settings, and we encourage the reader to return to John's account when they feel their focus has begun to shift away from the patient. Sadly the picture painted in his chapter is by no means unique, and it serves as a salutary reminder that no one is far from potential crisis. John has used his difficult personal experience to illustrate how healthcare professionals must pay attention to people as individuals rather than offenders. The need for holistic care is never more evident than within the confines of a prison. We believe that including an 'expert by experience' view offers a context within which to examine our own beliefs, attitudes and behaviours.

The first half of this book moves the reader along the health and justice pathway, from initial patient contact with nurses in police stations, to nursing care in courts, through prison nursing services and finally into the work of the multi-disciplinary team in the community, where nurses work alongside the Probation Service. The second half of the book addresses some of the broader issues facing nurses working in criminal justice settings, including governance, legal issues, professional development and caring for vulnerable people. We have bridged these two parts with a contribution from Professor Freshwater, who considers the nature of caring in criminal justice settings, and the importance of caring for each other. Readers will get the most out of this chapter if they read it in the light of their own practice. There is an opportunity here for some truly reflective thinking. Although the book is structured to reflect the criminal justice pathway, from police to probation, individual chapters can also be read on their own as stand-alone narratives.

Although many nurses have no direct involvement in criminal justice settings, the majority of nurses working in all areas of nursing will come into contact with patients or relatives of patients involved in criminal justice at some point. On wards where prisoners are receiving treatment whilst guarded by prison officers, in schools where children have a parent in prison, or in a GP practice where patients have substance misuse issues, nurses will come into contact with criminal justice. This book can therefore offer all nurses an understanding of nursing roles, nursing practice and the challenges of caring for offenders and those in contact with criminal justice.

As you read this book and consider the various contexts of care for those in contact with criminal justice, we hope you will recognise that good-quality nursing care can be provided within these settings, resulting in positive health outcomes for individuals whilst also promoting public safety.

## References

Bradley, K. (2009). *The Bradley Report*. London: Department of Health, The Stationery Office.

Byrt, R. (2013). Forensic nursing interventions with patients with personality disorder: a holistic approach. *Journal of Forensic Nursing*. **9** (3), 182–88.

Department of Health (2013). 'The NHS Constitution'. London: The Stationery Office.

'The Health and Social Care Act' (2012). London: The Stationery Office.

Hurley, J., Linsley, P., Elvins, M. & Jones, M. (2013). Nurses leading care in custody suite environments: A qualitative study from Scotland. *Journal of Forensic Nursing*. **9** (1), 45–51.

Martin, T., Maguire, T., Quinn, C., Ryan, J., Bawden, L., & Summers, M. (2013). Standards of practice for forensic mental health nurses – identifying contemporary practice. *Journal of Forensic Nursing*. **9** (3), 171–78.

NHS Commissioning Board (2013). 'Securing Excellence in Commissioning for Offender Health'.
http://www.england.nhs.uk/wp-content/uploads/2013/03/offender-commissioning.pdf
(Last accessed 12 June 2014).

Norman, A. & Parrish, A. (2002). *Nursing in Prison*. Oxford: Wiley Blackwell.

Royal College of Nursing (2014). http://www.rcn.org.uk/development/communities/rcn_forum_communities/prison_nurses/nursing_in_cjs_principles_of_nursing_practice
(Last accessed: 7 May 2014).

Trujillo, A.C., Delap, T.D. & Hendrix, T.J. (2014). A practical guide to prevention for forensic nursing. *Journal of Forensic Nursing*. **10** (1), 20–26

# Recovery and redemption

John Walker

I was one of five children born into a very deprived working-class area in one England's major cities. I was second youngest, with a younger brother and three older sisters, and in the late 1970s and early 80s life was pretty tough for most people where I lived.

My parents are Roman Catholic but never practised or went to church. My mum stayed at home and my dad was a career criminal, like his father before him and most of his side of the family. Serious criminality was his life – armed robbery, gun running, drug dealing and violence was the way he earned his living. This gave us a better standard of living than some around us but with that came many, many problems.

My earliest memories are from when I was four years old and it's the noise (more than anything) that sticks in my mind. Sounds played a large part in my childhood but this was the first of many times I can remember the noise of sledgehammers slamming against our front door. To me as a little boy, hearing this for the first time felt like monsters or giants kicking in your house to get you and eat you up! I can remember being curled up under my blankets, screaming with fright. Then it stopped for what felt like an eternity but could only have been a second or two because what sounded like horses running up the stairs replaced that moment of silence. There was another loud bang as my bedroom door slammed open and what followed was the first time I had a loaded gun pointed at me by a man dressed all in black with just his eyes visible; sadly this was not going to be the last. If my father had time he would fight them (and we did too when we got older) but most times my parents were too busy shoving drugs or guns in our underwear.

These raids by the police were just one aspect of my childhood that shaped my life. They never got any less frightening but I did get a thrill out of hitting a police officer without him being able to do anything about it. No matter what my father had done, I hated the police for what they were doing. I watched them beat my dad mercilessly with the butts of their guns while I was being held back and they were smiling and laughing as they did it.

My issues with authority started then, but the violence I witnessed because of what my father did outside the home wasn't the only abuse I suffered. My dad was also extremely violent towards us, his own family.

Most of it was directed at my mum but he wasn't scared to attack his children either. The sounds of my mum being beaten will never leave me and no matter how loud we screamed it could never drown my mum's cries. When he'd finished with her, my sisters came next, then my brother and me, but sometimes he had worn himself out so much that we got missed out. Waiting to get beaten while hearing what was coming was horrendous. I don't know how I coped but I did do things that I later found out were obsessive compulsive disorder (OCD) behaviour.

The abuse wasn't just physical; it was emotional, mental and psychological, and my father never showed remorse or said sorry and everything had to remain a secret. Sometimes Mum would take the girls and run away but my brother and I always remained and that was her reason for always coming back. My brother and I did run away to a neighbour's house on many occasions but we suffered sexual abuse at that house too so my early years were pretty extreme.

School was my only sanctuary but there were also times when I was abused there. I went to a Roman Catholic school that in the early years was run by nuns. Religion was number one and the methods they used on anyone who questioned anything are what the Geneva Convention would call torture! What happened at home sort of didn't tally with what I was being taught at school, and from an early age I became convinced that what I was being told wasn't the truth as I was being abused a lot at school too.

I did like primary school though, in spite of the abuse. I topped the class in all subjects except religion, was a good footballer and an excellent runner. My teachers couldn't understand why such an intelligent child refused to believe in God but I didn't and it caused all sorts of problems for me.

The headmistress was a small flame-haired lady and what she lacked in stature she more than made up for in aggression. She was Old Testament, fire and brimstone, and if you crossed her you were in trouble. I developed a special relationship with her because every Monday she would go round each classroom, pull the kids who hadn't been to church on Sunday to the front of the class, and humiliate them in front of their friends and peers. Every Monday morning I would endure this but, because I was never intimidated, cried or seemed affected, she would almost explode with rage! Compared to what was going on at home, that sort of abuse and the physical punishments were easier to bear.

When Mum ran away, Dad wouldn't take us to school so my brother and I had huge gaps in our education. Instead he'd take us to the pub and leave us there while he went to earn his money. Of all the places we spent many hours in, we never got abused in the pubs. In fact we were well looked after because my father's reputation instilled fear in most people. These gaps in our schooling could last weeks or months and we had to come up with a story to explain why we hadn't been to school when we eventually got back. But things were different then and I doubt you could get away with it now.

With the criminality came the money, and we had all the toys any kids would dream of. But I knew they were the product of a guilty conscience and I preferred being outside in the trees or reading. I got into books quite early. I suppose it was a way I could escape from my world for a while. The only true escape from the horrors at home came when my father was sent to prison. The contrast was stark. To get that respite at home was the only saving grace. It gave us a chance to relax a bit and I feel the happiest moments of my childhood were when my dad was locked up. I think for most it would be the opposite but it was difficult too because money would be tight and the violence from one parent was replaced with that of the other. It was never on the same scale as that of my dad, but my mum could be extremely violent towards us, especially my brother and me.

I developed an introverted personality and was very quiet. Although I did have friends, nobody was allowed to come round, and I got into a fair few fights, which again my teachers couldn't understand. As well as all the psychological problems I developed, I also had a strong belief in right and wrong, fairness and justice, and hated bullies, so conflict with others was always based on these principles. I always felt alone, even amongst friends, and still do now to some extent.

I left primary school to go to a secondary school that was also religious but in the first year everything seemed fine. My dad was locked up and it was new and exciting. I made lots of new friends and I started taking more notice of girls. Before my dad got out the following summer, I had grown a lot and was becoming a young man and gaining some confidence. I hoped he would see me in a different way and maybe leave us alone but I was very wrong about that. He had become even worse and the little confidence I had built up was smashed out of me before too long. School then became a place of total rebellion for me. I started to play truant and the little time I spent there I wasted mucking about or fighting. I was the first and only pupil I know of to be banned from doing religious studies and I wore that badge with pride. Although I never had a go at anyone, I just wouldn't be forced into faith.

As I started to mature further, my relationship with my father did start to change – in some ways for the better but mostly for the opposite. I knew my apprenticeship would start one day and shortly after my thirteenth birthday my dad let me hold a gun for the first time (unloaded, I may add, as if that made any difference!). I can remember being overcome by the sense of power and the knowledge that I could end a life with just a squeeze of the trigger. Over the next couple of years I started dealing drugs for him, using drugs with him, not going to school and slowly but surely turning into his image. I remember every Sunday my mum would be cooking the roast in the kitchen downstairs while I was getting high with my father upstairs in their bedroom. These are the only times I actually enjoyed being in his company. Sadly, the only quality time we had together was when we did drugs and I was just a kid!

Dealing drugs was just a way of making money; I never got any excitement from it. But when my Dad was locked up now and again I had to find a new way to make some cash. I started to shoplift and found I got a huge rush from it. I became good at it relatively quickly and was making way more money than when I was selling drugs for my dad. I used to go to school in the morning, get signed in, then walk straight out and catch a bus to the city centre and spend the day shoplifting and using drugs.

The first time I got arrested was for shoplifting. My dad was out of prison so I was up to everything and doing all right for myself, but I made a fatal error in a particular store by going back in after I had just been in and got something. That was my first lesson in what can happen if you are greedy. I got jumped on by the staff, arrested, then taken to the nearest police station. The police tried to intimidate me by acting aggressive and threatening but I wasn't fazed by them and my respect for the police was zero, based on my experience up to that point. The only thing that did scare me was my dad because he didn't know I was shoplifting and I knew he was on his way to pick me up.

After being processed I met my dad at the front desk and was expecting a beating when we got in the car but he was smiling and seemed in a good mood. I was a bit puzzled at first but on the way home he said, 'What the #@?% are you doing robbing out of shops? You should be robbing security vans, cash in transit lad! #@?%ing shoplifting!' That was it! That was my reprimand, that was my punishment but it was also the first time he was genuinely proud of me. I feel quite sad about it as I write because while other children were making their parents proud playing football or doing well at school I had to get arrested to achieve that. The actual experience of being put in a cell for the first time didn't scare me. I always loved being on my own and the officers were not pointing guns at me like they did at home.

Over this period of time, I was brought deeper and deeper into my dad's world, and the deeper I got, the less I liked it. He would take me on little errands and I started getting introduced to all the other gangsters and villains. They all seemed to be in awe of him and constantly told me how great my dad was. It became almost impossible to bear when I knew the truth about just what sort of man he was. At the same time he was beating my mum more severely. She had been admitted to hospital in the past but it was on every occasion now, and he totally left my brother and me alone. My siblings and I had a meeting one day after we had seen a film called 'The right to kill', which depicted the sort of abuse that we had been enduring all these years, and the son shot his father dead with his own gun. I am getting emotional as I write this because five children actually discussed killing one of their parents!!

Can you imagine that? I was chosen because I knew how to use a gun and I had been sneaking into his room, stealing drugs and money for ages. Although he kept his guns locked in a safe, maybe he would make a mistake one day. That day never came but I started to step in when the beatings started, and he would start to back off when I put myself in the middle. I knew the day was coming when I would have to stop him from killing Mum.

I was just fifteen when one day I was coming home, after skipping school as usual, and I could hear my sister and my mum screaming. I ran into the house to find my sister on the floor screaming in pain. She had been attacked with a baseball bat and had multiple fractures and there in the living room my mum was fighting for her life while my dad was trying to stab her to death! Blood was everywhere, even on the ceiling.

I didn't think. I just dived on her, crashing us both to the floor. I was lucky I landed on top of her so he couldn't bring the knife down on her! I don't know what we screamed but we did scream until he stepped back. With no emotion whatsoever, he just calmly said, 'Son get off your mum and come here.' I remember saying, 'No, you are going to kill Mum!' He told me he wouldn't and I did as he said. I got off my blood-soaked, crying mother, turned to face him and walked over to him. I looked at the blood-drenched knife. It was huge and dripping. He was holding it out as if to offer it. I looked up into his eyes, more scared than I have ever been before or since. They weren't my dad's eyes I was staring into. What I saw in those eyes wasn't human, it was almost animal-like, and he said as calmly as he did before, 'Take this knife, Son, because if you don't, I will kill everyone in this house!' I remember saying, 'No, Dad, please', but he placed it in my hands, then walked out of the house. I didn't know it then but it would be five years before I saw my dad again.

Within hours of that horrible incident, I had decided never to show my face in school again. I was now the man of the house. I knew how to make money, as I was involved in more serious and more lucrative criminality at that time. So that was it. Dad was gone, Mum was safe and I had to look after her from now on. What I didn't know was what all this was doing to my mental health. I always found it hard making friends, and girlfriends seemed to be even harder. I could have girlfriends round now but I didn't know I was suffering from depression, anxiety, panic attacks, OCD, paranoia and post-traumatic stress disorder (PTSD). I thought that was just how I was. I didn't know any different so girlfriends were off and on. Also, getting a job, without any bit of paper to say you had ever gone to school, was going to be pretty difficult.

Crime was the only answer and remained so until I got to about nineteen, when a friend who worked at a factory nearby got me a job there. I loved it immediately. The atmosphere was great and the humour as dark as it gets, which really suited me. The wages were rubbish but I was still drug dealing so I didn't care. After a year or so went by and I was firmly established, I felt more confident than ever before. I was still having mental health issues but I still thought it was just me.

My father, on the other hand, had been serving another sentence and had been released about this time and paid a visit to my sister's house. I was sitting in the living room when he walked in. I had an extreme mixture of emotions running through me but I stood and said hello. We were never touchy-feely in our house. We didn't say we loved each other or hug or anything like that and I was certainly not going to even shake his hand. But he said, 'What are you doing with yourself, Son?'

I told him I was working at a place nearby and that I liked it. He looked me up and down with utter disgust and spat, '#@?%ing working at some factory! I never brought you up like that!' He then began to laugh and I felt as if my world had just ended there and then. I put my coat on while he was still laughing. When he stopped and looked at me, I told him, 'You never brought me up to do something different, Dad, but I did.' With that, I walked out and went to where one of my most trusted friends lived and cried my eyes out. At that moment, I had never hated my dad more! Confidence and self-esteem were always a problem. Whenever I could just see the light at the end of the tunnel it always seemed that down came some huge boulders to keep me trapped.

I stuck with the factory job though, and within a few weeks met the girl who would become the mother of our daughter.

I had had my fair share of girlfriends through my teens but I didn't know my mental health was the reason I could never build a relationship. Something about this one was different from all the rest. I had met her before, a couple of years earlier, but only in passing. We were placed together at work and we hit it off straight away. At first it was just fun but we found out we both liked drugs, had both been abused and she had previously self-harmed and was on medication. I had never self-harmed but had thought about suicide many times, even when I was very young. As before, I thought this was normal and just how I was. But as the relationship deepened, so did our drug use and soon we were spiralling out of control together. We got fired from our jobs after being caught using drugs at work. By that time, we had set up home together in a little bedsit. We had to earn money somehow so back to crime I went, this time with a partner.

After a year or so of constant drug abuse, our relationship was about as stormy as you can get, until the day we found out that we were having a baby. This really came as a big shock! And it brought us to our senses. Over the next nine months we got ourselves a little house, I found a job that was somewhere between legal and not legal, which paid very well, and when our daughter was born we were ready to be a little family.

Almost immediately something became very apparent and extremely worrying for me. The birth itself was traumatic. The baby was breech and my partner struggled like hell but I was so proud of her. The ordeal took a massive toll on my girlfriend and she rejected our daughter the moment she got home. I totally understood, considering what she had been through. I thought it might last a couple of weeks and then we could be a family. But the fortnight never ended. My girlfriend not only distanced herself from our daughter but also from me. She would disappear for weeks and then come home, then go again. I decided to leave my job and stay at home with my daughter. I couldn't spend ten hours a day, six days a week, away from her. She needed a parent and I was her only one for the time being.

Over the first three years of my daughter's life, I was there every day. Her mum came and went. The relationship I had with her was non-existent but I always wanted her back and would constantly try to bring us together but to no avail. I also got 50 per cent custody of my daughter in court but we hid her mum's true behaviour and said it was to make sure we didn't need to do it in the future under bad terms.

During this time I was getting involved in serious crime again, as it took less time to earn money. I had given up using drugs at this point and was trying to slowly build a future but it was extremely hard. My mental health was still suffering and, due to criminal disputes, my life came under threat. I decided enough was enough – my daughter was starting nursery. There was no way I could put my life at risk so I tried to get a job and succeeded!

There was another dispute that had been simmering. Although this wasn't business, it was very personal and my life came under threat again! The boulders were trapping me in the tunnel again and – two weeks into my new job – my world ended! For some reason I woke up that Friday morning with a sense of dread and it didn't shift all through the day. I came home from work and before the phone rang I already knew what was coming. I picked up and received a threat to my life! I don't quite know exactly why, even to this day, but I went and met the threat head on, in the knowledge that one or both of us could end up dead.

The amount of pressure I was feeling in the build-up to these events and my whole life previously had led me to the point where I was taking part in a fight to the death! The outcome was tragic for all concerned. I came out with minimal injuries but my victim was seriously hurt and I was arrested, put before the courts and sentenced to four and a half years. My daughter, who I wanted to be kept with my family, went straight to her mum, with us having the custody agreement. I worried myself to a breakdown in the first few months of being in prison. The only thing that helped, and it's sad to say, is that my daughter and her mum moved to the other side of the country and I hoped it would help my little girl to forget about her dad.

Although this was my first time in prison (amazingly!), I had visited my dad there many times and family members too. It's just a case of getting used to it and trying to make it as easy as you can. I never got that 'It's them and us' thing. I just wanted to get out and see my daughter again so I knuckled down and got on with it, one day at a time. My mental health was flagged up as an issue pretty early. I was assessed by a forensic psychologist for about half an hour, then by a doctor who put me on a prescription of anti-depressants and sleeping tablets. The next couple of months I have no memory of. I must have been a zombie – I needed help to go and get my dinner because I was so out of it. I didn't know but the doses I was on were extremely high. It was only with the help of a cellmate that I able to stop taking them and decided to go to the gym and feel better that way. Reading also helped, like it did when I was young. I was reading a book a day (all subjects, all genres); I just devoured the information, ever hungry for more. I came across a couple of psychology books and worked out that almost all my problems were psychological. I knew then that I needed help.

After a short time in prison, you find that primary healthcare is not easy to access. It's only in emergencies that you get seen within three to six months. For doctors and dentists the waiting lists are endless, and psychology didn't exist as far as I could gather. So I decided to seek help for my mental health when I got out. I did have to do courses to get my parole but these were sentence-based, not therapy. I know I would have benefited from the treatment I later received if that had been available in prison at that time. But I know things really are improving now so that's very positive.

I do have a horror story about my experience of primary healthcare in prison, or the lack of it. As I said before, the dentist waiting lists are very long, and I developed an abscess in my tooth and gum. You have to put in an application, which has to be processed, and then you go on the list. I was given painkillers by the officers and basically had to put up with it until my appointment in the distant future. For three months I had to drain my abscess every morning by squeezing my gums. The pain is difficult to describe. It was unbelievable but I did get used to it and it was purely survival instinct kicking in. By this time, I understood what septicaemia was.

About fourteen weeks in, with a large hole in my gum, which felt as if it was collapsing in on itself, I was told I was being moved to another prison – with immediate effect. This can happen and did so a couple of times for me, but I couldn't have been more than another week away from seeing the dentist. The process started again and when I did finally get to see the dentist in my new prison, months later, he took one look, winced and said, 'This is going to hurt!' I didn't care. I just told him to sort it out. He put his fingers in my mouth to feel the offending tooth and just plucked it out! There was nothing left but the top of the tooth! I could have done that myself, I thought, but the abscess had eaten part of the jaw away and my gums took months to recover. Improvements can and should be made. Everyone should have access to good healthcare – even prisoners. We are all human beings.

To balance that story, I sustained an injury in the gym once that needed hospital treatment. I was taken to the prison healthcare unit and sat in a room with some of the prison nurses while waiting for a taxi, believe it or not! An officer was there with me but the atmosphere in that room was totally different to the rest of the prison. It was just so normal, warm, friendly and very relaxed and I must have forgotten what that was like because I was taken aback by it. When the taxi arrived I was double-cuffed on to a long chain that had an officer attached at the other end, as if I was a dog and he was my master.

Going from a very human experience to this was very demeaning for me but off we went with another officer to the hospital, and when we got to the A&E department the whole waiting room turned and stared at me. I actually felt like an animal, with all those eyes on me, like I was being paraded for their judgement. I gave them what they wanted and glared back at each and every single one of them. One by one, they averted their gaze but I didn't feel better. I felt even more like an animal until I got into a room to have my injury looked at by a nurse. Something amazing happened.

The female nurse came in, all smiling, and said, 'John, is it?' I didn't answer. I wasn't sure if she was talking to one of the officers. She said it again, this time staring at me and nodding as if to say 'You are John'. I *was* John but no one had called me that for quite some time because your first name doesn't get used in prison – it's your surname and a number and that's it. It seems such a small thing but to be treated like a human being again, even on the end of a chain, was a beautiful thing for me, considering I was being treated like an animal only moments earlier. The small things really do make big differences!

I was released on parole early and was determined to seek treatment for my mental health problems, try to get a job and get in contact with my daughter again. From the outset, all three aims became more difficult than I could have imagined. Seeing my daughter again was the hardest part because, to get any contact again, I would have to go through the courts and straight away it was made clear that I wasn't welcome in my daughter's life. I was not up for the fight. I didn't want it to be like that. I just wanted to see her, but I knew I wasn't strong enough to cope with the battles that would ensue so I had to give up on what mattered most in my life, my daughter!

Under that level of stress, and with no support from probation, I started using drugs again but still tried to achieve my other targets. The job search was like banging my head against a brick wall. More often than not, I would receive no replies to my applications, and when I did reach interview stage it was pointless trying to tell them why I had no qualifications and explain the offences of which I had been convicted.

My health was worse than ever by this stage but I did start to make some progress on getting treated. I had some sessions with a therapist, and built a rapport with her. But when I started opening up, she referred me to a psychiatric ward as an out-patient. I was disappointed by this, because I had enjoyed the earlier sessions, but I went along with it. I had two half-hour long sessions with a consultant over a period of about a year, which was no use to me as far as I could see. Then I was referred on again, this time to a more secure unit, which frightened the life out of me! Was I that ill? Would they lock me up forever? Was I a lunatic? All these questions and fears built up until I totally disengaged and went back to taking drugs and committing crimes.

Four years in the wilderness followed, with my health deteriorating to the point where I started to plan how to take my own life. With the drugs I was using, I knew an overdose would do the job, and I planned it with precision, step by step, so I wouldn't make any mistakes. I didn't want to fail. I wanted it to be foolproof. I needed my way out to be a sure thing because it gave me some piece of mind knowing that I had an exit. During this period I was a total recluse and started building my own theories on the nature of reality and researching conspiracies and a host of other weird stuff. I became convinced that this human experience was not real and therefore exiting from life didn't seem such a hard thing to do.

13

On the rare occasions when I did go out, it was usually to buy some drugs. I always bought a month's worth at a time, which meant not going out much and getting more for my money.

It was just a normal day, having just bought my drugs, and I wasn't paying much attention when I bumped into an old criminal associate and stopped for a chat. A few seconds later five big guys rushed us and started shouting at us to get on the floor! They looked just like us but they were undercover police and had been watching my friend for some time. We were standing in an alleyway and it must have looked as if a deal was being done. But I had my stuff on me that was for my own personal use and he had nothing but a pack of cigarettes on him.

On my way to the police station in that van I thought, 'How unlucky is that?' I had stopped for a few moments and lost all my drugs, which I still had to pay for. I couldn't believe it. My mate lit a cigarette and strolled off, chuckling to himself, while I was being shoved in a van.

At the police station it was the same procedure I had been through many times and I didn't want to be there any longer than I had to. I refused a solicitor, as I had started studying Law for my own protection over the years. There's no point being a criminal if you don't know the law, I always thought. Ignorance is no defence. While giving my details, my mental health was flagged up on the computer and this confused the desk sergeant who thought I was somehow wasting his time! 'You look all right to me, wasting my time having to get a doctor out for you!' He obviously had no understanding of mental illness and I told him I was sorry for wasting his time and I didn't want to see the doctor, as that would add two hours to my stay. An hour or two later the ignorant sergeant opened my cell door and said, 'The doctor's arrived. Now get going, you little time-wasting #@?%'

I did actually feel like I was a waste of time – not just his but my own – but I had to concentrate, as I didn't want to be sectioned! The chat with the doctor lasted ten minutes, and that was as long as it took to educate this ignorant officer. He stood in the doorway smirking at first, with his arms crossed, possibly waiting for the doctor to turn round and say, 'He's wasting my time too!' But over that short period of time, I watched his whole body language change from dismissive to genuinely interested, and on the way back to my cell he apologised for treating me so badly and hoped I would forgive him! I said 'Of course I would' and he gave me what felt like a fatherly squeeze on the shoulders. My own father had never given me one of those and I thought something deep and meaningful had happened there. In just ten minutes somebody was educated enough to see his error and immediately acted with humility. It's something I think about a lot now, just how much we can change in so short a time.

I was charged and bailed and was given a court date, which became the most important date of my life so far.

Building up to that day, I had settled it within myself that if it didn't go well in court this would be the deciding factor. I could cope with a fine if it wasn't too extortionate, but prison or a community sentence would push me over the edge and give me the incentive I needed to take my own life.

I was ready when the day came, just a matter of hours from the ultimate self-destruction! I was eerily at peace when I walked into the court building. I was more than capable of representing myself but I thought, 'Let the courts do their dark work and unknowingly sentence me to death!'

There, at the lowest point I have ever reached in a place of darkness, I sat waiting to be called, unaware of anyone around me. Lost in this spinning vortex, a face came into view, a kind face, a face shining with humanity and concern for someone other than himself. 'Hello, John.' I'd heard that before somewhere. 'I am a nurse, can we have a chat?' The suit was fooling me at first but he was for real. He couldn't have stood out more in this place if he'd tried! For some reason I trusted him immediately and followed him into a room, where I learned the reason he was here was to help me. His compassion and knowledge and willingness to listen in such a short space of time gave me hope, where minutes earlier I had nothing but despair! That nurse, that man, that human being, actually saved my life and he didn't even know. He was just doing what came naturally to him because he cared.

He was working as a court liaison for a new programme that was seeking to treat people in the criminal justice system with mental health issues and help them to recover. He actually spoke in court for me and I can say with certainty that I would not be here today without him. I walked out of court with a probation order, with treatment engagement tied in. This was very new and something I didn't expect, but I also walked out with hope in my heart!

Almost two years on, after a year of treatment with a superb psychologist, I now work for the same programme that saved me! I volunteer as much time as I can and love what I do. I now help people to benefit from the amazing service that saved my life, and I hope to take it as far as I can and be an advocate for what works and for a good service. No offending, no drug abuse, a new passion for life! In fact what I found at the end of treatment was myself. I found the young boy who didn't get to grow up and be something different. Now I *am* something different and I hope to make a difference in others. I aim to be like the nurse who saved me every single day. Everybody can be a nurse in their hearts. I cared about things when I was young and now I do again.

# 3

# Nursing in police custody

Jennie Smith and Karen Swinson

## Context

Country borders separate police forces in the UK. In England, there are 39 forces, while Wales has four. Prior to April 2013, there were eight legacy forces in Scotland. However the Scottish government amalgamated them into a single force, known as Police Scotland. Finally, Northern Ireland has a single police force. There are also other forces across the country, some of which are local (such as Port of Liverpool Police and Port of Dover Police). Others are national and these include, for example, the UK Border Agency (UKBA), Her Majesty's Revenue and Customs (HMRC) and British Transport Police.

In England and Wales, policing is governed by the Police and Criminal Evidence (PACE) Act 1984 (Home Office 1984). In Northern Ireland, policing is governed by the Police and Criminal Evidence Order 1989. All police officers must comply with these pieces of legislation, and their codes of practice. Meanwhile, Scottish police forces are governed and advised by the Criminal Procedure (Scotland) Act 1995.

Government policy requires the provision of safe, supportive and humane custody environments that balance the needs of the criminal justice system with health imperatives. The NHS responds to this policy by trying to respect the rights and requirements of the individual and the public, as well as the police, nurses and other professionals involved in the criminal justice system (De Viggiani 2013).

The Police and Criminal Evidence Act 1984 (Home Office 1984) and its codes of practice provide the framework for police powers and safeguards in England and Wales. These concern practices such as stop and search, arrest, detention, investigation, identification and interviewing detainees. Code C governs the detention of people in custody and their treatment. This code sets out the requirements for the detention, treatment and questioning of suspects not related to terrorism in police custody. This section of PACE gives clear guidance on all aspects of custody, including the rights of detained persons. It also includes explicit guidance on healthcare.

PACE, Code C, paragraph 9.5 states:

> **The custody officer must make sure a detainee receives appropriate clinical attention as soon as reasonably practicable if the person:**
>
> **(a) Appears to be suffering from physical illness;**
>
> **(b) Or is injured;**
>
> **(c) Or appears to be suffering from a mental disorder;**
>
> **(d) Or appears to need clinical attention.**

In some areas, the custody sergeant will perform a risk assessment as part of the booking-in process. If they feel the detainee fits any of the above criteria, they will arrange for a healthcare professional to attend and assess them. In other areas, the nurse on duty will work closely alongside the sergeant to ensure that every individual coming into custody is triaged.

Before 2000, healthcare services within UK custody suites were delivered by Forensic Medical Examiners (FMEs) and arrangements differed from one area to another. Anecdotally, we believe the chief officer usually requested the assistance of a local doctor (often known to them) on an ad-hoc basis, to attend to detainees. Decades later, the numbers of detainees grew, and the complex and increased healthcare needs of this group led to more formal contracts being offered. The majority of doctors who worked as FMEs did so on a part-time basis. They were often General Practitioners and some practised hospital medicine.

Despite the existence of formal contracts, there was little monitoring of the quality of the service at this time. In its 1998 report 'The Doctor's Bill', the Audit Commission concluded that radical changes were needed to meet the complex demands of modern policing and to provide a cost-effective custodial and forensic medical service. This White Paper specifically criticised the quality of care and excessive costs. Following this, government proposals were made, specifying other healthcare professionals who could carry out this role to improve clinical care and provide a more cost-efficient service. There was a perception that the former medical approach to healthcare provision in police custody was inadequate in addressing the complex healthcare needs of some patients/detainees.

In 2000 Home Office pilots were launched, introducing custody nurses in Kent and the Metropolitan Police. The success of this highly innovative approach to care in custody challenged existing government policy, legislation and clinical practice. These changes could not have occurred without significant amendments to areas of legislation, such as medicines administration within the custody setting and existing police codes of practice. These were fully amended in 2003 to recognise nurses and paramedics, in addition to FMEs, as healthcare professionals who could practise in this unique environment. Since 2003, the majority of police forces have had a combination of nurses and

FMEs providing healthcare in custody suites. Since 2003, many forces have started outsourcing this area of healthcare to private providers, while others have continued to contract their own FMEs and also employ nurses. In the future, police custody healthcare will be commissioned by the NHS.

# The role of the police custody nurse

A disproportionate number of people enter custody with significant health and social care needs, mental illness and drug and/or alcohol dependency. In view of this, reducing the risk of death in custody is a particular political and professional concern.

An on-site nursing team, with a clinical screening and monitoring function, aims to safeguard the health and welfare of prisoners. However, it should be remembered that when a person enters custody they are 'a detainee' (rather than 'a prisoner') because they are suspected of having committed a criminal offence but they are not guilty, at the point of contact. The on-site nursing team can offer significant support to custody sergeants in their hugely demanding role, and this has led to the continuation of the service nationally. Hurley *et al.* (2013) evaluated the impact of nursing leadership roles in delivering primary care within police custody suites in Scotland, and noted the positive outcomes for all key stakeholders with a nurse-led healthcare service in police custody.

The nurse's responsibilities in the police custody setting can include: assessing the fitness of detainees for detention and interview; treating minor illnesses and minor injuries; caring for detainees with a wide variety of illnesses, infections and diseases; managing the care of drug and alcohol abusers; assessing mental health; taking forensic samples; and verifying that life is extinct when a sudden death has occurred.

Clinical assessments in custody are often complex, as detainees will regularly present with multiple issues and therefore require a breadth of skill, knowledge and experience to manage. Often the clinical symptoms of these conditions are subtle, whilst at other times they may be acute and unpredictable. Hurley *et al.* (2013) suggest that part of the difficulty in implementing evidence-based healthcare practice in police custody is that so little research has been done on this subject within the UK. What *is* recognised is that detainees have higher levels of mental health problems and substance misuse issues than the general public and are considered to be more vulnerable as a result (Cummins 2007, cited by Hurley *et al.* 2013). Many are not receiving appropriate care in the community, which can lead to low levels of concordance and compliance in medicine taking and/or restricted access to treatment (Hurley *et al.* 2013).

Through their proximity and involvement in caring for detainees, many police custody nurses have gained significant understanding of subjects such as investigative interviewing techniques, presentation of evidence at court and criminal law.

There are some health-related roles that, at the time of writing, still require a Forensic Medical Examiner (FME). For example, according to the Road Traffic Act (RTA) Section 4, an FME is required to assess those whose driving may have been impaired by taking a drug which may be prescribed but could also be an illegal drug. However, the North Report (North 2010) recommends that nurses can undertake this procedure as well as RTA Section 5 procedures in hospital.

Another area in which most police services have yet to introduce nurses is that of persons detained under the Terrorism Act. The PACE codes of practice support nurses providing care and taking samples from detainees arrested under terrorism legislation. However, given the relatively small numbers of detainees involved, it would be more appropriate to allocate this work to specialist teams of nurses in the future.

Healthcare responsibilities across most police services now are commonly shared between nurses and FMEs, and either an FME or a nurse may be present in the custody suite, according to location and/or rosters. This type of joint working has enabled frameworks to be created, including, for example, Medicines Management, Clinical Practice and Performance, and Risk Management. These are comparable with clinical governance frameworks in the NHS.

Clinical skills are the key attributes required to work in the custody environment. The clinical ability and suitability of nurses working in this area may vary from one police service to another. There is little national guidance as to the essential and desirable qualities any police custody nurse should possess. The 'Guidance on the Safer Detention and Handling of Persons in Police Custody' document (National Policing Improvement Agency 2102) advises that nurses should have at least four years' post-qualification experience. It also says that it is desirable for them to hold an emergency nurse practitioner qualification. In addition, it could be argued that any police custody nurse should have passed the clinical diagnostics and clinical examination skills modules.

Other nursing skills that are more likely to be called upon in a police custody setting are those pertaining to the criminal justice process. Part of the role is to obtain forensic samples, whether non-intimate or intimate swabs. Whilst the collection of evidence by swabs is not a difficult procedure, it is vital that the evidence is obtained in line with current recommendations and guidelines. It is often more serious cases, such as wounding or sexual assault, that require forensic samples to be taken. These cases highlight the importance of clinical skills, and show that suitable training is vital in order to equip custody nurses with the correct skills to safeguard the criminal justice process.

In custody nursing there is always the possibility that any patient being cared for may be involved in a criminal proceeding. A police custody nurse must therefore be equipped with the skills to provide a comprehensive statement, based upon contemporaneous notes taken at the time of assessment. The giving of evidence should be a key component of any induction into the role. However if the custody nurse is called as a witness, it is also important to be confident when giving evidence.

There are three types of witness: witness of fact, professional witness and expert witness. A witness of fact would be a member of the public, who would quite simply give the facts of any incident as they saw it, whereas an expert witness is a person recognised in their field. They are likely to be published and have local, national and even international renown as experts on their subject. Nurses fall into the category of professional witness, and would therefore be expected to give an account of any medical assessment they undertook. In Scotland, forensic examinations are undertaken by nurses when an opinion is not likely to be sought in court. If a serious indictable offence has been committed, such as murder or rape, then a forensic physician would be better placed to undertake the assessment and write a report. This is the current advice from the Faculty of Forensic and Legal Medicine (FFLM) and the Crown Office and Procurator Fiscal Service (COPFS), although this may change as services develop.

## The value of nursing in police custody

The Royal College of Nursing (RCN) document 'Health and nursing care in the Criminal Justice Service' (RCN 2009) states that the current government policy for offender healthcare is based on the principle of equivalence, which means that standards of healthcare for people in custody should be the same as for people in the wider community. According to the 'Guidance on the Safer Detention and Handling of Persons in Police Custody' document (National Policing Improvement Agency 2012), 'a healthcare professional' means a clinically qualified person working within the scope of practice determined by the relevant professional body. This is supported by a similar recommendation in PACE (Code C, Paragraph 9 note 9A). This has led to a move to a nursing-based service in recent years.

West (2006) refers to the role of nurses being dynamic. In its 'Comprehensive Critical Care' review (DH 2000), the Department of Health suggests that improving and developing nurses' ability to recognise clinical deterioration is an important principle of the health agenda. This is a view carried forward into the 'NHS Improvement Plan: Putting people at the heart of public services' (DH 2004), which stipulates that nurses should be expected to increase their skills in practice in line with the needs of their patients. Based upon these comments, and the fact that in recent years nurses have moved into more autonomous practitioner roles, the value of police custody nurses seems clear.

All nurses in the UK must comply with the Nursing and Midwifery Council (NMC) Code (NMC 2008) and all aspects of the NMC code are relevant to our work as nurses. However, there are three key points to note:

- The people in your care must be able to trust you with their health and well-being.
- You must have the knowledge and skills needed for safe and effective practice when working without direct supervision.
- You must recognise and work within the limits of your competence.

Based on the expectations set out by the NMC and the work being done nationally by organisations such as the Royal College of Nursing (RCN) and the UK Association of Forensic Nurses, the role of police custody nurses seems set to expand, and the value of nurses within this environment should continue to be recognised.

The following case studies give some insight into the work of custody nurses.

## Case study one

The custody nurse was contacted via the central call centre to attend one of the police custody suites to assess a young man for 'fitness for detention'. This is the most common reason for calling a healthcare practitioner to see a detainee. The nurse arrived at the custody suite and the detainee was brought to the medical room for the assessment to be carried out. Consent was gained for the assessment before it began.

The detainee was a 27-year-old male who had no recent injuries, and was usually fit and well, apart from asthma, which had been diagnosed by his GP two years earlier. He stated that he was alcohol-dependent, drinking approximately three to four cans of 9 per cent alcohol strength lager per day. This was a pattern of drinking that had evolved over the previous three to four months. He reported that he had never suffered withdrawal symptoms before, and that he had drunk two cans that day. He also disclosed that he was being prescribed methadone (40ml daily), but he was using street heroin as well. He had last used heroin two days before his arrest. The detainee had no allergies of note and stated that his only medications were his asthma inhalers. He reported that he had no learning needs and that he was currently living in a hostel.

He appeared to be unwell and said that for five days he had been suffering from diarrhoea, vomiting, general cold and flu-like symptoms and some chest pain. He had been self-medicating with paracetamol (to little effect) and he rated the severity of his symptoms 7/10. The detainee had a hacking productive cough, which was painful, and this discomfort was clearly seen during the assessment.

In relation to his mental health, the patient hesitated to admit that he suffered from anxiety and depression, but suggested he was open to mental health services treatment with regular visits from a community psychiatric nurse. He mentioned that he had been told he might be schizophrenic but this had not been formally diagnosed. At one point, he had been prescribed antipsychotics but not currently. He stated that he had self-harmed in the past, by cutting himself. The last episode was four years ago, but he would give no assurance that he would not harm himself whilst in his cell.

was normal, and there was no inflammation, tonsillar or uvular swelling or deformity. No exudate was seen on either tonsil and he did not have any trismus. An ear examination was not possible, as auriscopes are not available in this custody suite, but he did have tonsillar and anterior chain lymphadenopathy.

Finally chest auscultation was performed. Air entry could be heard across all lobes of both lungs. There were clear wheezes on the left upper lobe, but it was the right lung that gave cause for concern. There were widespread added sounds across all lobes. The detainee also commented that his right-sided chest wall was tender to touch. His observations were all within normal parameters apart from his saturation. This was 95 per cent, which was low for a man of his age. He presented as clearly unwell and was rather tearful during the assessment, saying that he could not ever remember feeling so poorly. He was given some pain relief for his chest. In view of the history and the findings of the physical examination, the custody staff were advised that he was not fit for either detention or interview and that arrangements must be made to take him to the local hospital for assessment and further treatment.

This transfer to hospital was arranged. There he was diagnosed with pneumonia and subsequently admitted to a medical ward for treatment.

## Case study two

The custody nurse was contacted via the central call centre to attend one of the police custody suites to assess a young man and to administer medication. The nurse arrived at the custody suite and the detainee was brought to the medical room for the assessment to be carried out. Consent was gained before the assessment began.

The detainee was a 35-year-old man who had suffered no injuries. He stated that he had had cardiac problems as a child, including surgery, but was unable to give further details of the diagnosis. Apart from slight shortness of breath on exertion, his prior cardiac problems were not acute. He said that he was not alcohol-dependent but would drink when he had money. It was during discussion about his mental health that concern was raised.

The detainee cried throughout the entire assessment, which initially raised the alarm. When asked whether he had any formal mental health diagnosis, he said no. However, he became very distressed and started to describe an incident that had occurred one month prior to his arrest. He explained that he had 'lost the plot' in his kitchen for approximately thirty minutes. He did not give any specific details about what that had entailed. He stated that afterwards his head was trying to take him somewhere else, to a place full of fields and bright colours, but he had managed to stop it and stay in his kitchen.

He also described a change in his sense of taste and smell since this incident. He was unable to give specifics about the tastes or smells but did state that they were not nice, and they bothered him. He also explained that he had had no respite from these sensations. When asked if he was currently receiving treatment from mental health services, he said that he was not. But he had been seen around two months previously by the crisis team at the city centre hospital, following an incident where he sat on a main road flyover and was considering jumping off. The flyover in question is in the city centre, and is over an extremely busy main thoroughfare into the city. He stated that he had never been an in-patient in a mental health ward, but had a feeling he would end up in one soon. He said he was being prescribed an anti-depressant and had taken this until the day before his arrest.

The answers to the other assessment questions did not arouse concern, and his observations were normal. He was able to read and write, with no learning needs, and was living with his parents. Physically this young man was stable but his mental health was of concern.

This assessment was performed on a Saturday evening and he was in custody until his appearance in court on Monday morning, so he was effectively in a place of safety. This case was discussed with the doctor on duty, who was also a psychiatrist. They advised that the on-call member of the Criminal Justice Mental Health Team (CJMHT) be contacted the following morning and asked to do an assessment. This plan was handed over and discussed with the sergeant in charge of the detainee. The following day the plan was implemented and he was seen by the CJMHT.

Following his assessment, the feedback received was that this had been an appropriate referral. The CJMHT nurse felt that he did not require admission at that point but that, following the assessment, he would be referred to mental health services and followed up in the next couple of days or weeks. The nurse also commented that had this young man been managed differently he almost certainly would have presented at a later date with much more severe symptoms, and been more seriously ill.

## Case study three

The detainee was arrested for an assault on a member of the public, and presented with a head injury to his left forehead and a contusion to the left side of his face, with no open wounds or bleeding. On arrest, officers believed he was drunk, because of his aggressive behaviour and the smell of alcohol. He was clearly agitated on arrival and had a 30-minute wait before being booked in. When booking in, he did not appear to remember who he was, and was experiencing memory lapses. The Designated Detention Officer immediately alerted the nurse to this behaviour and the detainee was taken to the Medical Assessment Room.

The initial clinical assessment was that his balance was fine, he could walk unaided, and, whilst his speech was slow, it was coherent. Within three minutes of the assessment commencing, the detainee became increasingly drowsy and then unresponsive. He did not respond to voice or pain, and was assisted to the floor. His observations were recorded. His pupils were sluggish, and oxygen was commenced, as his saturation levels were 90 per cent. He was tachycardic and hypertensive. The ambulance service was called. On departure from the custody suite, the detainee started to fit. He was transported into the ambulance, where intravenous diazepam was given, which did not appear to impact on the seizure. The detainee was taken to hospital, where he was found to have a subdural haematoma. He went on to have surgery and made a full recovery.

The signs and symptoms of head injuries can often be masked by those of intoxication. The history of events can often assist but can sometimes be misleading to the healthcare professional carrying out a clinical examination.

## Case study four

A 30-year-old female was arrested for a serious offence in a public place. She was brought into a police custody suite, which was exceptionally busy at the time. This case was extremely high profile and therefore attracted a lot of public and media attention. The female was seen by a custody nurse, who felt she needed more support, and referred the case to a nurse manager. The nurse manager immediately contacted mental health services, who attended the custody suite and sectioned the detainee. Unfortunately there were no high-security beds in the area, and the mental health team were unable to transfer within an acceptable timeframe. Despite many phone calls across the wider area, the mental health teams were unable to transfer this detainee until the following afternoon.

Healthcare professionals felt this was unacceptable, as this lady was extremely unwell and the custody environment was detrimental to her health, causing her to react by shouting and screeching. Liaison also took place with the senior managers at the local mental health trust. Unfortunately, despite everyone's concerns for the detainee, it was decided that she would need to remain in custody until transfer to hospital.

The healthcare team (including the FME, the nurse manager and the custody nurse) created an emergency care plan to deliver the best care they were able to provide for this detainee in this unsuitable environment. They arranged for the detainee to be seen in custody by a consultant psychiatrist, who prescribed appropriate medication. Whilst the situation was far from ideal, the team were able to manage the detainee safely during the time she spent in custody.

## A different dynamic from prison

Nursing in a police custody environment is rather different from nursing within a prison setting, for several reasons. Firstly, custody nursing can be, but is not exclusively, a more acute service. Whilst the range of medical conditions seen will be similar, the presentations of these conditions can be vastly different. For example, alcohol-dependent detainees can often be intoxicated in custody, but by the time they arrive at prison they may be some way through their withdrawal and will have been given several doses of medication to combat their symptoms. Drug users would often be in a comparable situation.

The skills required by custody nurses can be different to those required in prison. Detainees in custody are invariably still subject to ongoing investigations regarding the offence for which they have been arrested. Nurses may therefore be called upon to collect forensic evidence – for instance, by swabbing the individual concerned. This is a specific job that is associated with the custody nurse role.

It is essential for custody nurses to have a working knowledge of PACE, whereas prison nurses do not need this. Detainees are not convicted prisoners and their treatment is subject to specific rules, which custody nurses need to be aware of. These rules are completely different to those governing convicted prisoners. When prisoners are brought into custody for questioning they are treated as PACE prisoners, but there is no legal requirement to do this.

Custody nursing is a specialist field, which requires a specific education programme. This initial training should include, as a minimum, an overview of the Police and Criminal Evidence Act (Home Office 1984), forensic sampling, knowledge of substance misuse and the documenting of injuries. This should ensure nurses working in the field can provide the quality of healthcare that is expected of them. At present, this is predominantly provided by the specific healthcare provider or police force. However, more and more national specialist programmes are being introduced.

## Challenging issues for custody nurses

As stated earlier, nurses working in the UK have to comply with the Nursing and Midwifery Council's Code of Conduct (NMC 2008), as well as the laws of the country in which they practise. Nurses are aware that they are accountable for their own actions and omissions.

Care provided in police custody settings is governed by the NMC code and there are no questions about compliance. However, police officers may occasionally give orders to nurses. For example, they could ask a nurse to assess and deal with a wound on a detainee who is being held down by officers, due to violent behaviour.

Under police regulations, police officers can be issued with orders, which are generally defined as lawful, provided that they are for police purposes and will not render the individual liable to any criminal, civil or disciplinary action. The question then remains, are nurses obliged to carry out an order issued by a police officer? Furthermore, would carrying out the order, as in the example above, contravene the NMC code, as the detainee would clearly not be consenting to assessment and/or treatment? It might be argued that nurses employed directly by police forces would be more obliged to carry out the order than those working for a private healthcare provider. As with any nursing role, the individual needs to evaluate the situation and decide:

- Is this lawful?
- Is it in the best interests of the patient/detainee?
- And is it in keeping with the NMC code of conduct?

If the person believes they can answer 'Yes' to the above questions, they will be able to defend their decisions appropriately.

These Home Office codes complement other areas of legislation pertaining to healthcare in police custody. This has been particularly challenging in recent years with, for example, the complexities of medicines management, including the use of Patient Group Directions (PGD) by nurses. A PGD, signed by a doctor and agreed by a pharmacist, can act as an instruction to a nurse to supply and/ or administer prescription-only medicines (POMs) to patients, using their own assessment of patient need, without necessarily referring back to a doctor for an individual prescription.

## Conclusion

Custody nurses clearly need to have a thorough knowledge of a wide range of clinical presentations. Experience in accident and emergency, walk-in centres and primary care nursing can all provide a solid basis for working in the custodial environment. Custody nursing requires competent, confident nurses who can work as part of a team but also autonomously, as the majority of the time in the job may be spent working independently.

Custody is a very different environment from that in which most nurses will have previously practised. The thought of this type of work may be daunting but the reality is very different. As with any job, it is full of challenges but it is also extremely rewarding, providing the best possible care for very chaotic and often vulnerable people.

The custody environment is a relatively new clinical area for nurses. However it is a specialty that is growing quickly, not only in terms of the numbers of nurses working in these settings, but also in view of the expanded roles and responsibilities these nurses are undertaking. With ongoing reviews of the law and changes possibly being implemented that will allow these nurses to extend their capabilities, the value of nurses in custody care can only continue to grow.

# References

Audit Commission (1998). *The Doctor's Bill. The Provision of Forensic Medical Services to the Police*. London: Audit Commission.

Baksheev G.N., Thomas, S.D.M. & Ogloff, J.R.P. (2010). Psychiatric disorders and unmet needs in Australian police cells. *Australian and New Zealand Journal of Psychiatry*. **44**, 1043–51.

De Viggiani N (2013). A clean bill of health? The efficacy of an NHS commissioned outsourced police custody healthcare service. *Journal of Legal and Forensic Medicine*. **20**, 610–17.

Department of Health (2000). *Comprehensive Critical Care: a review of adult critical care services*. London: DH.

Department of Health (2004). *The NHS Improvement Plan: Putting people at the heart of public services*. London: DH.

Elvins, M., Gao, C., Hurley, J., Jones, M., Linsley, P. & Petrie, D. (2012). 'Provision of healthcare and forensic medical services in Tayside police custody settings. An evaluation of a partnership agreement between NHS Rayside and Tayside Police (2009–2011)'. The Scottish Institute for Policing Research.

Faculty of Legal and Forensic Medicine (2013). http://fflm.ac.uk/

Home Office (1984). *Police and Criminal Evidence Act*. London: The Stationery Office.

Hurley, J., Linsley, P., Elvins, M. & Jones, M. (2013). Nurses leading care in custody suite environments: A qualitative study from Scotland. *Journal of Forensic Nursing*. **9**, 1–7.

Loucks, N. (2007). *Prisoners with Learning Difficulties and Learning Disabilities – Review of prevalence and associated needs*. London. Prison Reform Trust.

Loucks, N. & Talbot, J. (2007). *No one knows: identifying and supporting prisoners with learning difficulties and learning disabilities: the views of prison staff in Scotland*. Prison Reform Trust.

National Policing Improvement Agency (2012). *Guidance on the Safer Detention and Handling of Persons in Police Custody*. 2nd ed. London: National Policing Improvement Agency.

North, P. (2010). *Report of the Review of Drink and Drug Driving Law*. London: The Stationery Office.

Nursing and Midwifery Council (2008). *The Code*. London: NMC.

Payne, James J. (2010). Clinical risk and detainees in police custody. *Clinical Risk*. **16**, 56–60.

Payne, James J., Anderson, W.R., Green, P.G. & Johnston, A. (2009). Provision of forensic medical services to police custody suites in England and Wales: Current Practice. *Journal of Forensic and Legal Medicine*. **16**, 189–95.

Royal College of Nursing (2009). *Health and Nursing Care in the Criminal Justice Service*. London: RCN.

Scottish Government (2008). *Equally Well. Report of the ministerial task force on health inequalities*. **2**. Edinburgh, Scottish Government.

West, S.L. (2006). Physical assessment: whose role is in anyway? *Nursing in Critical Care*. **11** (4), 161–67.

# 4

# Forensic nurse examiners: Caring for victims of sexual assault

Emma Durmaz

Rape and sexual violence are crimes that are massively unreported, and some studies have shown that between 80 and 90 per cent of victims never disclose their abuse. Male rape survivors are significantly less likely to report the crime than female survivors. Male rape accounts for 12 per cent of all reported rapes (Survivors Trust 2014).

The consequences of sexual violence can be devastating for the individual and their family and indeed society as a whole. The cost of healthcare and long-term support for individuals with mental health problems caused by sexual violence far outweighs the cost of any initial support that can be provided.

The long-term effects of rape can include depression, anxiety, post-traumatic stress disorder (PTSD), drug and substance misuse, self-harm and suicide, and the government has recognised the importance of offering support straight away: 'The simple fact is that when victims receive the support they need when they need it, they are more likely to take positive steps to recovery. This should be our goal' (Home Office 2011).

In 2010, the Home Office estimated that the average cost to the state of a single rape victim was £96,000 (Home Office 2010). This represented a significant increase on the previous figure of £73,487 (2003/04) and was updated to take into account the growth in nominal income as negative health impacts rise in line with real income. Year on year, this figure will continue to increase. The cost to the individual and the impact on families and communities is much higher.

Rape victims are 6.4 times more likely to use Class A drugs. It is estimated that 50–75 per cent of women in substance misuse treatment programmes are survivors of sexual violence. Research suggests that 50–60 per cent of in-patients and 40–60 per cent of out-patients in Mental Health Services were victims of sexual violence and/or child sexual abuse (Itzin 2008).

A review carried out by Westmarland et al. (2012) suggests that, if received soon after a traumatic sexual experience, therapeutic interventions can prevent the onset of chronic post-traumatic stress disorder and reduce the symptoms in women already presenting with the disorder. This highlights the need for all victims, irrespective of age or sex, to be able to access and receive effective therapeutic support in the immediate aftermath of a sexually traumatic event.

Many people who have suffered sexual violence have pre-existing vulnerabilities, and there is evidence that certain population groups are more vulnerable to sexual assault. These groups include adolescents, young women, those with disabilities, homeless people, sex workers, women on low incomes, women who were previously victims of sexual abuse or assaults, and lesbian, gay, bisexual, transgender and intersex people (COSAI 2013). The COSAI document is a review of literature and concerns only women and sexual violence. However, we know that sexual violence does not respect age or gender, and can also be perpetrated against children, older people, men and boys.

## Sexual assault referral centres (SARCs)

A SARC is a 'one-stop shop' to support victims of sexual violence, where they can access care and services to meet their health and well-being needs, and where they can attend for a forensic clinical examination if appropriate. Across the United Kingdom, there are 44 SARCs. Some of these are jointly commissioned by the NHS and the police, while some run alongside existing NHS services. Each SARC aims to provide all the therapeutic support required immediately following an assault, such as HIV prophylaxis and emergency contraception. Advice regarding aftercare services is also offered at the first attendance. This includes information about access to counselling, an Independent Sexual Violence Adviser (ISVA) and contact details for Sexual Health Services. If the victim wishes, the SARC can make appointments on their behalf and liaise with other agencies to ensure that the correct support is put in place and maintained.

Sexual offence examinations used to be undertaken by doctors acting in the role of police surgeons. These examinations took place in GPs' surgeries, or Accident and Emergency Departments, both of which were inappropriate venues for this type of examination.

Most of the medical examiners used to be male and there was often little or no therapeutic aftercare available. The SARC now provides all the services needed under one roof, in a forensically 'clean' environment, with access to aftercare rooms that are welcoming and safe.

SARCs provide care and support for anyone who is a victim of acute or historic sexual violence. As we have seen, rape and sexual violence can affect all members of society, whatever their age, gender, socioeconomic group, nationality, ethnicity or religion (Rights of Women 2011).

## Forensic examinations and the criminal justice system

We know there is a huge discrepancy between reported cases of sexual assault and rates of conviction (Temin & Krahe 2008). Many cases never progress from reporting sexual assault to actually going to court. This may be due to many factors, such as the victim not wishing to undertake an examination, or the victim withdrawing their complaint (Cybulska 2007).

Many victims liken the examination to a further assault (Kelly & Regan 2003). According to Heenan and Murray (2006), there is a widely held perception that refusing an examination will cause professionals to doubt the veracity of the complaint.

In 2010, Baroness Stern stressed that the prosecution process should be part of a therapeutic intervention (Home Office 2010). Sadly, this is not usually the case. The victim is frequently merely seen as a witness in the case for the prosecution, assuming that the case progresses as far as this. In future, if forensic examinations became more therapeutically focused (rather than process-orientated, with the sole goal of collecting evidence), victims might feel more willing to undergo such examinations.

A forensic examination should therefore be both therapeutic and forensically sound. It should be carried out in a forensically clean environment, to reduce the potential for DNA contamination to a minimum. This is crucial, as any breach in the forensic integrity of the environment could impede successful prosecution.

The aim of the examination, from a forensic point of view, is to consider the persistence of DNA in the mouth, vagina and anus and from sexual touching. Based on this information, we can decide which samples will need to be taken. For example, we know that DNA can be found in the vagina up to seven days after the offence, but in the anus for up to three days (Faculty of Forensic & Legal Medicine 2014). Any evidence collected as part of this forensic examination will be handled according to strict protocols, and secured to ensure continuity of evidence that will stand up in a court of law.

If the victim does not wish to report to the police, who refer victims to the SARC, then the SARC will offer a further option – self-referral. The client will access the SARC through a 24-hour emergency number and speak to a crisis worker, who can support them and advise them about their options. If the victim requests a forensic examination, they can still access this service through the SARC and their evidence will be frozen, under strict chain of evidence conditions. If they later decide they wish to report to the police, the evidence will still be available to support their individual disclosure.

Staff at the SARC will also take a statement from the victim at the time of examination and obtain photographic evidence. Sometimes the forensic evidence can be anonymously submitted to the forensic laboratory, which may, for instance, reveal foreign DNA or date rape drugs in the blood sample. Knowing that this evidence has been tested may help the individual decide whether or not to report their assault.

# The development of the Forensic Nurse Examiner (FNE)

As previously mentioned, sexual assault examinations were historically carried out by doctors, known as Forensic Medical Examiners (FMEs). With the relatively recent introduction of nurses working in police custody environments, some nurses have become involved in sexual offences examinations. Other nurses may have come to this role from previous work within Sexual Health Services, accident and emergency nursing or primary care nursing.

As nursing roles have developed, more registered nurses have started to undertake this role. Now that there is a multidisciplinary approach to the process, it is expected that it will also incorporate a therapeutic element (Kelly & Regan 2003). It is essential that anyone examining the victims of sexual violence realises that the therapeutic element is equally, if not more, important as the forensic element. Poor therapeutic care can have lifelong implications for the victim, leading, for example, to unwanted pregnancy, HIV sero-conversion, self-harm and suicide.

The forensic examination is commonly thought to be a difficult experience for the victim, as it can involve lengthy delays, victim blaming and ill-informed responses from forensic examiners (Campbell 2006). Victims often feel that the medical examination can be intrusive at best and almost abusive at worst. The provision of highly trained, empathic and knowledgeable FMEs is fragmented across the country (Coy et al. 2007). Whilst there are pockets of excellent practice, there are many areas where the standard of care is in need of further improvement.

Nurses bring a more holistic approach to the forensic examination; indeed, doctors working in the sexual offences field have commented that they find nurses well trained and sufficiently sensitive to fulfil these roles well. Most nurses undertaking this role are passionate about the care they give the victim and are committed to their continued professional development as required by the nursing regulator. Forensic Nurse Examiners (FNEs) have been independently conducting forensic examinations for the survivors of rape and sexual assault since 2001 (Rees & Jamieson 2012).

# The Forensic Nurse Examiner's role

The FNE role seems to have largely developed in response to the lack of suitably qualified doctors and the lack of female practitioners in this field. Indeed, there has been some criticism of doctors' roles in cases where their lack of experience and poor training have affected legal outcomes within the criminal justice system (Campbell 2011).

The FNE for Sexual Offences is responsible for carrying out a forensic and therapeutic examination of the victim of rape or sexual assault. FNEs will work in a SARC, alongside a crisis worker, police officers, social workers and staff from external agencies, who are all involved in supporting the victim.

The examination begins with the FNE spending time with the victim, getting to know them and building a therapeutic relationship based on honesty and trust. Anyone who has been raped has had control taken away from them so it is important that the FNE offers them choices and the opportunity to make decisions about the examination and their treatment plan.

Knowledge of the psychological response to sexual trauma is imperative, if the FNE is to understand how the individual may react. For example, many people would say, 'If someone tried to rape me I would run away.' However, once someone is in that situation, the brain considers what action is most likely to bring about survival. If submission is most likely to make you survive, then that is what the brain tells you to do. After the event, victims will often ask themselves why they didn't run away. They will then find a way to justify (wrongly) what has happened by blaming themselves (Lodrick 2007).

The first part of the examination involves taking an initial disclosure from the police officer or, in the case of a self-referral, from the crisis worker. The purpose of the initial disclosure is to establish the nature of the offence that has occurred, thus enabling the FNE to consider both therapeutic and forensic elements that will need to be taken into account during the examination. The FNE will discuss the examination with the victim and ensure that they have a thorough understanding of the process and any statement or disclosure the FNE may have to make to the police or in court. For example, the victim will need to be aware of how confidential information will be disseminated and how this may be used in a court setting. Consent for DVD evidence or photography will be discussed. Explaining to the victim about the rationale for taking swabs is important, so that they feel they are in control of the examination and have a complete understanding of why certain procedures need to take place.

The forensic examination is a thorough and detailed physical examination, which covers every part of the body and involves taking forensic swabs where indicated. The FNE collects hair, nail samples and nail scrapings, draws a body map and swabs any injuries or areas where the victim indicates the perpetrator may have touched. They also examine the external and internal genitalia. For females, the FNE would use a speculum to examine the high vagina and swab the endo-cervical canal. For males, the penis and surrounding area is examined and swabbed; and in the case of anal rape, anal and rectal swabs are taken. If a victim refuses an internal examination, the FNE can take 'blind' swabs (where a swab is inserted without instrumentation, such as a speculum or proctoscope). In all these cases, it is important that consent is sought and the victim is given a choice, as this enables them to take back some control.

Any injuries will be body-mapped and consent will be sought to have a Scenes of Crime Officer (SOCO) photograph the injuries. If the examination is as a result of a self-referral, most SARC staff have been trained to take photographic evidence of injuries. The FNE would be expected to provide a professional opinion to the investigating officer regarding any injuries found, in terms of their age and provenance. Clothing and underwear may also be kept and, along with the forensic swabs, this would be submitted as evidence for forensic analysis in a specialist laboratory.

Pre-pubertal children have an external examination of the genitalia, which includes commenting on any hymenal injury or anal abnormalities. The examination of pre-pubertal children is a speciality within sexual offences medicine, and is often carried out jointly by a Consultant Paediatrician and a Forensic Medical Examiner. The interpretation of paediatric genital findings can be difficult, with many different potential diagnoses complicating the findings. It takes a lot of support, supervision and experience to undertake this type of examination.

The therapeutic aspect of the examination includes risk assessment for self-harm, and any safeguarding concerns or child sexual exploitation indicators. The FNE will administer emergency hormonal contraception and prophylaxis against HIV (HIV PEP or Post Exposure Prophylaxis) and begin an accelerated course of Hepatitis B vaccine. The FNE will also refer the victim on to a General Practitioner, Sexual Health Services, Mental Health Services, Counselling, and a team of Independent Sexual Violence Advisers. Ideally, the FNE will be a supplementary and independent prescriber. This will enable the nurse to work completely autonomously and will ensure continuity of care.

The FNE may also be required to provide a statement (CJ ACT 1967, s9, MC Rules 1981, r70), (Crown Prosecution Service 2014). This will form part of the police submission to the Crown Prosecution Service (CPS). The CPS will then make a decision regarding prosecution. If a case goes to trial, the FNE may be required to give evidence. This may be as a professional or expert witness, depending on the FNE's experience and qualifications.

Traditionally, only doctors have been able to provide an expert opinion (Pyrek 2006). However, now that nurses have more experience as well as recognised forensic qualifications, this is set to change. The *Criminal Procedure Rules* Sec 33.2 (Ministry of Justice 2013) outline the qualities of an expert witness: '…an expert must help the court to achieve the overriding objective by giving objective, unbiased opinions on matters within his expertise…' In Section 33.3, the text continues: 'the report will contain the experience and qualifications of the individual expert along with relevant literature to support the opinion and ensure the facts stated in the report are within the expert's own knowledge'.

Not all FMEs or FNEs will necessarily fit this profile, and individual nurses therefore need to understand what is required of a professional or expert witness. Specific court-room training and statement-writing skills are a mandatory part of the FNE training. Gee (1996) suggests that this training should be both theoretical and experiential, including actual experience of standing in the witness box and being cross-examined in a courtroom.

## Challenges of the FNE's role

There is always a tension between the needs of the criminal justice system, the needs of the victim and the demands of the nurse's professional code. The FNE is obliged to be objective and balanced, whilst acting as an agent of the court. However, the victim is owed a high degree of professionalism by the FNE, in terms of knowledge base and the quality of care provided. This tension is particularly acute during the disclosure of evidence and the content of medical/nursing notes.

When consent is requested, it is made very clear to the individual that they are not only consenting to the examination, but also to the disclosure of information by means of a report or statement. The FNE will have two sets of notes, one of which covers the forensic part of the examination. This provides all the information needed to support a written statement and/or disclosure of the notes in court. The second, separate set of notes, 'Confidential Medical Aftercare', deals entirely with the therapeutic aspects of the examination and consultation. The criminal justice system is aware that these notes exist but would rarely ask to see them, and if so it would be at the direction of a judge. Technically, however, all medical records may be disclosed – even notes held by an individual GP. Occasionally, where an individual's well-being is of concern (for example, when safeguarding a child), the FNE may have to break that confidentiality and escalate those concerns to a higher level of authority.

More than anything, any victim of sexual violence wants to be believed. If they report to the police, they will immediately be asked to undertake a medical examination. Victims often feel that they cannot say no to this, as otherwise they will not be believed. Therefore, throughout the criminal justice process, the victim may have to agree to things they may not wish to happen – in order to ensure that people will believe them. The benefit of the self-referral option can be clearly seen here. With self-referral, the individual is in control of the process. If they want a medical examination, this will be made available to them. If they do not, that is a choice that they are free to make. Victims are always reassured by the FNE that they are believed, whatever decision they make.

## Professional development and training

Training and continuing professional development are important in this area of practice and it is recommended that all healthcare practitioners undertaking this work have a robust induction from their employer as well as regular supervision and appropriate updates (Crilly & Combes *et al.* 2011). The induction course should cover all aspects of the sexual offences examination, including an overview of the Sexual Offences Act, anatomy and physiology and therapeutic aspects of care. A forensic scientist will provide practical training on the labelling and chain of custody elements of evidence collection, and theoretical input regarding the specific scientific foundations of forensic sampling. Separate courtroom training will be provided by barristers; this will include statement-writing and experience in giving evidence and being cross-examined.

The psychological aspects of sexual violence will be covered by an experienced psychologist. This is an important and often undervalued aspect of the training. It equips FNEs with an understanding of why victims react to sexual violence in a particular way psychologically and emotionally. As in any speciality, training is an important aspect of professional development. Training to deal with sexual offences also covers child and adult safeguarding, consent and child sexual exploitation. Local training in SARC-related issues is provided, and this includes practical training in the use of colposcopic evidence collection, along with local referral pathways.

Once the induction programme has been completed, the FNE will be required to shadow an experienced examiner, gradually taking greater responsibility for the examination and assessment for therapeutic aftercare. Alongside this, they will complete a skills-based training log. This training log can mirror the Compendium of Validated Evidence, which is a requirement of the Diploma in Forensic and Clinical Aspects of Sexual Assault (DFCASA) examination. All FNEs must undertake a recognised Sexual Offences Qualification, and it is recommended that by 2015 all Forensic Examiners should have the DFCASA.

## Conclusion

Nurses currently practising as FNEs are gaining experience and expertise; and, as more nurses enter this area of practice, it is likely that the majority of sexual offences examinations will be undertaken by nurses. A study by Cowley *et al.* (2014) examined UK forensic nurses' experiences of their role. Based on this study, there is a collective view that being an FNE is about putting the health and well-being of the individual victim first. Respondents also emphasised the importance of empathy and therapeutic intervention in their work. Whilst FNEs understand their obligation to be objective and act as agents of the court, it is clear that they can also provide a holistic, compassionate assessment of the individual. An experienced nurse, with good physical assessment skills and a prescribing qualification, has the perfect background to work with victims of sexual violence (Waszak 2013).

The challenge to all FNEs is to ensure that they constantly strive to develop their skills and their knowledge base. This involves taking a victim-focused approach to sexual violence as well as undertaking further quantitative and qualitative research, which can enhance the current evidence base. It is imperative for the FNE community to keep expanding the evidence base in order to underpin and develop the care provided.

# References

Campbell, D. (3 October 2011). Rapists escaping justice because police surgeons not up to the job, say critics. *The Guardian*. http://www.theguardian.com/lifeandstyle/2011/oct/03/police-surgeons-letting-rapists-free (Last accessed 12 August 2013).

Campbell, R. (2006). Rape survivors' experiences with legal and medical systems: Do rape victim advocates make a difference? *Violence Against Women*. **12** (1), 30–45.

COSAI (2013). Models of intervention for women who have been sexually assaulted in Europe – A review of the literature. http://www.cosai.eu/products/documents/literature-review.html (Last accessed: 15 May 2014).

Cowley, R., Walsh, E. & Horrocks, J. (2014). The role of the sexual assault nurse examiner in England: Nurse experiences and perspectives. *Journal of Forensic Nursing*. **10** (2), 77–83.

Coy, M., Kelly, L. & Foord, J. (2007). *Map of Gaps: The postcode lottery of Violence Against Women support services*. London: End Violence Against Women.

Crilly, T., Combes, G., Davidson, D., Joyner, O. & Doidge, S. (2011). *Feasibility of Transferring Budget & Commissioning Responsibility for Forensic Sexual Offences Examination Work from the Police to NHS: Evidence Base to Support the Impact Assessment.* University of Birmingham & Tavistock Institute.

Crown Prosecution Service (2014). http://www.cps.gov.uk/legal/d_to_g/evidence_admiting_evidence_under_the_cja (Last accessed 18 May 2014).

Cybulska, B. (2007). Sexual assault key issues. *Journal of the Royal Society of Medicine*. **100**, 321–24.

Faculty of Forensic and Legal Medicine (2014). *Recommendations for the collection of forensic specimens from Complainants and Suspects*. http://fflm.ac.uk/librarydetail/4000068 (Last accessed 12 May 2014).

Gee, D.J. (1996). 'Chapter 8: Training the medical witness' in *Limitations of Expert Evidence*. London: Royal College of Physicians.

Heenan, M. & Murray, S. (2006). Study of reported rapes in Victoria 2000–2003. Summary research report, Melbourne, Victoria. State-wide steering committee to Reduce Sexual Assault.

Home Office (2010). Interim Government Response to the Stern Review 2010. http://webarchive.nationalarchives.gov.uk/20100418065537/http://equalities.gov.uk/pdf/Response_to_Stern_finalWeb.pdf (Last accessed 25 March 2014).

Home Office (2011). Government Response to the Stern Review 2011. (Last accessed 25 March 2014).

Itzin, C. (2008). Tackling the health and mental health effects of domestic and sexual violence and childhood sexual abuse. *Psychiatric Bulletin*. **32**, 448–50.

Kelly, L. & Regan, L. (2003). *Good Practice in Medical Responses to Recently Reported Rape, Especially Forensic Examinations: A Briefing Paper for the Daphne Strengthening the Linkages Project*. London: Child and Woman Abuse Studies Unit, London Metropolitan University.

Lodrick, Z. (2007). Psychological trauma – what every trauma worker should know. *The British Journal of Psychotherapy Integration*. **4** (2), 1–19.

Ministry of Justice (2013). *Criminal Procedure Rules*. https://www.gov.uk/government/uploads/system/uploads/attachment_data/file/97907/government-stern-review.pdf (Last accessed 12 May 2014).

Pyrek, A. (2006). *Forensic Nursing*. Florida, USA: CRC Press.

Rees, G. & Jamieson, L. (2012). *The Role and Work of Forensic Nurses in Sexual Assault Cases: An International Comparative Approach: ESRC Impact Report, RES-000-22-4084*. Swindon: ESRC.

Regan, L. & Lovett, J. (2004). *Forensic nursing: an option for improving responses to reported rape and sexual assault*. Home Office Development and Practice Report 31. London: Home Office, Research Development & Statistics Directorate.

Rights of Women (2011). *From Report to Court: A handbook for the adult survivors of sexual violence*. London: Rights of Women.

Survivors Trust UK (2014).
http://www.thesurvivorstrust.org/latest-news/funding-announced-help-male-victims-sexual-violence
(Last accessed 12 May 2014).

Temkin, J. & Krahe, B. (2008). *Sexual Assault and the JusticeGap: A question of attitude.* London: Hart.

Waszak, D. (2013). S.A.N.E Sexual Assault Nurse Examiner, RN + CSI = SANE. http://www.workingnurse.com/articles/S-A-N-E-Sexual-Assault-Nurse-Examiner (Last accessed 5 May 2014).

Westmarland, N., Alderson, S. & Kirkham, L. (2012). *The Health, Mental Health and Well-being Benefits of Rape Crisis Counselling.* Durham: Durham University and Northern Rock Foundation.

# 5

# Caring in court

Richard Evans

This chapter considers actual and potential roles for nurses in assessing, supporting and caring for individuals appearing in court settings. It looks at nurses' relationships with non-health and social care professionals and organisations working in the court environment, and explores the complex dynamics that often exist in these relationships. The unique and fascinating scenarios that arise in court are discussed in the context of the nursing role. Confidentiality and the sharing of information are key considerations in all health and social care settings (Nursing and Midwifery Council 2008), and these issues present significant and unique challenges for the nurse in court. All relevant areas of nursing care are explored, including physical health, mental health and learning disability. Wider considerations include discussion of mental capacity, the court structure and the emergence of liaison and diversion services across the country.

There is a dearth of literature associated with the role of the nurse in court. However, in addition to my own experiences as a mental health nurse working in the court environment, I have been able to garner information and opinion from my nursing colleagues and from wider criminal justice agencies who work alongside us in the courts. This has included discussions with solicitors, legal advisers, district judges, probation staff and other court staff personnel. Perhaps most significantly, I have borne in mind the feedback and views of the service users I have encountered whilst working in the courts.

## Changes in nursing in the court

In terms of the nursing role, the court has seen significant change and development over the past decade. This has been particularly evident since the Bradley Report (2009) and the governmental interest and funding that followed its publication. Lord Bradley's review of the treatment of people with mental health problems or learning disabilities in the criminal justice system appears to have generated sufficient support to initiate meaningful change in the provision of healthcare across the criminal justice pathway, including the courts.

There is growing evidence suggesting that financial savings can be made by identifying appropriate health and social care pathways as alternatives to custody or as supplements to traditional community sentences (Sainsbury Centre 2009). Recent research indicates that service users are more likely to engage with health and social care services if they are also engaged with the Probation Service (Byng *et al.* 2012). This highlights the need for health and social care services to actively participate and contribute to the court process, where key decisions that impact an individual's future are being made. The court is a place where health services, in conjunction with criminal justice agencies, can introduce measures that may significantly improve the lives of those individuals. Across the country, nurses are increasingly meeting this need by performing a role that is becoming an integral and familiar part of daily court proceedings.

The specific roles and responsibilities of the nurse in court will form the greater part of this chapter. However, I will begin with a brief outline of the environment and context in which the work of the nurse takes place.

## The court environment

For the sake of simplicity, the legal and court system, including its structure, role and function, will be discussed here in the broadest terms. The legal system is fraught with technicalities and exceptions that do not required discussion and are not practically possible to cover in this chapter. Nevertheless, there is an evident benefit in knowing the basic foundations and principles of the law and the courts, in order to value and understand the role of the nurse.

The United Kingdom does not have a single unified legal system. Effectively, there are three separate systems, which are divided as follows: England and Wales; Scotland; and, thirdly, Ireland. All three systems are complex in nature and structure, and are made up of several divisions and tiers. There are many different types of court operating in the UK, each performing different roles within their specific jurisdictions. For the nurse in court, it is important to have a basic awareness of the wider court structure and have a deeper understanding of the specific area of work their role involves. However, there is no role-specific and nationally recognised training programme for healthcare professionals working within court settings. This need is met by locally devised, in-house training packages.

Broadly speaking, cases heard in courts can be divided into two categories: civil cases and criminal cases. Civil cases are predominantly, but not exclusively, heard at the County or Civil Court. Civil cases can relate to individuals or organisations and deal with matters such as land ownership, disputes between a landlord and a tenant, consumer disputes (such as faulty goods or services), and small claims. Criminal cases, where a specific crime is alleged to have taken place, are heard at the Magistrate's Court and the

Crown Court. All criminal cases begin at the Magistrate's Court and only the more serious cases are referred to the Crown Court for a trial by jury or for sentencing. This chapter will focus on the role of the nurse in criminal courts, namely the Magistrate's Court and Crown Court.

The Crown Court is an area of the criminal justice system that is frequently portrayed in television and film drama. Most people will be able to picture a courtroom, based on what they have seen on television – a judge in a gown and wig, presiding over a courtroom, complete with barristers, with a witness being cross-examined and a 12-person jury listening intently. By and large, this is quite an accurate picture.

However, the Magistrate's Court is perhaps less familiar and certainly not so widely portrayed in the media. The Magistrate's Court is less formal, with no requirement to wear court dress. There are no trials by jury and, rather than a judge, there are more likely to be three lay magistrates, who are volunteers from the local community and have no formal legal training. The magistrates are guided by a court-appointed legal adviser. Given that the Crown Court is far more familiar to the public and portrayed so widely in the media, it may come as a surprise to hear that, according to the Crown Prosecution Service (see www.cps.org.uk), 95 per cent of all criminal cases are actually dealt with at the Magistrate's Court. Only the most serious and complex of criminal cases are dealt with at the Crown Court. For this reason, discussion of the nursing role in clinical practice in this chapter will focus specifically on the Magistrate's Court.

As the Magistrate's Court is the starting point for all criminal cases, it is an ideal setting in which to identify those in need of support from health and social care services at an early stage. Court-based health services appear to be most effective when they have established links with health services operating in other criminal justice areas, such as police stations and prisons (James 1999). From this point of view, the Magistrate's Court provides a good opportunity for health services to intervene and assess for a wide variety of needs.

## Health services in court

The health and social well-being of people who come into contact with the criminal justice system is receiving great interest and increased attention, and it is now more common to take a holistic approach to the needs of these individuals. Many people believe that tackling their complex health and social care issues is likely to help reduce reoffending rates and engagement with services. However, although Lord Bradley alludes to the benefits associated with increased provision of healthcare services across criminal justice settings in his landmark report (Bradley 2009), there is insufficient evidence to quantify specific benefits such as reoffending rates. This lack of evidence has since been acknowledged by the Offender Health Research Network (2011) and Kane *et al.* (2012).

Time spent in court can usually be viewed as a relatively brief interim period before a period of prison custody, or between custody and release into the community. Access to healthcare services to address physical health concerns is readily available in the community and also at the prison. Consequently, nurses in the court provide minimal physical healthcare, as the window of opportunity is small. It can be assumed that anyone suffering from a significant physical health problem will have been identified, assessed and treated at the police station before they arrive at court. The question of whether the person is 'fit to be detained' and 'fit for interview' is a requirement under the Police and Criminal Evidence Act 1984 (PACE). It will therefore already have been established and addressed appropriately at the earliest stage at the police station. If the individual has arrived from prison, prison healthcare staff will have addressed any physical health need. PACE sets out the statutory requirement of the police to consider the health of an individual detained in custody. While at the court, PACE is no longer applicable.

Whilst the individual is at the court, which may range from 2 to 10 hours on a given day, their physical health needs are met by the court custody contractors, who include private security firms. This approach appears to rely on nurses, and other healthcare professionals at the police station or prison, planning interim management of physical health problems and providing a care plan for the court custody staff to follow. Court custody staff are trained in how to administer first aid, and sometimes (but not always) defibrillators are available and can be used in an emergency by custody staff. Some areas have an additional on-call facility to access support around physical health advice. However, this facility is not widely available and its provision appears to depend on individual contractor arrangements.

If an individual's physical health deteriorates in court, or in the event of an emergency, the emergency services would be called. Clearly, this is by no means a comprehensive way of delivering effective physical healthcare but the system is likely to remain as it is, due to the statutory measures put in place in police custody suites and prisons to assess, identify and treat physical health problems at the earliest opportunity. Physical health interventions required during the time in court and requiring custody staff to follow up, including administration of medication, should be recorded on the prisoner escort records. Local protocols will need to be in place for the administration of medication, to incorporate safe handling and storage.

The majority of individuals appearing in court do so either by summons or 'on bail' and arrive from the community, rather than from custody. Most of these individuals will have either been granted 'bail' by the police or will be attending their second or subsequent hearing as their case progresses. In practice, this means they will be walking in through the main entrance of the court, along with the general public. This is usually the case for those individuals whose criminal charges are deemed less serious or where no imminent risk of further offending has been identified (for example, those accused of driving offences).

When individuals appear in court 'on bail', there seems to be even less emphasis on their physical health needs. They are not considered to be within the remit of the court custody contractor because they are not actually in custody. As in any building used by the public, first aid provision must be available in the court. However, despite increased attention being focused on the health of individuals coming into contact with the criminal justice system, little research appears to have been done on the provision of physical healthcare in courts, especially when compared with mental health and learning disability services provision.

## Liaison and diversion

Mental health, learning disability and mental capacity are all factors that require consideration in criminal law. Consequently, when these issues arise during criminal proceedings they usually receive great emphasis and attention. The presence of a mental illness, learning disability or a lack of mental capacity may well affect the way an individual is dealt with by the criminal justice system, as outlined in the Criminal Justice Act (2003). When such a concern is raised, the requirement to assess the needs of the individual, and address any identified difficulties, becomes prominent in the minds of the defence solicitor, prosecutor and those responsible for passing sentence – both magistrates and judges. There are several stages in the court proceedings when these matters are questioned, discussed and addressed accordingly.

Historically, criminal courts have relied solely on expert psychiatric opinion – in the form of reports completed by psychiatrists. In order to obtain these reports, courts have used 'remand to custody' as a means to facilitate psychiatric assessment (Rickford & Edgar 2005). However, for many reasons (including difficulties in identifying suitable psychiatrists and issues around funding), such reports invariably take several months to complete, incur significant cost, and often vary in quality and usefulness (Hean et al. 2008). Consequently, there has been an increasing emphasis on the need for more timely and reliable interventions at the earliest opportunity along the criminal justice pathway (Centre for Mental Health 2014). Liaison and diversion services, predominantly managed and staffed by nurses (Kane et al. 2012), are specifically geared towards meeting the complex needs of the individuals who come into contact with criminal justice agencies, while liaising and sharing information with all those involved so that informed decisions can be made (Dean 2013, Hean et al. 2010).

At the time of writing, there is no official or agreed definition of the term 'liaison and diversion', although the concepts and ideals of the professionals working under this banner are widely understood. 'Liaison and diversion' is the overarching term used to describe the services that work along the criminal justice pathway, identifying, assessing and addressing the needs of individuals who present with mental health problems or learning disabilities. To be effective, these services must ensure fluid transfer of information between health and social care services and the criminal justice agencies, so that informed decisions can be made. There will be an emphasis on identifying meaningful and appropriate options for diversion away from the criminal justice system into areas where treatment, care and support are delivered.

The term 'diversion' was originally used to describe the redirecting of an individual from the criminal justice system into an appropriate health and social care setting. In more recent times, this term appears to have evolved to encompass something more complex. Diversion now includes cases where the health and criminal justice systems work alongside each other simultaneously. There are many examples of liaison and diversion services in practice (McMillan 2009, Centre for Mental Health 2014).

The recent surge in attention and funding being directed towards liaison and diversion services may imply that this has happened in response to a new way of thinking or due to the results of new research. However, the concept of liaison and diversion is actually not new at all. A number of court-based liaison and diversion services have been operational since the 1980s, and particularly the early 1990s, many of which were conceived as a consequence of the Home Office Circular 66/90 (Home Office 1990) and the Reed Report (1992). Both these influential publications advocated the implementation of specialist services to help divert people away from custody into hospitals and towards more appropriate types of care and treatment. This view has changed very little in over twenty years.

The idea of finding an alternative to prison for those identified as having a mental health problem or learning disabilities can in fact be traced even further back. John Howard, the eighteenth-century prison reformer who made revolutionary changes to the prison system, was particularly astute in identifying areas in need of improvement and development. He was perhaps the first to acknowledge the need for healthcare provision not only within prison but also as an alternative to prison. The following excerpt from his writings on the state of the prisons was used as evidence to a House of Commons Committee in 1784:

> **Many of the bridewells are crowded and offensive, because the rooms which were designed for prisoners are occupied by lunatics… No care is taken of them, although it is probable that by medicines, and proper regimen, some of them might be restored to their senses, and usefulness in life…**
>
> *(Howard 1784)*

The language used by Howard may well be archaic but the concerns remain very pertinent today.

## The role of the nurse in court

The court is a place where the details of individuals' offending, risk, health and social circumstances are discussed a great deal, as many decisions need to be made in the light of all these factors. In view of all this, the court is also often a place where issues and problems are raised. The impact of mental health, learning disability and mental capacity on behaviour is of particular interest and concern to the court. This is partly due to legal requirements that must be satisfied (the Powers of Criminal Courts (Sentencing) Act 2000), as well as moral and ethical factors that must be considered.

Consequently, the role of the nurse in court is mainly focused on addressing the mental health, learning disability and mental capacity needs of the individual. Nurses have been performing such roles in courts for over two decades, although not in all areas of the country. The role of the nurse in court falls firmly within the wider concept of 'liaison and diversion', which has returned to the fore in national debate in recent years, since Lord Keith Bradley carried out his review of people with mental health problems and learning disabilities in the criminal justice system (Bradley 2009). This review was commissioned in order to help determine the effectiveness of existing services in the diversion of offenders away from the criminal justice system into more appropriate settings and identify the barriers to such diversion.

The window of opportunity at the court is relatively small and so the type of work undertaken by the nurse is focused accordingly. There is no opportunity to deliver lengthy treatment or therapies during this period. The work of the nurse in court, in the context of a liaison and diversion service, can be divided into three key stages: early identification; assessment; and liaison. These stages will now be discussed in greater detail.

## Early identification

Identifying individuals who are likely to benefit from assessment, support and treatment at the earliest opportunity is a crucial task in a liaison and diversion service. The nurse in court is likely to be the only registered healthcare professional in the building and, as such, will often be viewed as the resident specialist and point of contact for all matters relating to health. There is a need to be mindful of one's own identity, values and code of practice as a nurse (Nursing and Midwifery Council 2008); otherwise there can be a risk of gravitating towards the values and ethics of other non-healthcare professionals.

The nurse should not rely solely on referrals from the court staff. The majority of liaison and diversion services implement some form of proactive identification of individuals who may benefit from health and social care services. For example, many nurses cross-check details of those appearing in court that day against local healthcare records in order to identify individuals known to be in current or previous contact with health services, such as the community mental health team.

The criminal courts are open between the set hours of 9am and 5pm, and the individual's attendance is geared towards the court hearing itself and not towards the activities of a health service. Delays and obstructions to the legal process are costly and frustrating for all involved; nurses must therefore be constantly mindful of all this and deliver their interventions in a timely fashion, so not to cause unnecessary disruption to the proceedings.

The court is usually a bustling environment, with a mix of professionals performing a variety of duties and holding differing responsibilities. Nurses need to understand and appreciate these other roles in order to work alongside other professionals effectively and cohesively. For this reason, it may be helpful to consider their roles in some detail.

# Solicitors

Solicitors are legally trained and focused on attaining the most positive (in their view) outcome for the individual they represent. They are often under pressure and have many clients to support on any one day. They can be adept at recognising when there is a clear difficulty with their client's capacity or mental health. The solicitor's desire to obtain the best possible outcome for their client may complement the nurse's need to assess, support and identify a care pathway for the individual. This usually means that the solicitor (and subsequently the court) will be willing to wait for the necessary health assessments and interventions to be completed.

At first glance, it would seem that the relationship between solicitor and court healthcare worker can only be a fruitful one. However, waiting for a mental health assessment to be completed is not always considered a priority in the court process, and an assessment will frequently be halted so that the court hearing can continue. In this respect, solicitors can sometimes obstruct the role of the nurse. Ultimately, there must be a balance between meeting the needs of the individual and allowing the court to continue in a timely manner. Solicitors, by their nature, are skilled and confident in debating and putting forward strong arguments for and against issues that, at times, overlap with the role and opinions of the nurse.

## Custody staff

Various private contractors operate this service across the country. Local agreements are often needed to ensure good working relationships and mutual understanding of roles and responsibilities. For instance, access to the individual and the prisoner escort records is essential. Information sharing helps produce improved risk assessments for the custody staff and the nurse.

## Court building security staff

Security staff are also provided by a private contractor, who may differ from the contractor who provides the custody staff. Court nurses have to work in isolation, away from the safety of a hospital ward or team base. They may therefore need to consult court security staff when seeing someone in an interview room that is separate from the custody area. The court security staff will be the first responders if an emergency situation occurs within an area of the court that is accessible to the public.

## Probation staff

Probation officers are often adept at assessing the needs and risks of offenders with complex presentations. Risk assessment is as important for probation officers as it is for healthcare professionals. In the National Probation Service (NPS), risk is assessed and measured with arguably more formal and recognised tools than those used by healthcare professionals. These tools include, for instance, the Offender Assessment System (OASys) used in England and Wales. The court is the place where mental health services have the first contact with the NPS. This provides an opportunity to create links between the community-based input from the mental health provider and the NPS as the offender manager. There are clear benefits to both services in maintaining this relationship, as their combined expertise will inevitably inform risk assessments, care planning and support the wider needs of the individual. Furthermore, a recent study by Byng *et al.* (2012) suggests that offenders who are managed by probation officers are more likely to engage with health and social care services in the community than those who are not.

Brooker *et al.* (2011) suggest that the mental health needs of offenders are still not being identified by probation services. The research highlighted that only 33 per cent of individuals assessed as having a psychotic disorder, by the mental health service, were also identified on probation records as having a psychotic disorder. This indicates that better inter-professional links still need to be made.

## Assessment and the nurse patient relationship

The nurse in court will routinely be required to complete assessments and to provide support without advance warning or prior knowledge of the individual. Issues and concerns often arise on the day of a court appearance and these concerns need to be addressed immediately.

Individuals appearing in court frequently present with complex and diverse needs. The nurse requires well-developed assessment skills to ensure that all their needs are identified and addressed. This is often difficult, as the nurse may only have access to limited historical information prior to the assessment. Safeguarding issues frequently arise from these assessments, and the nurse will need to make arrangements for these issues to be addressed.

The nurse working in court requires a wide and varied knowledge of both primary and secondary care services to ensure that appropriate onward referrals can be made in a timely fashion.

The assessment undertaken in court is not simply a process of gathering information, as the client may be at a point of crisis. The nurse will therefore need to ensure that there is a supportive element to the interaction at all stages: in court; in custody; and while the individual is on bail.

### In court

Individuals appearing in court may do so primarily in two ways – 'on bail' and 'in custody'. There is also a third, more modern possibility, in that courts now routinely use video links in certain types of hearing, where defendants are 'present' at their trial through the use of videoconferencing technology. Video link hearings usually take place between the prison and the court. Bear in mind that healthcare jargon and terminology may not be easily understood by those working in the criminal justice system. The ability to explain complex issues in a bite-sized, digestible manner, without using jargon, is essential in inter-professional working.

## In custody

The individual may well be frightened, confused and uncertain about what might happen. They will have already been in custody overnight, possibly for the first time, and the implications and magnitude of the previous day's incident, arrest, interview and charging may only just be sinking in. They may be apprehensive about appearing in a courtroom for the first time and may not have even sought legal advice and representation. The nurse will not only need to assess the individual's health needs but also utilise their understanding of the criminal justice process to support and empower the individual to make important decisions that may affect their liberty.

## On bail

The individual will be appearing of their own volition, even if they have been instructed to do so, and may have made arrangements for family members and friends to be present to support them. Conversely, this may be their second or third appearance in court as part of the ongoing criminal justice process. Only a minority of criminal cases are dealt with at one hearing at court. The majority require several hearings to consider all the available evidence, for a plea to be entered (Guilty or Not Guilty), for a trial to take place (witnesses will need to be called and time allowed for the court to complete this process), and for probation to assess the individual (post-conviction) and make recommendations in terms of sentencing options in the community.

There may well be times when the individual being supported attributes some of the sanctions being placed on them to the nurse. They may also see the role of the nurse as a failure if the criminal justice outcome is not the one they wanted. The criminal justice outcome will of course take into account the assessment and shared information, but decisions made by the courts are based on many other factors. Mental health is a contributing factor, not the only factor.

# Liaison in court

The nurse in court will routinely be asked to share information with the criminal justice agencies so that they are better able to make informed decisions. Consenting to share information, in order to manage risk and improve safeguarding, forms a key part of the nurse's role.

The nurse will be expected to have knowledge of, and access to, a multitude of care pathway options. They will also be required to identify appropriate avenues of care, support and treatment within a limited timeframe. There will invariably be times when the expectations of the court and wider criminal justice agencies exceed what is reasonably and clinically possible for the nurse to achieve. In such cases, it will be the role of the nurse to educate the court in this respect and to offer alternative options.

Establishing a good exchange of information between the nurse in court and other court professionals and agencies is fundamental to the success of the nurse's role and the nurse's ability to help service users. As in any area of healthcare, gaining the consent of the service user should always be the starting point, before any disclosures are made (Nursing and Midwifery Council 2008).

When information is being shared so frequently, it stands to reason that there should be protocols and guidelines in place to ensure that nurses deliver care safely. In situations where consent has not been gained, consideration must be given to the Mental Capacity Act (2005) and *The Code* (Nursing and Midwifery Council 2008) to determine whether it is in the public interest to share certain information. The nurse's ability to clearly assess and identify risk will be key in deciding whether to share information without consent. Locally agreed information-sharing protocols and service level agreements, which stipulate the boundaries within which healthcare professionals must work when collecting, storing and distributing confidential information, should also be in place.

In addition, the nurse should consider the format in which information is shared. Clarity often comes with familiarity, so it may be preferable for the same formats to be consistently used when presenting information. For example, information-sharing may take the form of a letter or a written report (such as a Health and Social Circumstance Report).

In order to put theory in the context of practice, the following two case studies are presented for reflection.

## Case study one

A district judge halts a sentencing hearing at a Magistrate's Court due to concerns relating to the offender's mental health. The judge asks for a mental health assessment to be completed. The mental health nurse based at the Magistrate's Court is called to the courtroom and informed of the concerns. The case is temporarily adjourned to allow the assessment to take place. The offender is agreeable to being seen and the assessment takes place the same day.

The mental health nurse forms an opinion with regard to presenting problems and appropriate care pathways, and promptly puts this in writing. Having gained consent from the individual, the court reconvenes to consider the outcome of the assessment. In this case, the pathway identified is an onward referral to a community mental health team, with a view to further assessment and treatment as appropriate.

The court decides to postpone sentencing to hear about the individual's progress in a month's time. After a month, the court reconvenes to consider the case. The nurse provides feedback relating to the subsequent engagement with community services and the long-term treatment plan. The court considers this information and passes a sentence that is appropriate and proportionate, given the individual's mental health problems and the severity and nature of the offence.

## Case study two

An individual known to local mental health services is present in the court custody area, having been arrested and charged with an offence the previous day. The nurse has identified the individual by proactively screening the names of all individuals in the court that day and cross-checking with local health records. The nurse is also approached by the individual's legal representative. The nurse attends the custody area and offers the individual an opportunity to be assessed. Although initially reluctant, the individual eventually agrees to be seen.

The assessment is completed and evidence of serious mental illness is identified. Following discussion with the court legal adviser and local mental health services, a further assessment under the Mental Health Act is indicated. The nurse initiates arrangements for the assessment to take place at the court the same day. The nurse is informed by the court that they wish to hear the outcome of the Mental Health Act assessment and that this will inform their decision. The nurse confirms with the Crown Prosecution Service that there will be no opposition to the individual being detained under the Mental Health Act and transferred to hospital. The magistrates adjourn the case, to be reviewed at a later date.

## Conclusion

The emergence of liaison and diversion services has provided a way for nurses to perform a pivotal and influential role within the criminal courts. Nurses are increasingly seen as a lynchpin, interfacing between the key decision-makers in the courts and the health and social care services responsible for providing treatment and support. It is hoped that the rapid growth of such services, supported by the recommendations made in *The Bradley Report* (2009), will be approved by the government in due course. Governmental approval of such services will pave the way for further expansion, national coverage and long-term commitment to the role of nurses in court.

In contrast, the physical health needs of the person in court are not so comprehensively met. Physical health needs are not considered in the same manner as issues relating to mental health and learning disability. However, in the light of the growing acceptance that the wider needs of offenders should be considered at any opportunity, it is possible that the role of nurses in court will develop further in the coming years, as their value and contribution to patient care is made explicit.

# References

Centre for Mental Health (2014). *Keys to diversion: Best practice for offenders with multiple needs.* London: Centre for Mental Health.

Criminal Justice Act (2003). http://www.legislation.gov.uk/ukpga/2003/44/contents  (Last accessed 1 July 2014).

Bradley, K. (2009). *The Bradley Report.* London: Department of Health, The Stationery Office.

Brooker, C., Sirdifield, C., Blizard, R., Maxwell-Harrison, D., Tetley, D., Moran, P., Pluck, G., Chafer, A., Denney, D. & Turner, M. (2011). *An Investigation into the Prevalence of Mental Health Disorder and Patterns of Health Service Access in a Probation Population.* Lincoln: University of Lincoln.

Byng, R., Quinn, C., Sheaff, R., Samele, C., Duggan, S., Harrison, D., Owens, C., Smithson, P., Annison, J., Brown, C., Taylor, R., Henley, W., Qureshi, A., Shenton, D., Porter, I., Warrington, C. & Campbell, J. (2012). Final report, care for offenders: continuity of access. London: National Institute for Health Research.

Dean, E. (2013). A nursing alternative to prison. *Nursing Standard.* **28** (6), 20–22.

Hean, S., Warr, J. & Staddon, S. (2008). *Report on Phase 1 Baseline of the Evaluation of the South West Mental Health Assessment and Advice Pilot.* Bournemouth: School of Health and Social Care, Bournemouth University.

Hean, S., Heaslip, S., Warr, J., Bell, H. & Staddon, S. (2010). A women's worker in court: A more appropriate service for women defendants with mental health issues? *Perspectives in Public Health.* **130** (2), 91–96.

Home Office (1990). *Provision for Mentally Disordered Offenders.* Home Office Circular 66/90. London: The Stationery Office.

Howard, J. (2010). *The State of Prisons in England and Wales* [1784]. 3rd ed. Warrington: Gale ECCO.

James, D. (1999). Court diversion at 10 years: Can it work, does it work and has it a future? *The Journal of Forensic Psychiatry.* **10** (3), 507–24.

Home Office (1984). *Police and Criminal Evidence Act.* London: The Stationery Office.

Kane, E., Jordan, M., Beeley, C., Huband, N., Roe, J. & Frew, S. (2012). *Liaison and Diversion: Narrative Review of the Literature.* Nottingham: Centre for Health and Justice, University of Nottingham and Nottinghamshire Healthcare NHS Trust.

McMillan, I. (July–August 2009). Disciplinary tactics. *Mental Health Today.* 10–12.

Mental Capacity Act 2005.  http://www.legislation.gov.uk/ukpga/2005/9/contents (Last accessed 1 July 2014).

Nursing and Midwifery Council (2008). *The Code: Standards of conduct, performance and ethics for nurses and midwives.* London: NMC.

Offender Health Research Network (2011). *Liaison and Diversion Services: Current practices and future directions.* Manchester: University of Manchester.

Reed, J. (1992). *Review of Mental Health and Social Services for Mentally Disordered Offenders and Others Requiring Similar Services, Vol. 1: Final summary report.* London: The Stationery Office.

Rickford, D. & Edgar, K. (2005). *Troubled Inside: Responding to the Mental Health Needs of Men in Prison.* London: Prison Reform Trust.

Sainsbury Centre for Mental Health (2009). *Diversion: a better way for criminal justice and mental health.* London: Centre for Mental Health.

Sly, K.A., Sharples, J., Lewin, T.J. & Bench, C.J. (2009). Court outcomes for clients referred to a community mental health court liaison service. *International Journal of Law and Psychiatry*. **32** (2), 92–100.

The Powers of Criminal Courts (Sentencing) Act (2000). http://www.legislation.gov.uk/ukpga/2000/6 (Last accessed 1 July 2014).

# 6

# Nursing in prison

Chrissy Reeves

This chapter gives a very broad overview of what it is like to be a nurse working in the prison environment. It takes the reader through the typical patient/prisoner journey, from reception to release from prison, whilst acknowledging that all prisons are different and contain different services and structures according to the needs of the population. However, people are complicated and do not always flow easily through the systems provided, and you are asked to acknowledge this as you journey through this chapter. The terms 'prisoner' and 'patient' have been used interchangeably throughout.

In May 2014, the UK prison population was approximately 84,000 with just under 4,000 females (Ministry of Justice 2014). There are 128 prisons in England and Wales and 12 immigration removal centres (IRCs), all of varying sizes with different functions (Ministry of Justice 2012a). There are also 16 prisons in Scotland (Scottish Prison Service 2012a), holding 7,830 prisoners (Scottish Prison Service 2012b) and three establishments in Northern Ireland (Department of Justice Northern Ireland 2011), containing approximately 1,700 prisoners (Northern Ireland Prison Service 2013). The turnover of prisoners is high, with nearly half of all people in prison in 2011 serving sentences of six months or less.

Security is clearly a major priority in any prison. Her Majesty's Prison Service (HMPS) also has a duty to look after prisoners with humanity and help them to lead law-abiding and useful lives in custody and after release (Ministry of Justice n.d.). In order to achieve this, HMPS must work collaboratively with health services in prison to get those in their charge first healthy and then able and willing to engage in education, resettlement and their sentence plans. Since 2003, there has been a joint health and prison policy to work towards health-promoting prisons in recognition of these challenges (Her Majesty's Prison Service 2003).

## Prison healthcare

The British prisoner population reportedly has significant healthcare needs, with 90 per cent of prisoners experiencing a mental health or substance misuse problem, or both (Sainsbury Centre for Mental Health 2009).

Over the last decade, prison health has developed into a functional primary care model, with healthcare professionals providing clinic-based care for the prison population, alongside Integrated Drug Treatment Services (IDTS) and prison in-reach mental health teams. National Health Service (NHS) provision within prisons has also developed significantly over the last ten years. Increased NHS involvement in prisons has been a positive step, both for nurses transferring to the NHS from the HMPS, and also for patients because it ensures that all aspects of clinical governance are adhered to, via internal structures and with the prison governors and primary care trusts (PCTs) overseeing the practice at partnership board level. In April 2013 the commissioning arrangements for prison health were significantly altered, as they have been elsewhere within the NHS (National Commissioning Board 2013).

The aim is that prison healthcare should be of an equal standard to that provided in the community. This has ensured that prison healthcare providers have been striving to improve quality, develop pathways and support new and existing nursing staff. These efforts have created some real opportunities for nurses to improve the care offered to patients coming into prison. Both prison and IRC healthcare providers are now monitored by the Care Quality Commission (CQC). Healthcare standards are also internally monitored by the providers themselves, and can be checked by inspectors. The CQC jointly inspects services with Her Majesty's Inspectorate of Prisons (HMIP).

## Primary healthcare

Prisoners should not be disadvantaged by their situation with regard to accessing primary healthcare. Primary healthcare providers in prison therefore aim to offer a service that is comparable with community-based care, where practice nurses or nurse practitioners will provide the bulk of care for patients with long-term conditions, and non-medical prescribing is becoming the norm.

On entering this field of practice, nurses may firstly find that there is no one model of care across HMPS. Every establishment is doing similar work, providing similar services, but sometimes in very different ways. Prison buildings vary from Victorian to state-of-the-art private sector establishments. This variation in itself does not enable the provision of a 'one size fits all' health service. Prison categories and security levels add another level of variation to service provision, with prisoners in open (category C or D) conditions tending to have very different health requirements from those imprisoned in a category B remand prison or a category A high-security establishment. There is no single overall policy that dictates what should be done and when. For example, some prisons screen every prisoner coming through the gate for learning disability, and have inbuilt services to meet this need, whilst others have learning disability services that are still in their infancy.

# Reception

Every prisoner received into prison custody (usually on remand) will go through a reception process, and their first contact with the health service inside is with a nurse who undertakes a health screen. A national standardised health-screening tool was developed and piloted from 1999 (Grubin *et al.* 2002) and rolled out across the prison estate in England and Wales. This screening focuses on immediate needs such as prescribed medication; acute and/or chronic physical or mental illness; risk to self; and, of course, the need for alcohol or drug detoxification. This screening is then followed up within 72 hours by a healthcare professional with a full assessment of the patient's health needs (Offender Health Research Network 2008).

*The Bradley Report* (Bradley 2009) suggests that by the time someone comes into prison they should already have been assessed for mental health or learning disabilities at least once, by the police, and then possibly by the courts. However, the systems are not well integrated and this information does not automatically follow the individual through their Criminal Justice Service (CJS) journey. Reception screening and the follow-up assessment processes include both mental health and learning disability assessment.

There is some difference of opinion as to which speciality of nursing is best placed to undertake reception screening. Anecdotally, some staff feel that nurses specialising in addictions are best placed for reception duties, due to the high numbers of people being received who require some form of detoxification. However, in an evaluation undertaken by the Offender Health Research Network (2008), some staff felt that the screening should be done by mental health nurses because of the risk people pose to themselves when coming in to prison, and the perceived high levels of mental illness this patient group has. Irrespective of which branch of nursing the nurse is trained in, an interest in both mental health and substance misuse will be required. Nurses working in prison need to have excellent assessment and engagement skills, as they are the first point of contact with the health service for patients coming into prison.

Staff must also have a genuine interest in health inequalities, as there is evidence that the majority of patients in prisons have poorer physical health, as well as high levels of mental ill health and are very likely to have some kind of substance misuse problem. Compared with the general public, prisoners are more likely to have been homeless, unemployed, abused, in care as a child and/or to have under-achieved in education (DH 2009). In fact child poverty generally can lead to unemployment, criminal activity and greater ill health (Her Majesty's Government 2010), and prisoners are less likely to have engaged with health services in the community prior to imprisonment. Their contact with prison nurses may be the first health contact they have had in years, which places the prison nurse in a strong position to make a considerable impact on health.

# Risk to self

Assuming a patient then moves into the main prison following their reception, they will usually move into a 'first night' or 'induction unit'. These units were developed across the prison estate as it became clear that coming into prison was a risky time for those new to custody, with an increased risk of suicide. These units tend to be smaller and have a higher staff-to-prisoner ratio, thus providing more support for prisoners.

In different prisons, there are different risks concerning safer custody and violence prevention. Women are more likely to hurt themselves than others, and female establishments have higher numbers of individuals managed via Assessment Care in Custody Teamwork (ACCT) processes, but men are more likely to succeed in committing suicide. Men are also more likely to hurt each other than themselves (unlike women). However, increasing numbers of men are using deliberate self-harm as a method of coping in prison (National Offender Management Service 2011).

The ACCT process is a national system of assessing, monitoring and supporting individuals who are at risk of hurting themselves. Since this system was introduced, the suicide rate in prison has dropped (Ministry of Justice 2012b). It is a prison service process, and has gradually become more multi-disciplinary over time. Nurses can therefore expect to be trained in the procedures during their induction. Some take part in the ACCT assessors' rota and become ACCT case managers for individual patients. They are then part of the team supporting the individual through their care map and in ongoing reviews.

In all areas of the prison, nurses can expect to encounter deliberate self-harm and suicide attempts. Very often, prison can remove people's coping mechanisms, leaving them vulnerable to developing new ways of coping. Self-harm is often one of these new coping mechanisms. Self-harm in prison can be dangerous, and should never be dismissed as trivial or attention-seeking. Minor self-harm can easily become major, due to the lack of sharps available, and the use of blunt, non-sterile objects, which can cause infections and even death.

One of the roles of the prison nurse is to provide the Emergency Medical Response (EMR) for the prison. Prison staff carry radios to communicate with each other, and the prison nurse will also have a radio. Different establishments will allocate different numbers of nurses to this role, and the EMR may or may not be accessible 24 hours per day. In remand jails, nurses can be called to respond to any medical emergencies and at times these will be incidents of deliberate self-harm or attempted suicide. Prison and nursing staff carry anti-ligature cut down tools. The prison nurse may therefore play a part in emergency care, providing follow-up for any injuries that may have been sustained, and also be part of the ACCT process.

Prisoners are not only supported by prison officers and healthcare staff at difficult times, but also by prison chaplains, by the Samaritans (via telephones) or by a team of Listeners, who are prisoners trained by the Samaritans and employed to support others.

# Social care in prisons

Access to social care has become a source of contention between HMPS and the NHS. Aging prisoners often need social care assistance that, in the community, would be provided by support workers employed by Social Services. This type of social care is not currently available in custody.

In some prisons, it has been noted that prisoners have been informally providing care for their cellmates in such situations. This is certainly comparable to the support provided in the community by 'carers' – employed or otherwise. However, these arrangements have not been formalised as yet, despite the recommendation from the Prison and Probation Ombudsman for England and Wales (2012) that prisoners should be offered training in health and social care, supported by appropriate staff, and paid for their contributions as they would be paid for other employment within the prison. If well managed, this scheme could work very well in supporting both the health and prison services in the future.

# Physical health in prisons

Long-term medical conditions and chronic disease are managed in prison by primary care teams. These conditions include respiratory disease, cardiovascular disease, neurological conditions, diabetes and so on. They are managed in the same way as they would be in the community, as per the specific NHS frameworks and National Institute for Clinical Excellence (NICE) guidance (Royal College of Nursing 2009). Prisons hold chronic disease registers and use the same Quality Outcomes Framework as any other primary care practice would.

Around 80 per cent of prisoners smoke (DH 2002) so respiratory disease is common, and the risk of cardiovascular disease is high. Many people who are in prison make poor dietary choices and take little exercise. Depending upon drug use, a large number of prisoners are either overweight or underweight. Many have had limited education about what it means to lead a healthy life, and prison is therefore a real opportunity to promote good health. In 2003, the national Prison Service signed up to 'Health in Prisons' (Møller et al. 2007) when these inequalities were recognised.

It has been suggested that prisoners are physiologically around ten years older than people in the community (Nacro 2009). Services have had to adapt to this, offering services for the aging prison population to those over 55 years old (rather than the usual over-65s). Prison healthcare services have end-of-life and palliative care policies (Her Majesty's Inspector of Prisons 2012) and the number of prisoners dying in custody from natural causes has risen over the last few years (Ministry of Justice 2012c). The institutions that mainly have to manage care for aging prisoners and palliative care for dying prisoners are the prisons that hold prisoners on life sentences or extended determinate sentences or indeterminate sentences for public protection (IPP). Even though IPP has now been abolished, prisoners remain in custody on these sentences at the time of writing.

## Infectious/Communicable diseases

Infectious diseases have higher rates in prison. For example, there is a high incidence of tuberculosis (TB) in prison than in the community (Health Protection Agency 2010). Any active cases of TB must be isolated and prisons must have sufficient space to allow for this. The changing epidemiology of TB suggests that this has become primarily a migrant disease, and UK vaccination is now based on risk assessment rather than a universal programme. Risk factors for TB include being a migrant, homeless, a drug user and a member of an immunosuppressed community (Health Protection Agency 2012). These risk factors apply to many people who make up the prison population.

Blood-borne viruses are also more common in prison than in the general community, due to the lives that people lead prior to imprisonment. Rates of sexually transmitted infections (STIs) are high, and most remand prisons have specific clinics set up to manage these. Nurses offer hepatitis B vaccination schedules to those who agree. However, completing the full schedule of three injections can be difficult in a remand prison, due to the instability of the population, with prisoners being released or moved to other prisons. Nevertheless, primary care teams remain responsive to the latest public health intelligence and priorities. For example, the latest drug therapies for hepatitis C are now routinely given in prison.

Infectious diseases outbreaks, such as influenza, norovirus and even chickenpox, are challenging to manage, given the close proximity of people in the prison community. Healthcare teams have to organise immunisation programmes for the whole population, whilst also managing staff anxiety regarding contagion.

## Neurological diseases

Neurological disease manifests itself differently in prisons, and nurses may be called to EMR due to a patient having 'a fit'. It has been reported that there is a higher rate of epilepsy amongst the prison population than in the general population. However, this report may rely more on the prescribing of anticonvulsants than actual symptomology (Fazel *et al.* 2002). It is not clear how community GPs corroborate a diagnosis of epilepsy or whether formal testing ever takes place. The patient presents their diagnosis of epilepsy (and their prescription) in prison, where the same is continued. These prescriptions could, however, relate back to some substance withdrawal and may have been continued on repeat without evidence of ongoing need. In prison, prescriptions are continued as per community GPs' reports. However, custody may present an ideal opportunity to review the need for such a prescription.

The medicines prescribed are commonly sedating and tradable. Most recently, female prisoners have been prescribed Clonazepam for their 'epilepsy', but this is not a medicine that most prisons would want readily available throughout their wings (England *et al.* 2012). It is often questionable whether the 'fits' that nurses are called to attend to are true fits, as patients may be fully recovered and well by the time the nurse arrives. A good knowledge of seizure presentation is therefore useful, in addition to immediate life support skills. There is some evidence now that 'pseudo-seizures' can be linked to high levels of stress or poor coping (Epilepsy Society 2012), which may be useful when considering neurological disease in the prison population.

Traumatic brain injury (TBI) is now being cited as a possible cause of delinquent or criminal behaviour, and one (self-reporting) study showed that 60 per cent of male prisoners in one establishment could identify a previous hefty blow to their head (Williams *et al.* 2010). Brain scans of children experiencing severe neglect in childhood also show that their brains develop very differently (Her Majesty's Government 2010), and their ability to manage their lives is likely to be very different from those with normal brain scans. Prisoners with these types of injuries may have behavioural difficulties and emotional or impulse control problems, which can in turn make their prison stays longer, due to them getting into trouble with prison authorities. They often find it a challenge to conform to the strict rules of prison life. Williams (2012) recommends a training package for all staff who work with this group of prisoners.

Routine primary care clinics provided in prisons range as widely as they do in the community. There are 'well man' and 'well woman' clinics; and smoking cessation, sleep and pain clinics are popular; respiratory disease and diabetes clinics are also on offer. Within the primary care nursing teams, different individuals generally offer different areas of expertise, and training and support for these nurses is usually provided in order to meet the needs of the prison population.

## Medicine management

Medicine management makes up a large part of the prison nurse's workload. Indeed, it often used to feel as if a nurse's whole working day was taken up with dispensing and administering medicines. It is now thought desirable for patients to manage their own health, to keep their medicines with them and take responsibility themselves (The Offender Health Research Network 2009). Nevertheless, patients in prison have to be risk assessed before being allowed to keep medicines in their own possession, and even after risk assessment they are only allowed to keep a limited amount of medicine.

Medicines in prison can become a source of currency, and they have much greater value than they do out in the community. Pharmacy technicians now also do some of the administration work. The medicine round remains a good time for nurses to engage with patients. Some prisoners will use these opportunities to raise other health issues. Anecdotally, we have found that nurse clinics have also become busier, as patients now have to book in to discuss other health issues.

Medicines can become an area of contention between nurses (and healthcare staff in general) and patients, with many patients taking higher doses in the community than they are actually prescribed, or using someone else's prescribed medication. As we have seen, prison can remove patients' usual coping mechanisms, however unhealthy they may be. For example, being in custody may leave some people vulnerable to deliberate self-harming or choosing harder drugs than they would ordinarily find acceptable – due to their availability. It is commonly believed that problems can be resolved with 'a pill' and prisoners may have high expectations of medication. Some medicines are particularly popular but these may change over time, with changes in doctors' prescribing patterns.

To access certain medications in prison, patients have to present with photographic identification. Some institutions use iris recognition systems to verify identity. Patients are observed when taking the medicine, not only by nursing staff but often by prison officers too. However, prescribed medication may still be traded, despite the vigilance of staff, and methods of storing and secreting medication for use at a later date, to trade or store to attempt suicide, become ever more creative. Nursing staff work directly with the prison security departments to try to monitor and curtail this, as part of their drug supply and reduction procedures.

Patient Group Directions issued for certain medicines mean that nurses can run clinics and give groups of prisoners prescription-only medicines for certain conditions. Staff receive training and support for these procedures, as they would in any other healthcare environment.

# Challenges to continuity of care

One of the challenges of providing high-quality healthcare in prison is the frequent transfer of prisoners between establishments, which sometimes happens at very short notice. This can be disruptive to all types of care the patient may be receiving, whether physical, psychiatric or addiction-related.

Another challenge is the impact of some prison regimes, which only allow prisoners out of their cells for certain periods in the day. Accessing patients may therefore be a problem outside the hours of 'unlock'. Under these circumstances, some establishments expect healthcare staff to work outside normal working hours in order to deliver care.

In addition, prisoners attending any non-healthcare-related activities get paid to do so, whereas attending healthcare services may not be a priority. Even though prison wages or benefits are very small, this money really matters in prison. For this reason, prisoners may not choose to miss work or education sessions in order to address their health issues.

## Substance misuse services

Around 24 per cent of people coming into prison have injected drugs, and of this group 20 per cent have hepatitis B and 30 per cent have hepatitis C (DH 2002).

The Integrated Drug Treatment Services (IDTS) were rolled out across the prison estate from 2009. This system offers a better model for working with addicts, particularly those on short sentences.

Around 50 per cent of prisoners' offences are drug-related crimes carried out to fund addiction. It is therefore vital to tackle drug use and addiction. Prison provides a real opportunity to engage with this group of patients, who are sometimes in a far more stable state of mind than usual, due to the rigidity of the custodial regime and the containment that this provides. IDTS enables prison staff, clinical staff and teams of psychosocial intervention (PSI) workers to collaboratively manage the care of patients coming into prison, where their needs are first stabilised, and then reviewed in partnership with the patient, leading to detoxification or a prescribed maintenance regime. IDTS is very much about working with people in recovery from addiction, and the service extends through the gate into community drug intervention programmes (DIPs).

IDTS are quite unlike addictions services in the community in a number of ways. The PSI team is separate from the clinical team, whereas in community detoxification units the clinical team would be carrying out such interventions themselves. This means that the nurses are mainly left to do the nursing care on the stabilisation units, dealing primarily with medicines management, physical health monitoring and wound care. Both nursing and PSI teams join together to review patient care in standardised 5-day, 28-day and then 13-week reviews, to provide a collaborative care plan for the patient. Some of the group work with the patients is also done jointly, but this may depend on the capacity and staffing levels of the unit.

A significant difference between community detoxification units/wards and prison stabilisation units/wings is the number of patients on the units. A community setting may have only 12 beds, whereas a prison wing may hold 60 patients or more. Another difference is that the patients in prison substance misuse wings have not chosen to come in and address their drug habits (as they will have opted to do in community rehabilitation placements) and many prisoners say that they do not think that their drug use is a problem.

Illicit drugs enter prisons in a variety of ways. Prison staff members are constantly trying to prevent and reduce the supply of illicit drugs. Although nurses do not monitor illicit drug use, it has huge implications for the clinical care provided. Prison nurses are therefore sensitive to the signs of drug use. The most common illicit drugs in the prison setting are opiates or cannabis (Prison Reform Trust 2010). Opiates present the biggest potential risk to the patient, especially if the patient is also taking legal methadone.

Prisons have Narcotics Anonymous (NA) and Alcoholics Anonymous (AA) meetings and patients engage well with these self-help programmes. A more recent development has been peer supporters for addictions patients. These peer supporters are patients who have been through the programmes and can share their lived experience of the services offered. These are paid jobs for prisoners.

Some prisons in England and Wales are currently participating in a trial in which patients are given a dose of Naloxone to take away with them when they are released from prison. This will counteract an opiate overdose as a result of reduced tolerance to opiates following a period of imprisonment (Strang *et al.* 2013). The period immediately following release has been found to be a time of increased risk of death for patients leaving prison. As a result of this research, considerable changes were made in prescribing practice and national policy in the early 2000s. Instead of all patients going through detoxification, maintenance on opiate substitutes was implemented, with patients given a choice as to their treatment for addiction.

Alcohol services in prison are grouped together within the Substance Misuse Services, and indeed the two groups of patients will be housed on the same unit for detoxification (or stabilisation), with some patients receiving both at the same time. Again, these patients should be assessed and the requirement for alcohol detoxification picked up in reception. Assessment can be more of a challenge with alcohol users, as patients do not always admit to the amount of alcohol they have been consuming before coming to prison.

Nurses can commence detoxification medication from the first night of custody, and most prisons will have this on a Patient Group Direction (PGD). This is vital, as withdrawal from alcohol can cause seizures and delirium tremens, both of which can be fatal. If a patient gets through the assessment and onto the stabilisation unit from reception, they can be monitored and observed closely during their detoxification and any adjustments to the prescribing regime will be made as required. Alcohol services receive very little funding and attention compared to other addiction services, and yet alcohol is linked to a high percentage of violent and high-profile crime (MacAskill *et al.* 2011).

## Dual diagnosis

Usually about 50 per cent of patients within the Substance Misuse Service will also have some kind of mental health problem, which is referred to as having 'a dual diagnosis'. It is also common for patients to experience mental ill health whilst they are detoxifying from substances. Stabilisation units have mental health staff working within them, and part of their role is to monitor and observe patients for any symptoms of mental illness and support them during this time.

Any patients coming in to prison who are already on the Care Programme Approach (CPA) will of course be referred to the Prison Community Mental Health Team (CMHT) or in-reach team. The addictions nurses refer anyone else who does not seem to be managing their detox, and who may be exhibiting acute symptoms of mental illness. The teams work together to assess and plan the care needed by these patients.

By the end of the detoxification period, the symptoms of distress may have dissipated, and patients will transfer into the main prison without any further problems. Meanwhile, some other patients only start to show signs of being mentally unwell once their detoxification is well underway or completed. In these cases, the drugs may actually have been keeping their mental disorder symptoms under control and, without them, they become unwell. In fact these patients are often dismissed by CMHTs in the community, as the CMHTs may have concluded that their problems are all drug related. It is sometimes only whilst they are contained in prison, with far less access to illicit drugs and alcohol, that their true mental illness becomes visible.

## Mental health

All Prisons have mental health in-reach teams in some form – whether they are full teams housed within the prison itself, or visiting teams from a local community health provider. Some prisons also have primary care mental health teams to deal with low-level depression and anxiety problems. These are equivalent to Assessment and Brief Treatment Teams in the community.

In-reach teams have gone from strength to strength in the last decade, as the high levels of mental disorder in prisons have been recognised (Forrester et al. 2013). Unlike community teams that have more recently split up into Home Treatment/Crisis Resolution Teams, Assertive Outreach Teams, Early Intervention Teams, personality disorder services and so on, the prison in-reach team remains the main mental health service for the populations they serve. Nurses (and the rest of the multi-disciplinary team members) working within these teams have a very wide remit and usually a large caseload. Referrals are made from anywhere in the prison.

All patients on CPA are referred automatically, and any patients who have been remanded for serious offences or sentenced to long periods in custody should also be referred, due to the potential risk they may pose to themselves, particularly in the early stages of custody. Working with the primary care nursing team is essential for the patients who need their physical health monitored, such as patients on long-term anti-psychotic medication. They must also work with the officers working on the prison wings, as it is they who will notice changes in the patients' behaviour, very often they who will be making the referrals, and they who will be asking for help in managing certain prisoners.

Apart from the caseload management, and liaising with community teams externally, the work can be divided between crisis intervention and supporting the prison staff with behaviour management. As previously discussed, patients can behave very differently in prison, and changes in their usual ways of coping can lead to behaviours that are challenging – not only for themselves but also for those around them.

The work of an in-reach team is varied. In one day alone, a nurse could be seeing a patient on one of the residential wings for an ACCT review with the rest of the multi-disciplinary team; attending a CPA meeting for a patient with a psychotic illness with visitors from a local CMHT and probation; writing a discharge summary; liaising with a court diversion team about a patient coming into prison; assessing a new patient who has just been sentenced to life in prison; or working with officers in the Segregation Unit on a behavioural management plan for an individual with complex personality disorder.

Some prisons have in-patient mental health units and these are used for patients who require a higher level of support and monitoring due to their illness. These units are usually much smaller than the main residential wings and are staffed by clinical staff and, sometimes, specialist prison officers. Admission to these units will usually be via the in-reach teams (which are equivalent to community services). However, patients are also sometimes admitted by order of the governor of the prison for their own safety.

Having a patient on these units enables staff to carry out a full longitudinal assessment of their mental health and a medication review if required. Very often, an in-patient mental health unit will be a safer option than the main residential wing, as there may be 'safer cells' with no ligature points and a higher staff to patient ratio. These units are very much like acute admissions wards in the community, although there may be patients who stay longer than you would expect in those wards, depending on their ability to function within the main prison regime, and on what other wings are available.

Some prisoners admitted to the in-patient units will have treatment and get better, resulting in their transfer back to the ordinary wings, returning to the support of the in-reach team, and/ or other health and prison teams. Other prisoners may refuse treatment in prison and may then require transfer to hospital under the Mental Health Act (MHA). Unlike acute admissions units in the community, prisons cannot force patients to undergo treatment under the MHA. As in all other services, the Mental Capacity Act (2005) is used in prison to make treatment decisions with patients, and this legislation helps guide professionals through clinical decision-making.

Given the fact that they are not able to use the MHA, prisons have to manage a lot of patients in very acute stages of mental ill health. If the patient presents too great a risk to themselves or others, this can result in them spending long periods in isolation, requiring a certain number of prison officers to be present prior to the patient being unlocked. This is quite different from acute admissions wards in the community, where any time spent in seclusion is very carefully and cautiously monitored. In prison, officers carry out all the control and restraint, whereas in hospitals nurses lead on this.

Nationally, the target for transferring prisoners to hospital from prison under the MHA is 14 days. This target is monitored by the prisons themselves, and yet the prisons do not have full control over it. Nursing and medical staff lead on the transfer procedure, which starts with inviting an external team to come in and agree that their patient needs to be admitted to hospital. If the patient is not known to services, or the external team have fixed ideas about the patient's problems being 'drug-related', this can be challenging.

Once teams have been in and agreed, there is then a discussion about the level of security the patient requires. The prison team may have their own ideas about this. However, it is the Ministry of Justice Mental Health Casework Section that makes the final decision, as different crimes are categorised in different ways. Patients either go to local intensive care units, low secure wards, medium secure wards or high secure wards. If the local prison team do not have their own suitable ward, the hospital team will visit the patient and undertake an admission assessment. In the community, patients in need of urgent admission get into hospital the same day. From prison, it can take an average of 37 days for women or longer for men (Bartlett *et al.* 2012).

Even in well-funded mental health teams in prisons, it is sometimes hard to see equivalence with community services (Forrester *et al.* 2013). Rates of mental illness in prison are far higher than the incidence that community mental health teams (CMHTs) would usually have to contend with. Psychosis and neurosis rates are higher, as are rates of borderline personality disorder. In 2008 it was estimated that expenditure on mental health in prisons was between four and seven times the amount spent on mental health in the community (Sainsbury Centre for Mental Health 2008). However, the level of spending is still not thought to be sufficient. We know that coming into prison is distressing in itself, even for mentally stable people, and there is great concern about its impact on those with diagnosed mental illness.

## Women

There are far fewer women's prisons than men's prisons, and this is because there are far fewer women in prison (5 per cent of all prisoners are women). There are obvious differences in the female prison estate. For example, some women's prisons have mother and baby units, and pregnancy units, and therefore have visiting midwives and health visitors. A lot of women prisoners are separated from their children when remanded into custody and this is traumatic in itself, particularly if they are the main carers for those children, and they are worried that their children may consequently end up in the care system. Around 60 per cent of women are on short sentences of less than six months, and 80 per cent are imprisoned for non-violent offences. Because there are fewer establishments for women, prisoners are around 60 miles away from home on average, and this makes visits from family, children and even social services less likely.

The distance prisoners are from home is likely to present an increasing challenge not only for the prisoners but for health and resettlement services, as prisons become less local. As the national prison service attempts to reduce costs and closes smaller establishments in favour of larger jails, there will be more external services to refer to and develop relationships with. This issue is already being faced, particularly by mental health services in women's prisons, as women are not local, and prisoners are spread out nationwide.

# Conclusion

Nursing in prison is hard work, and can be physically tiring and emotionally draining at times. Patients in prison can be very demanding – of medicines, and of staff time. They can be very focused on themselves and their own situation, with little regard for others around them. There is a certain amount of 'emotional labour' required, as nurses are expected to present a strong professional front and be non-judgemental, whilst remaining empathic to patients' needs (Walsh 2009).

All teams need to receive clinical supervision or reflective practice to support them in their work, with its high stress levels. Teams also need strong leaders who can support them on the ground and make their voices heard in this unusual healthcare environment, where nurses are outnumbered by prison staff, and the demands of healthcare sometimes compete with those of security.

Prison nurses generally feel safe. Although there are fights and assaults (Ministry of Justice, 2012b), it is rare for nursing staff to be the victims of aggression in prison. The skills that prove invaluable in all clinical areas are high-level interpersonal skills, assessment skills, crisis intervention, and the ability to respond to emergencies. Prison nurses need to be calm under pressure, assertive, aware of boundaries and confident in order to work in this challenging environment. They also need to be compassionate and caring without being judgemental. Nurses coming to work in prisons from accident and emergency departments or walk-on clinics tend to do well. When jobs are advertised in prisons, a huge number of mental health nurses apply, even if the adverts are for adult branch nurses; and it seems that traditionally prisons are felt to be more of a mental health environment. It's true that mental ill health is prevalent in prisons, but a full range of services equivalent to those available in community services have to be offered, so it stands to reason that skilled nurses are required from all areas.

The separate clinical teams within prisons need to work together and recognise that all their work is intrinsically linked. It will then be possible to provide more holistic care for patients. Integrated healthcare from one provider tends to lend itself to better working relationships and therefore lead to better care. However, this may be difficult to achieve in the competitive new commissioning world, so close working with other providers in delivering the care is paramount.

One huge area that calls for development is linking patients in with community services once they leave prison. Traditionally, mental health services are better at this, due to CPA. Likewise, addictions patients, who need a community prescription, get referred back to their DIP teams. But there are many patients who state that they have no GP and no address, and upon release there is no one to help with their health issues. In such cases, however good prison nurses may have been at supporting that patient with their diabetes, asthma, depression or binge drinking, it will be of little consequence when they get back out to the community. These prisoners often do not know how to register with a GP because they do not have an address and so the cycle starts again, possibly as a prelude to recidivism.

Prison health has developed significantly in recent years. Prison nurses can make a big difference to patients' lives, but the work has to continue through the prison gates if prison nurses are to make a difference to people in society. This is where prison health becomes public health. Prison nurses are often given valuable opportunities to work with individuals to make better health choices and give them a good experience of accessing health services. This should encourage them to engage with local community healthcare services upon their release.

# References

Bartlett, A., Somers, N., Reeves, C. & White, S. (2012). Women prisoners: an analysis of the process of hospital transfers. *Journal of Forensic Psychiatry and Psychology.* **23** (4), 538–53.

Bradley, K. (2009). *The Bradley Report.* London: Department of Health, The Stationery Office.

Detention Advice Service (2012). 'Foreign national prisoners: Meeting the challenges ahead'. Conference Report. http://www.detentionadvice.org.uk/uploads/1/0/4/1/10410823/detention_advice_service_conference_report_2012.pdf (Last accessed 3 August 2013).

Department of Health (2002). *Health Promoting Prisons: a shared approach.* London: The Stationery Office.

Department of Health (2009). *Improving Health Supporting Justice: The national plan of the health and criminal justice programme board.* London: The Stationery Office.

Department of Justice Northern Ireland (2011). *Northern Ireland Prison Service: Prison Estate.* http://www.dojni.gov.uk/index/ni-prison-service/prison-estate.htm (Last accessed 1 June 2013).

England, R., Dholakia, N., Tukmachi, E., Murphy de Souza, T., Moss, B. & Ovaisi, S. (2012). Prison environment and health. *British Medical Journal.* http://www.bmj.com/content/345/bmj.e5921/rr/614354 (Last accessed 8 June 2013).

Epilepsy Society (2012). *About Epilepsy.* http://www.epilepsysociety.org.uk/AboutEpilepsy/Associatedconditions/Non-epilepticseizures (Last accessed 8 June 2013).

Fazel, S., Vassos, E. & Danesh, J. (2002). Prevalence of epilepsy in prisoners: systemic review. *British Medical Journal.* **324**, 1495.

Forrester, A., Exworthy, T., Olumoroti, O., Sessay, M., Parrott, J., Spencer, S. & Whyte, S. (2013). Variations in prison mental health services in England and Wales. *International Journal of Law and Psychiatry.* **36**, 326–32.

Grubin, D., Carson, D. & Parsons, S. (2002). *Report on New Prisoners Reception Health Screening Arrangements: the results of a pilot study in ten prisons.* pb.rcpsych.org/content/27/7/251.full (Last accessed 8 June 2013).

Health Protection Agency (2010). *Guidance for Health Protection Units on responding to TB incidents and outbreaks in prisons.* London: Health Protection Agency.

Health Protection Agency (2012). *Tuberculosis in the UK: 2012 Report.* London: Health Protection Agency.

Her Majesty's Prison Service (2003). *Prison Service Order Number 3200: Health Promotion.* London: HM Prison Service

Her Majesty's Inspector of Prisons (2012). *Expectations: Criteria for assessing the treatment of prisoners and conditions in prisons.* London: HMIP.

Her Majesty's Government (2010). *The Foundation Years: preventing poor children becoming poor adults. The Report of the Independent Review on Poverty and Life Chances (Field Report).* London: Cabinet Office.

MacAskill, S., Parkes, T., Brooks, O., Graham, L., McAuley, A. & Brown, A. (2011). Assessment of alcohol problems using AUDIT in a prison setting: more than an 'aye or no' question. *BioMedicalCentral Public Health.* **11**, 865.

Ministry of Justice (2010). *Safety in Custody: Assaults in Prison Custody (England and Wales) [xls].* http://www.justice.gov.uk/downloads/statistics/prison-probation/safety-custody/saftey-custody-assaults-statistics-0710.xls (Last accessed 21 March 2013).

Ministry of Justice (2012a). *Prisons map*. http://www.justice.gov.uk/downloads/contacts/hmps/prison-finder/prisons-map.pdf (Last accessed 24 February 2013).

Ministry of Justice (2012b). *Safety in Custody Assaults Tables jan – march 2012*. http://www.justice.gov.uk/downloads/statistics/prison-probation/safety-custody/safety-custody-assaults-sep-12.xls (Last accessed 21 March 2013).

Ministry of Justice (2012c). *Safety in Custody: Deaths*.
http://www.justice.gov.uk/statistics/prisons-and-probation/safety-in-custody (Last accessed 21 March 2013).

Ministry of Justice (2014). *Prison Population Figures: Population Bulletin – weekly 9 May 2014*.
http://www.justice.gov.uk/statistics/prisons-and-probation/prison-population-figures(Last accessed 13 May 2014).

Ministry of Justice (n.d.) *Her Majesty's Prison Service*. http://www.justice.gov.uk/about/hmps (Last accessed 24 February 2013).

Møller, L., Stöver, H., Jürgens, R., Gatherer, A. & Nikogosian, H. (2007). *Health in Prisons: A WHO guide to the essentials in prison health*. Denmark: WHO Regional Office for Europe.

Nacro (2009). *A Resource Pack for Working with Older Prisoners*. London: Department of Health.

National Commissioning Board (2013). *Securing Excellence for Commissioning in Offender Health*.
http://www.england.nhs.uk/wp-content/uploads/2013/03/offender-commissioning.pdf (Last accessed 8 June 2013).

Northern Ireland Prison Service (2013). *Analysis of NIPS Prison Population from 01/01/2012 to 31/03/2013*. Northern Ireland: Department of Justice.

National Offender Management Service (2011). *Prison Service Instruction 64/2011: Management of prisoners at risk of harm to self, to others and from others (Safer Custody)*. London: Ministry of Justice.

Offender Health Research Network (2008). *An Evaluation of the Reception Screening Process used within Prisons in England and Wales*. Manchester: Offender Health Research Network

Offender Health Research Network (2009). *An evaluation of in-possession medication procedures within prisons in England and Wales: a report to the National Institute of Health Research*.
http://www.ohrn.nhs.uk/resource/Research/OHRNInpossessionMedication.pdf (Last accessed 8 June 2013).

Prison and Probation Ombudsman for England and Wales (2012). *Annual Report 2011–2012*. London: The Stationery Office.

Prison Reform Trust (2010). *Bromley Briefings Prison Factfile*. London: Prison Reform Trust.

Royal College of Nursing (2009). *Health and Nursing Care in the Criminal Justice Sector: RCN Guidance for Nursing Staff*. London: RCN.

Sainsbury Centre for Mental Health (2008). *Short-changed: Spending on Prison Mental Healthcare*. London: Sainsbury Centre for Mental Health.

Sainsbury Centre for Mental Health (2009). *Briefing 39: Mental Healthcare and the Criminal Justice System*. London: Sainsbury Centre for Mental Health.

Scottish Prison Service (2012a). http://www.sps.gov.uk/AboutUs/sps-about-us.aspx (Last accessed 1 June 2013).

Scottish Prison Service (2012b). *Publications: Scottish Prison Population*. http://www.sps.gov.uk/Publications/ScottishPrisonPopulation.aspx (Last accessed 8 June 2013).

Strang, J., Bird, S.M. & Parmar, M.K. (2013). Take-home emergency naloxone to prevent heroin overdose deaths after prison release: Rationale and practicalities for the N-ALIVE randomized trial. *Journal of Urban Health: Bulletin of the New York Academy of Medicine*. http://link.springer.com/content/pdf/10.1007%2Fs11524-013-9803-1.pdf (Last accessed 8 June 2013).

Walsh, E. (2009). The emotional labor of nurses working in Her Majesty's (HM) Prison Service. *Journal of Forensic Nursing*. **5** (3), 143–52.

Williams, H. (2012). *Repairing Shattered Lives: Brain injury and its implications for criminal justice*. UK: Barrow Cadbury Trust on behalf of Transition to Adulthood Alliance.

Williams, W.H., Mewse, A.J., Tonks, J., Mills, S., Burgess, C.N.W. & Cordan, G. (2010). Traumatic Brain Injury in a Prison Population: Prevalence and risk for re-offending. *Brain Injury Journal*. **24** (10), 1184–88.

# 7

# On the out: Supporting offenders in the community

Mark Warren

There has been considerable recent interest in providing mental health liaison and diversion services at the so-called 'front end' of the criminal justice system. Since the publication of *The Bradley Report* (Bradley 2009), NHS England has invested considerable sums of money in the setting up of criminal justice teams. Mental health nurses are at the forefront of providing assessment and treatment in police custody suites and Magistrates' Courts, and innovative pilot schemes are now being rolled out to provide mental health assessment before people get to police custody suites. Street triage schemes are being piloted across England, operating mainly in city areas. These involve mental health workers accompanying police officers in the community to provide early mental health assessment and intervention where needed, well before individuals experience detention in the police station.

At the Welsh Government's launch of its *Criminal Justice Liaison Services Guide* (2013), there was widespread agreement amongst several agencies that mental health assessment and intervention would be welcomed at an even earlier stage. This would involve anti-social behaviour teams having access to mental health workers in order to identify and target people with mental health problems who are just starting to appear on the radar of the police. The anti-social behaviour teams could then provide assessment, treatment and support to prevent these individuals entering the criminal justice system wherever possible.

Many liaison and diversion schemes were set up, operating from a base within the local Magistrate's Court. Since then, there has been an increasing demand for this type of service to be based within police custody suites. Police forces are systematically closing smaller custody suites and replacing them with larger purpose-built units. The nursing and medical care provided at these units clearly needs to be supplemented by specialist mental health teams to provide early assessment, treatment and diversion wherever possible. The latest government guidance, the *Mental Health Crisis*

*Care Concordat* (DH 2014), champions a collaborative approach between the police, NHS, Social Services and a wide range of other agencies to ensure that people experiencing a mental health crisis get access to the best possible care and treatment as quickly as possible. Having mental health nurses working within police custody suites allows early, direct access to specialist practitioners in order to identify and, when necessary, divert individuals to the most appropriate care.

## Mental health support for offenders after they leave prison

Whilst the principles of early intervention and diversion are laudable, there is a danger that service users who are already in the system and serving community-based sentences, or being released early from prison on licence, may not be able to access appropriate levels of mental healthcare. The all stages diversion model (Sainsbury Centre for Mental Health 2009) and the *Offender Healthcare Pathway* (DH 2005) both acknowledge that aftercare and community support are essential components of the Criminal Justice Liaison Service (CJLS) mental health model. However, the practicalities of providing support to this group remain challenging for practitioners on the ground.

All offenders on community-based orders, or released early on licence following a 12-month custodial sentence, will be subject to supervision by the Probation Service. Little research has been done on the mental health needs of this particular group. Brooker *et al.* (2012) estimated that 39 per cent of people on probation suffer from current mental health problems and a systematic review by Jones and Maynard (2013) shows that offenders released from prison are over six times more likely to commit suicide than the general population. In many ways this is not surprising, as the prison population has been shown to have very high levels of mental ill health. One hoped-for outcome of the development of criminal justice and mental health teams is a reduction in the number of mentally ill people entering prison. However, little consideration is given to support after release from prison.

Probation services do not generally have scope to commission mental health services; and it it could be argued that this group of offenders should access the same community mental health services as the general public. However, research has shown that newly released offenders face a number of challenges, compared to the general public, that hamper their opportunities to access healthcare. Williamson (2006) reports that 42 per cent of newly released prisoners are of no fixed abode and 50 per cent have no GP. They therefore show an increased incidence of morbidity and an increased level of risk and reoffending, which can lead to the whole cycle being repeated. In addition, the mental health needs of this group are frequently compounded by high levels of co-occurring substance misuse (Brooker *et al.* 2011).

It could equally well be argued that, by concentrating mental health services to provide support for this group of offenders, we are providing liaison and diversion from re-offending, thus completing the system's provision of Criminal Justice Liaison Services in the field of mental health.

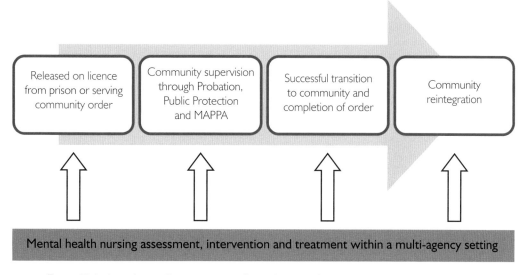

*Figure 7.1: A pathway for community-based criminal justice mental health practice.*

## Providing mental health services as part of a multi-agency approach

Healthcare in the Cwm Taf area of Wales is the responsibility of the Cwm Taf University Health Board, which covers the valley communities of the Rhondda, Cynon, Taff-Ely and Merthyr Tydfil. This will be discussed here as an example of a multi-agency approach to mental health service provision.

Positive multi-agency partnerships already exist in this area, created in order to tackle public protection and mental health issues. South Wales Police and the Wales Probation Trust welcomed the opportunity to have mental health nurses as part of these multi-agency teams to provide assessment, intervention, treatment and support for offenders with mental health needs. The service has been in existence since April 2011 and targets the following main groups:

- People with mental health needs who have been released from prison to serve the remainder of their sentence in the community
- People who have been sentenced directly to Community Orders and have mental health needs
- People under the management of the Police Public Protection Unit (PPU), who display behaviours that may indicate mental health problems and may benefit from assessment and treatment
- People with mental health problems who may fit into any of the above groups and are subject to Multi-Agency Public Protection Arrangements (MAPPA).

The service is a small one in terms of personnel, run by two mental health nurse practitioners experienced in working within the criminal justice system. The service offers:

- Assessment clinics taking direct referrals from probation officers, MAPPA and the Public Protection Unit. These clinics are held in Probation Services premises and provide mental health assessments without needing to navigate complex mental health referral systems.
- Direct liaison with prison mental health in-reach teams to ensure that service users being released from prison are proactively supported and managed
- Onward referral to local services, including primary and secondary mental health teams and the third sector
- Care coordination of complex, high-risk service users in cooperation with criminal justice partners
- Onward referral and access to regional South Wales Forensic Services for specialist assessment and advice
- Specialist mental health risk assessments (such as HCR-20) to inform risk management plans for service users
- Support to Beacon Integrated Offender Management (IOM) Teams as one of the partner agencies.

Beacon IOM teams are set up to manage prolific offenders in situations where a vast amount of crime is committed by a relatively small number of offenders. They are multi-agency in nature and operate by tackling issues such as drug and alcohol misuse, housing, criminal behaviour, finance and benefits and mental health within a dedicated service. These teams provide another context in which mental health nurses can contribute to improving the health of offenders whilst helping to create safer communities. Recent policy direction in the UK may see the provision of some of these schemes being transferred to new agencies outside the traditional Probation Service according to a policy known as 'Transforming Rehabilitation' (Ministry of Justice 2013).

## Case study: Bill

Bill was a 45-year-old man serving a six-year sentence for burglary, who was referred to the service by his probation officer. At the time of referral, he was coming up to his release date. Bill had spent much of the previous 27 years in prison, mainly for burglary. His pattern of behaviour was usually predictable. He would be released from custody and return to his home area, where he would be unable to manage the demands of everyday life. He would then reoffend and subsequently return to prison custody, where he felt safer and was under less stress and pressure.

Bill's probation officer was concerned that this cycle of behaviour would continue and was aware that Bill had had some contact with mental health services in the past. The probation officer requested an assessment from the Mental Health Liaison Service to ascertain if there was any support that could be offered on release. Due to his long periods of time in custody and frequent moves around the prison estate across England and Wales, very little information was available regarding Bill's mental health history. Bill was assessed whilst still in prison with the support of the mental health in-reach team and it became clear he had significant mental health problems, having seen a number of psychiatrists over the years, was currently on anti-psychotic medication and had received intensive psychotherapy during a previous sentence. His mental health needs were complex and significant, and the service agreed to support Bill on his release.

Bill was given assistance to register with a GP and help with accessing housing. He was also given an early appointment with a consultant psychiatrist in the local community mental health team and onward referral for trauma-focused therapy. He now has a care coordinator who is able to support him in conjunction with local probation and police staff and he has, so far, remained out of custody for the longest period of his adult life. Each week brings fresh challenges but, by using this targeted intervention, improvements have been made in Bill's mental health, which have reduced his offending behaviour. Bill has been able to develop a trusting relationship with the mental health team and has engaged with community health services for the first time.

## Multi-Agency Public Protection Arrangements (MAPPA)

The Criminal Justice Act 2003 requires local criminal justice agencies working in partnership to make arrangements to assess and manage the risk posed by sexual and violent offenders in their area. These arrangements are known as MAPPA (Multi-Agency Public Protection Arrangements). The Act also requires them to publish an annual report, setting out how the arrangements are working in their area. Partner agencies contributing to MAPPA include housing, social services and mental health services.

As MAPPA develop in each local area, there is considerable scope for mental health nurses to play a central role in managing people who are at high risk of offending and, as a group, have high levels of mental ill health. In the South Wales police area, a total of 1,222 people were deemed eligible for MAPPA by the end of 2011 (Ministry of Justice 2012). Using the data from the Brooker study (Brooker *et al.* 2012), it would be expected that between 450 and 470 of these people would be suffering from a current mental health problem.

In the Cwm Taf area, mental health nurses are an integral part of the MAPPA process, sitting as members of the MAPPA group and actively taking referrals for assessment and intervention. Between April 2012 and September 2013, a total of 370 referrals were discussed, and trends show a 50 per cent increase in referrals for 2013 compared with 2012. Ongoing research is being undertaken to identify the level of mental ill health in this particular group. From our own casework during the first two quarters of 2013, 166 MAPPA cases were heard, and 35.5 per cent of these individuals were found to have previous or current experience of mental ill health or a learning disability.

Mental health professionals are often cautious regarding the sharing of confidential information with non-health agencies, and working in this type of multi-agency setting (where the nurse may be the only health worker present) can be intimidating and a little daunting at first. Other professionals often expect the mental health nurse to be the expert in their field and careful professional judgement has to be exercised when an opinion is required.

MAPPA Guidance (Ministry of Justice 2012) enables mental health nurses to share all the information held by their organisation as long as this is lawful. The Criminal Justice Act 2003 allows member agencies to share information with each other in order to manage risk. At the same time, information sharing must be necessary and proportionate in order to meet the requirements of human rights legislation. Health professionals tend to see the duty of confidentiality as a cornerstone of practice. However, where there are clear issues of risk to the public there is a duty to disclose information in a multi-agency setting to enable all agencies to make considered, informed choices in order to manage risk. We perhaps need to consider the question: do healthcare professionals sometimes prioritise confidentiality too much? Countless enquiries into serious incidents concerning mental health service users have involved failures of communication and poor information sharing, and this has been replicated in the field of childcare. How many reports have been issued observing that too much (rather than too little) information has been shared?

## Mental health nursing and public protection

From the earliest days of psychiatry, mental health nurses were not only responsible for providing care and treatment for those in their charge but also for protecting the security of those individuals and the safety of the general public (Nolan 2000). Although the emphasis has changed greatly, with the move away from institutionalised care, nurses still have a responsibility, enshrined in the law and their own professional standards, to protect the people they care for and to protect the general public from harm.

In the United Kingdom, police forces have developed Public Protection Units (PPUs). One of the stated aims of these units is to liaise with mental health services in order to maintain the safety of the public. PPUs are usually the lead police presence on MAPPA panels and provide a natural link for mental health nurses when dealing with the police. PPUs also have a remit to assist local police officers with some of the most sensitive criminal investigations, providing strategic support and guidance in cases involving such issues as child protection, domestic abuse, sexual offences, missing people and mental health.

In the Cwm Taf area, working practices have developed alongside the MAPPA systems in order to provide mental health assessment and intervention for many offenders who are required to register as sex offenders. This is a developing area of practice that has challenged some nurses' attitudes and assumptions when working to improve the health of people who may have a mental health or learning disability and who have committed a serious sexual offence.

## Conclusion

The development of MAPPA and the creation of PPUs have created a framework within which mental health nurses can contribute in a direct, meaningful way to the assessment and treatment of people serving all or part of their sentences in the community. By working closely with criminal justice agencies, mental health nurses can also help reduce reoffending rates amongst some of the highest-risk offenders in our communities. Work continues on treating offenders with high-risk personality disorders in the community.

As these relationships and partnerships develop, mental health nurses may have opportunities to become team members in PPUs. Although these units are police led (and should remain so), there are many examples of effective multi-agency partnerships, including Multi-Agency Safeguarding Hub (MASH) teams in the field of child protection, adult protection and domestic abuse; and Beacon Integrated Offender Management (IOM) teams in the field of offender management. Beacon IOM teams include members from drug and alcohol services, probation, police, social services and mental health, who all work together as partners. As nurses, the challenge remains to provide the best possible care in an environment where the protection of the public is the overarching priority.

## References

Bradley, K. (2009). *The Bradley Report*. London: Department of Health, The Stationery Office.

Brooker, C., Sirdifield, C., Blizard,R., Maxwell-Harrison, D., Tetley, D., Moran, P., Pluck, G., Chafer, A., Denney, D. & Turner, M. (2011). *An Investigation into the Prevalence of Mental Health Disorder and Patterns of Health Service Access in a Probation Population*. Lincoln: University of Lincoln.

Brooker, C., Sirdifield, C., Blizard, R., Denney, D. & Pluck, G. (2012). Probation and Mental Illness. *Journal of Forensic Psychiatry and Psychology*. **23** (4), 522–37.

Department of Health (2005). *The Offender Mental Healthcare Pathway.* London: The Stationery Office.

Department of Health (2014). *Mental Health Crisis Care Concordat – Improving outcomes for people experiencing mental health crisis.* London: The Stationery Office.

Jones, D. & Maynard, A. (2013). Suicide in recently released prisoners: a systematic review. *Mental Health Practice.* **17** (3), 20–27.

Ministry of Justice (2011). *South Wales MAPPA Annual Report 2010–2011.*

Ministry of Justice, National Offender Management Service (2012). *Mappa Guidance 2012* version 4.

Ministry of Justice (2013). *Transforming Rehabilitation – a revolution in the way we manage offenders.*

Nolan, P. (2000). *A History of Mental Health Nursing.* London: Nelson Thorne.

Sainsbury Centre for Mental Health (2009). *Diversion.* London: Sainsbury Centre for Mental Health.

*The Criminal Justice Act 2003* (2003). London: The Stationery Office.

Welsh Government (2013). *Criminal Justice Liaison Services in Wales: Policy Implementation Guidance.*

Williamson, M. (2006). *Improving the Health and Social Outcomes of People Recently Released from Prisons in the UK: A Perspective from Primary Care.* London: Sainsbury Centre for Mental Health.

# 8

# Custodial caritas: Beyond rhetoric in caring and custody

Dawn Freshwater

This chapter explores the concepts of *caritas* (sometimes defined as 'Christian love or charity') and *agape* (often described as 'selfless, spiritual love of another') in relation to custodial care. The nature of human caring in custodial settings has been thoroughly debated, and has received much attention from researchers and practitioners. The relationships that develop in this context are often fraught with complexities.

Drawing upon the distinctive nursing theories of scholars such as Parse (1992) and Rogers (1970), as well as the practical science of Sister Simone Roach (2002), this chapter attempts to describe ways in which theories of human caring can be applied to the daily lives of practitioners working within offender health settings. In essence, I aim to re-establish the relevance of these theories to this professionally testing context, and to breathe life into the concept of human *agape* as understood in the context of custodial care. To do this, I draw upon such concepts as reflexivity and discourse (especially discourses of caring and custody and caring practices in custody). To truly engage with the material in this chapter requires a degree of interactive receptiveness that encourages the questioning of assumptions (Belenky *et al.* 1986). I begin by challenging the assumption that there is always a gap between theory and practice.

## Theory and practice in caring and custody

Many notable authors, including those mentioned in this text (such as Holmes *et al.* 2012, Walsh 2012, and Walsh & Freshwater 2009), have theorised about caring practices in custodial care. For this reason, I do not intend to rehearse the caring–custody debate here. Suffice to say that this caring–custody dichotomy has been subjected to substantial interrogation in recent years.

However, I do wish to dwell for a moment on the age-old concept of the theory–practice divide. Practice is sometimes differentiated from theory because it is seen as *doing* something (as opposed to *thinking* about something). However, this so-called distinction can be over-stated. Thoughts also *do* something, and doing can involve *thinking* – through mindfulness. Action and thought are interactive. Practices are grounded in understandings that people have about the world; and these understandings are in turn influenced by the effect of their practices and actions on the world. Hence, our understandings of the world of custodial care, and our actions and practices in that world, are inextricably linked.

If we take a reflexive approach to both our understandings of our world (our theories) and the ways in which we practise and act (our practices), we are likely to be challenged by an ever-changing dynamic that constitutes 'the dance of custodial care'. However, it is also, of course, possible to practise in a way that supports our personal (unconscious) theories. We may have such unshakable beliefs that, even when challenged with evidence to the contrary, our theories drive our practices, which in turn confirm our personal theories. In other words, we look at any additional evidence to confirm the opinion to which we are already committed! Many of us look for new ways to evaluate complex interventions in offender health settings, but do we view caring practices in offender health settings as complex interventions in themselves and evaluate them as such? What, if anything, makes caring in offender health settings different from working in any other type of healthcare setting?

## Back to the future

The distinctive nursing and caring theories of scholars such as Parse (1992), Newman (1994), Rogers (1970) and Watson (1998), as well as the practical science of Sister Simone Roach, describe how the experience of human caring provides opportunities for deep connections between individuals and greater insights into oneself. Many of these theorists have considered the concepts of *caritas* and *agape* for decades, and have thus developed a 'science of caring'. Nevertheless, it is only relatively recently that we have begun to think about these theories in the context of correctional care and the dominant discourses surrounding caring and custody (Walsh & Freshwater 2009).

For the purposes of this chapter, 'discourse' is defined as 'a set of rules and assumptions for organising and interpreting the subject matter of an academic or practice discipline, or a field of study' (Freshwater *et al.* 2013). Many discourses contain certain assumptions that only become apparent under stress or in crisis situations. In addition, members of the discourse discipline may find it difficult to challenge or deconstruct these deep-rooted assumptions, and indeed are often complicit in perpetuating them (Freshwater *et al.* 2013).

# Discourses of caring practices

The practice of caring has consistently avoided being subjected to deconstruction, despite challenges to engrained assumptions, such as the ideas that nurses are always good, feel compassion and act with integrity. Indeed, the terms 'care' and 'nursing' are often used almost interchangeably in the literature. The word 'care' actually refers to affective (emotional) components of the concept of nursing. In contrast, the term 'nursing', according to Florence Nightingale (1859), was originally more of a call to duty and carried spiritual connotations. Clearly, these concepts have been iterated and developed over time until we have what we now call '21st-century nursing practice'. This contemporary version of nursing does not shy away from the previously unmentionable subject of love: love for the patient; love of the patient; love of care; love for the carer (Freshwater & Esterhuizen 2009).

Indeed, Roach (2002) argues that the desire to love and be loved is at the heart of the human condition. She goes on to say that it is a 'prevailing undercurrent so easily missed in the needs of persons suffering from illness, disease and disability'. The desire to love and be loved is by no means confined to traditional marital, civil and familial relationships. It also, of course, occurs naturally in caring and fiduciary and filial relationships (Briant & Freshwater 1998). In her seminal text *Caring: The Human Mode of Being*, Dr Roach (2002) borrows from theology the terms *agape* and *caritas* in order to illuminate her points. Watson (1998) too, in her reflections on caring theory, suggests that using a reflective model of caring enables the formation of a link between caring and love, opening up the concept of 'clinical caritas' (Watson 1998, p. 218).

# *Caritas* and *agape*

The terms *agape* and *caritas* provide a lens through which love can be explored in the context of therapeutic alliances, such as those created in healthcare settings, including offender health and correctional services.

*Agape*, translated from the Greek, is described as 'an affection of the heart', whereas the Latin *caritas* was understood by the medieval theologian Thomas Aquinas to be 'the friendship of man for God'. Watson (1998) and Noddings (1984) have argued that *caritas*, which is often interpreted using words such as 'charity', 'caring' and 'cherish', is enacted through regard, affection, esteem and love. Such virtues have, as Watson and Noddings remind us, 'the connotation of preciousness'. In her early musings in this area, Noddings (1984) acknowledges the force of love and moreover the desire to come into direct undiluted contact with the human aspects of the other. This brings us to reflections on the relationship between self and other, and self and self, and specifically the ethical nature of those relationships.

Australian ethicist Stan Van Hooft (1995) does much to expose some of the questions around caring as a virtue in his thesis *Caring: An essay in the philosophy of ethics*. He contends that caring is 'a model of human agency and motivation (interpersonal and interactive, social). It is part of human structure and takes at least two forms: caring for self and caring for others. These two forms of caring are expressed in a variety of ways and functions at four levels, all of which can be applied to offender health and correctional settings. These are:

- The biological level, in which caring is expressed as the instinct to survive and nurture
- The perceptual level, in which caring is expressed as emotion and contains cultural constructions of the world
- The evaluative level, in which caring is expressed as pragmatic projects and social solidarity
- The spiritual level, in which caring is expressed as ethics and morality.

Thus, rather like Maslow (1970) with his hierarchy of need, Van Hooft (1995) seems to argue that it is difficult to concentrate on spiritual care giving when one is engaged in trying to survive at a physical level. We might think about this in the context of offenders' experience of incarceration and also in the experience of carers and health professionals who have to deliver care in professionally testing environments. In addition, the instability of health and correctional systems means that care-giving often becomes fragmented and fractured rather than holistic and dynamic, and care values may be subordinated to target-driven outcomes.

Stability is always, of course, an illusion to some extent. Broken continuity (or continuous fragmentation) is the best we can hope for. We are all broken and human; we are all inconsistent, complex, incongruent and ambiguous. Criminality, violence, hate, terrorism – these are not new phenomena. History paints for us the ambiguity and paradox of the human condition, and the stark contrast between violent acts and compassionate deeds. The so-called 'caring professions' are by no means excluded from causing suffering. We only need to look at the professional jealousy and professional terrorism that can take place in health-related professions to understand that such acts of uncaring are part and parcel of the human condition. Healthcare literature contains plentiful descriptions of overt and covert non-physical hostility, including sabotage, scapegoating, back-stabbing and negative criticism, failure to respect privacy and keep confidences, non-verbal innuendos and lack of openness and other such behaviours (Freshwater 2000).

It is paradoxical, though not surprising, that – within a discipline that has caring for others as its main focus – employee relationships are frequently so poor. The discourse of care is tested even further when practitioners challenge the generally held belief that nurses and health professionals do not engage in non-caring behaviours and criminal or deviant activities – especially those that inflict harm on someone in their charge. The so-called 'stable discourse' is challenged by such examples.

Current discourses of clinical practice emphasise regulation, safety and managed care, with financial and political drivers constraining practitioners to concentrate on focused care and dehumanised, depersonalised, rather than evidence-based, personalised, relational care (Walsh *et al.* 2013). Tensions between the ecologies and economies of performance can lead to an apparent impasse between judgemental policy reports, such as the Francis Report on the Mid-Staffordshire Inquiry (2013), and staff members' internalised experience of distress. This distress is most often related to the degree of compromise required to manage the level of cognitive dissonance experienced by the practitioner on a daily basis (Freshwater & Cahill 2011). Unfortunately a great deal of practice is shaped by discourses that simultaneously value and impede critical thinking. For example, pressures of time and space in the clinical environment are often presented as reasons not to allow time out for critical thinking and deconstruction of practice. However, lack of opportunities for reflection can result in self-justification and unhealthy ways of reducing the cognitive dissonance created by the tensions between espoused theories and values and what actually happens in practice.

## 'Flat pack care' versus values-based care

In February 2013, the final report of the Mid-Staffordshire NHS Foundation Trust Public Inquiry was published. This investigated complaints regarding standards of care in the Staffordshire Hospital. The report revealed that, while the Trust appeared to be complying with the standards set by official regulating bodies, 'appalling conditions of care were able to flourish'. This was partly attributed to a culture that prioritised targets over care, resulting in neglect of older patients. The regulatory mechanisms had clearly failed to ensure 'compassionate care', a value that was subordinated to the pressures of complying with managerial targets (Fisher & Freshwater 2013).

The dangers of poor care will always be present in situations where the values of care are outweighed by instrumental rationality, as evidenced through the pressure to meet often unrealistic targets. And the views put forward in the Francis Report (2013) are therefore welcome. Blaming individuals for systematic failures is generally fruitless. As Fisher and Freshwater (2013) note, the report advocates a route towards compassionate care through the enforcement of professional values associated with 'strong leadership' and 'the rigorous policing of fundamental standards'.

The Francis Report has received much international praise, and could consequently be regarded as a 'critical moment' exposing, as it did, a 'crisis of care'. The warning signs had in fact been evident for some time. In 1995, *The Crisis of Care* (Phillips & Benner 1995) highlighted how the moral obligation to show compassion and goodness was being eclipsed by depersonalised procedures and market imperatives in the USA, Canada and Australia. The US Institute of Medicine Report (IOM 2000) demonstrated the magnitude of the health and safety problem, revealing that the majority of deaths from unintended consequences of healthcare interventions occurred because of inadequate communication and the poor quality of working relationships. Similarly in Australia, the Australian Commission on Safety and Quality in Healthcare (ACSQHC 2011) was set up as an independent body, born out of widespread concern about uncoordinated approaches to healthcare. A key aspect of the commission's responsibility is to help senior clinicians develop leadership skills to support patient care.

Further, it has become clear that it is difficult to fulfil the ideal of 'cross-disciplinary working in order to deliver seamless services' against a backdrop of collaborative failures (Freshwater et al. 2013). The 2013 report by the Office of the Correctional Investigator in Canada, Risky Business, highlights the important principle of collaborative working between interdisciplinary teams. However, this investigation revealed considerable tension between members of different teams – particularly the mental health and security staff who worked together on the multidisciplinary team. It was not only staff who revealed these tensions, and the subsequent failures in care. Female prisoners interviewed as part of the investigation also commented that they learnt to deal with conflict between mental health professionals and security staff by developing covert coping strategies so as to avoid segregation when they were in need of physical and psychological care.

The pursuit of organisational targets and outcomes in health and social care organisations operating according to quasi-market forms of accountability has led to an increase in managed care (Weber 1978), which is directly at odds with the drive to a more compassionate model of care as prescribed by Francis (2013). Little space is left for personal emotion or compassion. And human *agape* and clinical *caritas* are seen as abstract concepts that cannot be measured, are not quantifiable, but experiential and, as such, are of little use to the policy maker or politician who needs hard evidence of targets being met in order to be re-elected. Practising in this context alone is challenging. Add to this the complexity of working in a marginalised healthcare setting, with marginalised social groups, and it becomes even more difficult to meet the challenge of delivering compassion in everyday care, and being human in the act of caring.

## The 'human mode of being'

I will now turn to what Simone Roach defines as the 'human mode of being' and use this as a lens through which to view the remainder of this chapter. Dr Roach (2002) identifies six key aspects of the human mode of being: compassion, comportment, conscience, confidence, competence and commitment. For the purpose of this chapter, I will emphasise the concepts of compassion and competence. I define compassion, which is central to the context of clinical *caritas*, as 'to suffer with and have sensitivity to the suffering of others'.

Competence is, in practice, the appropriate use of the tension between power and caring. This is not a simple tension to manage, as is evident in the large volume of literature related to power (Freshwater 2010). Sellman (2011) recently argued that the term 'competence' has been misappropriated, as it is now used to refer to ritualised, prescriptive protocols and pathways – what could be called formulaic and mechanistic approaches to care, a type of 'machine consciousness' adopted in order to appear competent. However, such appearances can be deceptive, as they divide the individual (see my earlier comment regarding the gap between theories and practices), team, organisations and practices. Divided and dividing practices are based on cognitive dissonance, most notably a dissonance between caring and power. Whilst dissonance is uncomfortable, often forcing us to search for resolutions quickly, the experience of uncertainty and the challenge to our preferred way of viewing the world is also an interesting and potentially creative space within which to dwell. Despite (or because of) the apparent contradictions that we are at first confronted with, such 'tense spaces' can provide us with a new and illuminating vantage point.

An example of divided and dividing practice can be seen in the French film *Amour*, in which the idealistic love most often portrayed in Hollywood romances is challenged and laid open to scrutiny. The plot line of the film, which closely resembles real-world research, articulates the narrative experience of an enduring devotion and duty of love between two people who have been inseparable for several decades. The storyline highlights something of the complexity of human caring, and the myriad emotions and dynamics that underlie any caring relationship.

In another French film *The Intouchables*, which is based on a true story, a quadriplegic aristocrat hires a young man from 'the projects' to be his caretaker. As the plot of the film unfolds, the audience is given the opportunity to reflect on their own values and beliefs regarding caring as well as the traditional, polarised and somewhat dichotomised discourses of lawlessness and love. The way in which caring is portrayed – within this intimate, unusual alliance of aristocrat and delinquent – is curiously gripping. The concept of reciprocity, as traditionally held, is questioned and interrogated, albeit subtly throughout the story. Such wise reciprocity between strangers, each essentially a stranger to the other, yet each with a gift of wisdom to share with the other, is (or should be) a fundamental tenet of clinical care.

As qualified and trained caring professionals, we may think we know about caring. Indeed, there is a wealth of literature and research available, identifying the nature of a caring epistemology, the ontology of caring, and even the ontical level (the latter being how we live and our statement of ethical obligation). But to what extent do we live out the theory of compassionate care, and how can this become an underpinning element of custodial and correctional practice?

Perhaps we could consider the value of Roslyn Bologh's (2009) feminist understanding of a 'sociability of care' within custodial caring contexts. In a recent paper, it was suggested that compassionate care requires an enlarged understanding of rationality, one that prioritises the importance of relationships (Fisher & Freshwater 2013). From a feminist perspective, the value of what Bologh terms 'aesthetic rationality' should be acknowledged in order to engender a sociability of compassion within care environments. Bologh argues that dominant organisational understandings of rationality need to be extended in ways that acknowledge the importance of compassionate care, and this is enacted within social relationships. However, this requires a degree of authentic emotional engagement on the part of formal caregivers that is more typically associated with relationships in the private sphere. Instead, the model that often prevails is one of the lone practitioner, isolated from colleagues, alienated from the organisation, and subjugated by a disciplinary culture of targets to be met.

Bologh sees aesthetic rationality as a mainly unacknowledged female form of rationality (in the sense that it is associated with domestic and communal relations). Aesthetic rationality is appreciative of, and responsive to, beauty. It joins together mind, body, feelings and senses and seeks to create a world that enriches and empowers people, and, in this respect, it is concerned with recognition of our humanity. In other words, the ultimate gain is the realisation of a subjective sense of well-being – physical, social and emotional. As Fisher and Freshwater (2013) note, 'This would include tending to the body in physically sensitive ways or invoking well-being through the organisation of playful or social activities, or simply listening attentively and responding in ways that foster a person's sense of belonging.'

The inclusion of the emotional dimension in Bologh's thinking is of particular significance to organisations that run caring businesses. In an age of algorithms of care, one might reasonably ask what model of care might be needed to ensure that aesthetic rationality is accorded equal importance to other forms of rationality, with a view to creating a relational ethic between these seemingly competing versions of caring. Fisher and Freshwater (2013) propose a 'sociability of care', based on dialogue and aesthetic rationality, arguing that this type of care cannot be conjured up or enforced through the imposition of authority: 'it requires a deeply embedded change of culture that is achieved though collective commitment'. And there again is a key concept from Roach's (2002) human mode of being – commitment. Aesthetic rationality might be a good starting place for developing not only commitment, but also compassion and competence.

For a sociability of care to take hold, critical dialogue is essential in the caring context – specifically in custodial settings. That dialogue is between wisdom and courage, and takes a form that is rather akin to David Bohm's notion of dialogue (Bohm 2004). That is, a common participation in which we are not playing a game *against* each other, but *with* each other, where the object of the dialogue is not to analyse or win an argument or even to exchange opinions. Rather, it is to suspend our opinions and to listen to those of others; then to suspend them all and to see what they all mean.

## Conclusion

Nursing is a social intervention that involves the actions of people. Understanding human intentions and motivations is therefore essential to understanding the implementation and subsequent evaluation of nursing. At each stage, any social intervention could either work as expected or misfire. In caring environments that are professionally testing, such as those that sit between the domains of custody and caring, there is a higher chance of those social interactions misfiring. The individuals, the institution and infrastructure create a system that can, if it is an open system, feed back on itself, with the aim of learning, reflecting and improving care.

In this sense, we all have a collective capacity and responsibility to question assumptions about the nature and consequences of social power relations within seemingly competing systems and paradigms that form the custody and caring dichotomy. We all have a responsibility to care for this dichotomy and for the opportunities for creative tension that it provides.

This chapter has provided an opportunity to reflect on the dialogue between our understandings of the world of custody and care, and our practices and actions in that world. The aim has also been to expand consciousness, to examine caring as a process of being and becoming, and to reflect on ways of responding in professionally testing situations. By caring for your theories and practices, you can care for and expand yourself, and in that process, unify theories and practices in order to improve the experience of patients. Gage (2003) proposed that caring science consisted of nurses creating their art and practising their science. I would argue that this can only be achieved in the context of relationships, and a sociability of care constructed through an aesthetic rationality and a human mode of being.

# References

Australian Commission on Safety and Quality in Healthcare (2013). Annual Report 2012/2013 Sydney: ACSQHC. http://www.safetyandquality.gov.au/wp-content/uploads/2012/10/ACSQHC-Annual-Report-2011-2012-web-version (Last accessed: 11 August 2014).

Belenky, M.F., Clinchy, B.M., Goldberger N.R. & Tarule, J.M. (1986). *Women's Ways of Knowing*. New York: Basic Books.

Bohm, D. (2004). *On Dialogue*. Oxford: Routledge.

Bologh, R.W. (2009). *Love or Greatness: Max Weber and Masculine Thinking – a Feminist Enquiry*. London: Taylor & Francis.

Briant, S. & Freshwater, D. (1998). Exploring mutuality within the nurse-patient relationship, *British Journal of Nursing*. **7** (4), 204–11.

Fisher, P. & Freshwater, D. (2013). *Towards compassionate care through aesthetic rationality*. (In press).

Francis, R. (2013). *The Mid Staffordshire NHS Foundation Trust Public Inquiry*. http://www.midstaffspublicinquiry.com/report (Last accessed on 7 July 2014).

Freshwater, D. (2000). Crosscurrents: against cultural narration in nursing. *Journal of Advanced Nursing*. **32** (2), 481–84.

Freshwater, D. (2010) *Power and Caring: The thorn in the side of nursing?* Asian Pacific Nursing Conference Invited Keynote Speaker, Singapore June 30.

Freshwater, D. & Cahill, J. (2011). Care and compromise: Developing a conceptual framework for work-related stress. *Journal of Research in Nursing*. **15** (6), 497–508.

Freshwater, D., Cahill, J. & Essen, C. (2013). Narratives of collaborative failure: Identity role and discourse in an interdisciplinary world. *Nursing Inquiry*. **21** (1), 59–68.

Freshwater, D. & Esterhuizen, P. (2009). 'Speaking the unspeakable: What's love got to do with it' in Warne, T. & McAndrew, S. (eds.) *Creative Approaches in Health and Social Care Education and Practice: Knowing me, understanding you*. London: Palgrave Macmillan.

Gage, J. (2003). Embracing the art and science of nursing. *Kai Tiaki Nursing New Zealand.* **9** (10), 18–19.

Holmes, D., Rudge, T. & Perron, A. (2012). *(Re)Thinking Violence in Healthcare Settings.* Burlington, USA: Ashgate.

Institute of Medicine (2010). The future of nursing: Leading change, advancing health. http://www.iom.edu/Reports/2010/the-future-of-nursing-leading-change-advancing-health.aspx (Last accessed: 11 August 2014).

Maslow, A. (1970). *Motivation and Personality.* (2nd ed.) New York: Harper and Row.

Newman, M. (1994). *Health as Expanding Consciousness.* 2nd ed. New York: National League for Nursing Press.

Nightingale, F. (1859). *Notes on Nursing: What it is, and What it is Not.* Edinburgh: Wadman.

Noddings, N. (1984). *Caring: A feminine approach to ethics and moral education.* Berkeley: University of California Press.

Office of the Correctional Investigator, Canada (2013) http://www.oci-bec.gc.ca/cnt/rpt/oth-aut/oth-aut20130930-eng.aspx

Parse, R.R. (1992). Human becoming: Parse's theory of nursing. *Nursing Science Quarterly.* Philadelphia: Saunders.

Phillips, S.S. & Benner, P.E. eds (1995). *The Crisis of Care: Affirming and Restoring Caring Practices in the Helping Professions.* Washington, DC: Georgetown University Press.

Roach, M. Simone (2002). *Caring, The human mode of being.* (2nd ed.) Ottawa: Canadian Healthcare Association Press.

Rogers, M.E. (1970) *An Introduction to the Theoretical Basis of Nursing.* New York: F.A. Davis.

Sellman, D. (2010). *What makes a Good Nurse: Why virtues are important for nursing.* London: Jessica Kingsley.

Van Hooft, S. (1995). *Caring: An essay in the philosophy of ethics.* Colorado: University Press of Colorado.

Walsh, E. (2012). 'Prison Nursing: Managing the threats to caring' in Holmes, D., Rudge, T. & Perron, A. (2012). *(Re)Thinking Violence in Healthcare Settings.* Burlington, USA: Ashgate, 281–97.

Walsh, E. & Freshwater, D. (2009). Developing the mental health awareness of prison staff in England and Wales. *Journal of Correctional Healthcare.* **15** (4), 302–309.

Walsh, E., Freshwater, D. & Fisher, P. (2013). Mindful practice: Caring for prisoners. *Journal of Research in Nursing.* **18** (2), 158–68.

Watson, J. (1998). 'Chapter 18: A Meta-Reflection on Reflective Practice and Caring Theory' in Johns, C. & Freshwater, D. (eds.) *Transforming Nursing Through Reflective Practice.* Oxford: Blackwell.

Weber, M. (1978). *Economy and Society.* Los Angeles and London: University of California Press.

# 9

# Caring for vulnerable people: Intellectual disability in the criminal justice system

Colin Dale and Pamela Inglis

Certain groups of people are particularly vulnerable when navigating the criminal justice system (CJS). This may be due to their low status in society, their physical or mental vulnerability and their lack of recourse. These vulnerable groups include: children, remand prisoners, women, those with mental health problems, the elderly, foreign prisoners, minority populations and those with an intellectual disability (ID) (Prison Fellowship International 2013).

This chapter considers the experiences of people with an ID, exploring the difficulties they face in gaining appropriate access and direction through the CJS, policy and practice in this field, and barriers to effective treatment.

The chapter begins by defining intellectual disability and considers some of the issues that are particularly relevant to vulnerable people. It outlines the characteristics of offenders with an intellectual disability and considers some of the crimes that lead them into the CJS.

## Vulnerability and its effects

Vulnerability is a word that is used often in our society, and its meaning can be broad. The online Oxford English Dictionary (2013) defines it as: 'exposed to the possibility of being attacked or harmed, either physically or emotionally. (of a person) in need of special care, support, or protection because of age, disability, or risk of abuse or neglect'.

Vulnerable people who are in contact with the CJS may also be easily swayed or led astray, often because they lack support, wisdom or experience, or lack understanding of the legal system, or social rules. People with an intellectual disability are most often defined by deficits. For example, they may be viewed as having an Intelligence Quotient (IQ) below 70, lack of communication skills, inability to understand and express emotions appropriately, poor memory, low literacy level, difficulty with understanding the consequences of their behaviour, naivety, lack of social and emotional support, isolation, and lack of financial support.

Such characteristics can easily be viewed as ones that would make someone vulnerable, rather than those that would usually be attributed to a habitual offender. Indeed, people with an intellectual disability are more likely to have offences such as assault and burglary committed against them, rather than becoming offenders themselves.

ID not only affects the individual's intellect but may also have wider consequences, such as behavioural and social challenges. It is commonly associated with health needs that are often not effectively met (MENCAP 2004, UKLDCNN 2005, Michael 2008). ID spans a wide range of ability, from people who are severely physically or sensorily impaired (some of whom require 24-hour support) to the majority, who require little support to get on with their everyday lives.

Most of the issues affecting people with an ID are not related to their intellectual impairment, but may be associated with the way they are treated by society. For example they, along with other underprivileged groups, are commonly vulnerable to social disadvantages such as: poverty, unstable family backgrounds, lack of optimum education opportunities, unemployment, and mental health issues.

Few positive facets tend to be described for this population, but – given the right education, support and access – people with ID are often described as proficient, trustworthy and enthusiastic employees who make other workers enjoy their work (Inglis 2010, Down's Syndrome Association 2007, *Personnel Today* 2007). Importantly, disabled people add something positive to society by increasing its diversity (Swain & French 2000, Smith 2000).

Additionally, despite a CJS that aims to protect vulnerable people, they are more likely to suffer from exploitation, physical and sexual assault, robbery, theft and burglary than the rest of the population (Wilson & Brewer 1992, Brown *et al.* 1995, Quarmby 2008).

## Prevalence of ID amongst offenders

Intellectual disability has long been associated with criminality, although true historical figures remain unknown (Lindsay & Taylor 2005, Riding *et al.* 2005). A longitudinal study in Sweden found that men with an intellectual disability were three times more likely to offend and five times more likely to have violent convictions than non-disabled people (Hodgins 1992). Fazel *et al.* (2008) conducted a systematic review across four countries but found that it was not possible to calculate prevalence because of the diversity of calculations used. They concluded that 0.5–1.5 per cent of all prisoners were diagnosed with ID. This constitutes a considerable number of prisoners, and therefore has great implications for policy as well as practice.

The negativity associated with ID may be strengthened when people with ID have an offending history, as this supports some of the myths associated with criminality and appears to justify the fear and scorn often directed towards this population (Inglis & Dale 2010). In addition, the crimes for which people with an ID are held may seem to confirm some of the worst assumptions about this group. For example, sex offenders seem to be over-represented in this population (Day 1994). However, other studies have shown that the overall prevalence of offenders is in fact similar or lower in people with an ID when compared to the general population, but that they may be more easily detected. Furthermore, their offences tend to be less violent than those of their non-disabled counterparts and their sexual crimes are less likely to involve penetration. Nevertheless, they are more likely to be given a custodial sentence for such crimes (Wilson & Brewer 1992, Brown et al. 1995).

The literature states different rates of prevalence of ID across the CJS, because the data are collected at various stages of the pathway and use a range of criteria for detecting ID, none of which are adequate to make a formal diagnosis (Beail 2004). The World Health Organisation (1992) found only 1 per cent of people with an ID committed an offence (this classification of ID was based on the International Classification of Diseases definition of ID as described in ICD-10), but McBrien (2003) reviewed other studies and found the prevalence of ID in the offending population to be between 2 and 9.7 per cent. More recent figures from the Prison Reform Trust (2007a) state a prevalence of between 1 per cent and 10 per cent in the prison population.

A more recent study of the prison population in England discovered 7 per cent of prisoners had an IQ of less than 70, and a further 25 per cent had an IQ of less than 80 (Mottram 2007). This figure has been found to be higher for certain prison populations, with 23 per cent of juvenile prisoners found to have an IQ of less than 70 (Harrington & Bailey et al. 2005).

The Prison Reform Trust, in their 2007 study, discovered that 20 per cent of the prison population has some form of 'hidden disability' that affects their ability to work and participate in education (Rack 2005, cited in Prison Reform Trust 2007a). It has been suggested that between 20 and 50 per cent of men in prison have a specific intellectual disability (Disability Rights Commission 2005 memorandum to the Commons Select Committee on prison education, cited in Prison Reform Trust 2007a).

- Assuming a prison population of 82,000, this equates to an estimated: 5,740 men, women and children with very low IQs (of less than 70)
- 20,500 individuals with IQs between 71 and 80
- 16,400 with a 'hidden disability' that 'will affect and undermine their performance in both education and work settings.'

What remains unknown, due to a lack of research data, is how many more people with an ID are currently engaged with police custody, the courts and the probation services. Whether the conviction rates mirror prevalence is also unknown. It is possible that people with an ID are more likely to be detected and subsequently convicted because of their disability. What is certain, though, is that people with an ID are often treated differently in the CJS from the outset, and this has a significant impact on their experiences in the CJS.

## Characteristics of intellectually disabled offenders

Offenders with an ID often share characteristics with the general population of offenders, as they are from younger age groups and tend to be male.

In addition, offenders with an ID often present with:

- Challenging behaviours
- A level of functioning in the 70–90 IQ range (often described as mild/borderline ID)
- Reduced social skills
- Familial and financial difficulties
- A frequent history of childhood behaviour disorder and criminal behaviour
- A deprived or abusive background
- High rates of co-morbidity with other psychiatric diagnoses, with a 13–37 per cent rate of dual diagnosis
- Higher rates of epilepsy than the general population
- Excess of speech/language dysfunction even when IQ is corrected for
- Difficulty in getting an accurate diagnosis
- Poor verbal skills, with difficulty recognising and articulating what they are feeling (Day 1994, Seaward & Rees 2001, Gunn 1994, Holland et al. 2002).

Whilst some of these characteristics are shared with the general prison population, people with a mild or borderline ID will not usually be eligible for community health service provision and so will not be known to services. They consequently risk passing unidentified through the CJS system. There is still a lack of support available to people with ID in the criminal justice system, and they remain excluded from activities and opportunities available to others due to their literacy and concentration limitations and a lack of modification of activities by prison staff (Prison Reform Trust 2007b).

In particular, their vulnerability factors include: impaired self-control; naivety or gullibility; the leading of chaotic lives; often being homeless and substance abusers; commonly having a recent history of major life events and an inability to adequately/appropriately express emotions, dissent, anger or frustration (Winter et al. 1997).

Unlike the average prison inmate, the most common form of behaviour in those with ID that results in convictions is aggression, followed by sexual behaviour and then self-harm (Seaward & Rees

2001). Prior to arrest, prisoners with an ID were almost twice as likely as the comparison group to have been unemployed, and were three times as likely to have been excluded from school; over half said they had attended a special school.

## Types of offending behaviour

People with an ID get caught up in the CJS for a number of reasons. For some, it is curiosity or gullibility that draws them into offending, whilst for others there may be more conscious thought and planning involved in their offending behaviour. Walker (1991) provides a useful framework for considering the level of consciousness in offending, which he describes as 'Risky Typologies':

- Type 1: Bad luck gives rise to provocation or temptation
- Type 2: Individual seeks out 'risky situations' by choice
- Type 3: Individual constantly vigilant for opportunities to offend
- Type 4: Individual contrives to create offending situations

Day (1994) suggested that, amongst ID offenders, too many arson and sex offenders were diverted from the CJS and forcibly hospitalised. More recently, however, Taylor (2013) has described the evidence base for this assumption as poor, with a dearth of control studies, including reference groups. However, offenders with ID are possibly under-represented in more serious and violent crimes, including homicide.

## Detecting intellectual disability in the CJS

In order to meet the needs of people with ID in the criminal justice system, ID offenders need to be directly referred at the outset, as soon as they are identified in the CJS pathway. This process includes the police services; the courts; and the prison service itself, through the prison healthcare provider, through an intellectual disability clinic or through the use of Complex Case Forums. All these agencies need to cooperate to create a more natural convergence of services for people with ID, forming pathways across these estates and/or back into the community.

The *Healthy Children: Safer Communities* initiative (DH 2009) highlighted the way youth justice screening tools often overlook physical health problems and underestimate the incidence of mental health problems in children who offend. Furthermore, these tools do not screen for intellectual disability, for speech, language and communication needs, or for conduct disorder (Prison Reform Trust 2007a). The study also found evidence that dyslexia is three to four times more common amongst prisoners than within the general population (Prison Reform Trust 2007a).

The Prison Reform Trust (2007a) suggests that, although there is much that prisons could do locally to improve things for offenders with ID by ensuring that staff are aware of what support is available and how to access it, commitment and leadership are needed across government departments in order to improve upon the current state of affairs.

The shift in commissioning priorities has picked up momentum over the last few years, through publications such as *The Bradley Report* (Bradley 2009) and more recently the Centre for Mental Health report *Blurring the Boundaries* (Rutherford 2010). Both these national drivers extol the virtues of multi-agency cooperation between all organisations working within the criminal justice system, in order to deliver more positive experiences for those people who are primarily seen as vulnerable and mentally disordered. However, all interventions and policy are useless unless the ID and vulnerability are detected early in the person's contact with the CJS.

## Coming into contact with the criminal justice system

From first contact with the CJS, people with ID may be treated differently from the general population (if their disability is detected). As the Criminal Procedure (Insanity) Act 1964 states: 'Mental disability (as in the MHA) on the part of the defendant may affect the outcome of a case in three ways.' These three ways are listed as follows:

- Mental disability at committal may mean that the person is 'unfit to be tried'.
- Mental disability at the time of the offence may give rise to the defence of insanity (or, alternatively, diminished responsibility in a murder case).
- Mental disability at the time of conviction may require hospital admission under the remit of the MHA (1983), section 37, sub-section 1.

This different treatment is sometimes viewed as advantageous for detainees, but it can disadvantage them. The *No One Knows* report (Prison Reform Trust, 2007a) states that police officers commonly prefer that no further action is taken for people with ID. This may seem advantageous but those officers proceeding to charges often do so to ensure the person receives proper treatment and support. Diversion to healthcare is usually the preferred option with mentally disordered offenders (Bradley 2009).

If the person with ID is not diverted, their experiences within the criminal justice system follow a familiar pattern. They usually report feeling overwhelmed by police presence and may try to flee, thus appearing guilty. They often pretend to know more than they really do (sometimes deliberately hiding their disability). They also may not fully understand the implications of the offence, and can therefore appear to have no remorse. This may affect the way they are viewed and subsequently treated in the CJS.

They commonly have a desire to please people in authority, including nursing staff, and often rely heavily on authority figures (Inglis 2010). Their tendency to acquiesce may mean they are overly willing to confess. In addition, memory problems can make traditional interviewing techniques inadequate, and may mean that false confessions are made to nursing staff.

Often, because of their naivety they have accomplices who blame them. This is now commonly described as 'mate crime', where friends or relatives take advantage of the disabled person (Thomas 2011). Additionally, people with an ID are often unable to understand the legal process, but they may be hiding their disability and, because police officers lack training in this area, the disability may not be detected. A study conducted in the USA by a national advocacy service demonstrated the naivety of people with ID. In the USA, the intellectual disability group 'The Arc' found that 38 per cent of people with an ID thought they could be arrested for having a disability; 50 per cent said they would tell someone they had a disability when arrested; 58 per cent said they would talk to the police before talking to a lawyer; and 68 per cent said they believed that the arresting officer would protect them (The Arc 2006). Further, in Inglis & Dale (2010), the men with ID believed that they were 'locked-up' because of their ID.

## First contact with the CJS

From their first contact with the CJS, people with ID are commonly disadvantaged. Firstly, the caution is a long statement, with many different and complex parts, that many people don't understand. Indeed, it is not only people with ID who are confused by cautions. BSL interpreters also have difficulty in translating convoluted speech to D/deaf suspects: as in the following description: 'The officer is speaking the exact words of a densely written construction that is far from natural spoken English' (Hann & Tate 2010, p. 2).

Furthermore, the provision of an 'appropriate adult' (AA) is not consistent across police forces and local authorities, and this can lead to anomalies in practice. Many commentators believe that AA attendance should be mandatory where concerns are sufficient to request the involvement of healthcare professionals, and that this should be a statutory provision rather than left to the voluntary sector. Half of prisoners with a possible ID said they did not know what would happen to them once they had been charged, and they were more likely to say they received help from a solicitor (Talbot 2008).

## At the police station

According to a study by Talbot (2008), less than a third of prisoners received support from an AA during police interviews and none appeared to have benefited from special measures such as the support of an intermediary.

In another study (Prison Reform Trust, 2007a), people with ID said they had been beaten or handled roughly by the police. They reported feeling suicidal or considering self-harm and felt manipulated into agreeing to a police interview without support. They also reported that they were denied their medication whilst in police custody.

# Barriers and strategies

Autistic spectrum disorders (ASD) may cause specific difficulties. Even though people with ASD are no more likely to commit crimes than the general population, their inability to deal with certain types of stimulation and understand social situations means that police officers might benefit from altering their approach (Gomez de la Cuesta & Mason 2010). Again, if the ASD/ID or vulnerability is identified early, then simple measures may help to avoid escalation of tension. These could include, for instance:

- Switching off sirens and flashing lights
- Keeping calm when approaching the individual, as anxiety can often be sensed in others
- Ensuring that personal space is understood (people with ASD/ID may require more space or may invade others' space unknowingly)
- Keeping facial expressions and gestures to a minimum (some people with ASD/ID have difficulty understanding emotions)
- Using the person's name
- Giving slow, clear and direct instructions and using other media if possible (people with ID often understand visual information better)
- Allowing time for people to process information
- Not expecting an immediate response to instructions or questions
- Avoiding sarcasm, metaphors and irony (they may be taken literally)
- Not attempting to stop idiosyncratic behaviours (such as rocking or hand-flapping or other repetitive or ritualistic movements, as these are often used to lower anxiety).

*(The National Autistic Society 2006)*

At the point of arrest, the custody officer is responsible for identifying whether the detainee needs further professional assessment. The custody officer first has to recognise the signs of ID in order to refer the individual. The custody officer then reads the offender their rights and gives them a leaflet outlining their rights. Of course this is useless if the detainee does not possess sufficient literacy to be able to understand the leaflet. The custody officer is then required to check the detainee's level of understanding, as they may not understand that they have the right to remain silent and to see a solicitor.

Obviously if the person arrested has ID they may not be capable of consenting to being questioned, requesting a solicitor or waiving any rights. Only if ID is identified can the person be treated fairly but this relies upon the ability to recognise ID, which suggests the need for highly trained police officers (Hayes 2002). In recent years, there have been several attempts to develop a simple screening instrument for use within the CJS. However, research to date has suggested that the tools developed are difficult to apply, as the most valid, for example the WAIS-III (Kaufman & Litchtenberger 1999), is not suitable for routine screening in prisons (Prison Reform Trust 2007a, Mottram 2007). The follow-through of a suspect's right to legal advice is sometimes poor, but extremely effective when carried out well:

> Though many criticisms have been made of the competence and effectiveness of legal advisers… there is overwhelming evidence that suspects who receive such help are less likely to make self-incriminating confessions, and more likely to exercise their right to silence.
>
> *(Clare 2003)*

## Interviewing witnesses with an intellectual disability

When acting as witnesses or suspects, people with ID have protection under the Police and Criminal Evidence Act (PACE) Codes of Practice. This is important to note for nurses, who may be accompanying suspects or acting as an 'appropriate adult' in such circumstances. When giving statements, the reliability of witnesses with ID is often questioned because of assumptions about impaired memory, vulnerability and difficulties in coping with the uncertainty of questioning (Gudjonsson & Henry 2003). However, studies have in fact shown that people with ID can give sound testimonies (Kebbell & Hatton 1999), especially when the interviewer uses open questions and structures interviews carefully (guidance by Tully & Cahill 1984, summarised in Grant *et al.* 2005).

Furthermore, use of the Gudjonsson Suggestibility Scale (GSS) (Gudjonsson 1997) may be particularly useful when accompanying suspects to legal interviews, as it scores the ability of the witness to resist suggestibility. Beail (2002) reports that the lower suggestibility scores in people with ID are based upon assessing their memory for facts. However, people with an intellectual disability actually have better episodic memory. This is confirmed by a study by White and Willner (2003) who found that the recall was higher, and the suggestibility lower, in people with ID who had witnessed an event, rather than just been told about it. Therefore, it seems that false statements and confessions may actually be *less* likely in people with ID.

Due to the intellectual deficits associated with ID, gaining accurate and detailed information from these witnesses may pose particular problems. Studies have shown how the interviewer's behaviour, the form and content of the interviews, and the types of questions and how they are asked, may all influence the interviewee's ability to give valid answers and provide valid information about their well-being, their history, their relationships and their needs (Prosser & Bromley 2012). As a consequence of fine-tuning interview techniques, people with ID are more likely to receive the appropriate help/treatment and be supported in their rights. When satisfaction is increased in this way, it may lead to increased compliance with regimes.

As we have seen, people with ID occasionally have a tendency to acquiesce, especially to closed (yes and no) questions. Acquiescence is obvious when they give an affirmative response to two conflicting questions, or when they simply agree with whatever statement is given. People are thought to acquiesce because they have ID or for social desirability – in other words, seeking social approval by agreeing. They may believe that disagreeing will displease the interviewer. Indeed, research by Sigelman et al. (1981, cited in Prosser & Bromley 2012) suggests that acquiescence is negatively correlated with IQ. Acquiescence may be minimised by using certain interview techniques, some of which are highlighted here, and may be useful to nursing staff when ensuring that a person in their care is treated fairly.

When planning any interview, but particularly with people with ID as they may require more resources than an ordinary suspected offender, it is important to consider who will be present and where the interview will be conducted. For instance, a nurse with whom the individual is familiar may act as a third party to support them. Likewise, conducting the interview in a familiar setting may help put them at ease. A relaxed, informal, conversational atmosphere boosts confidence, reduces anxiety and contributes to a more productive interview. Bear in mind that the person with ID may have had poor experiences of interviews previously – with confidentiality broken and severe life changes made because of information they disclosed.

It is important to note that different levels of disability require a range of communication styles. For instance, someone with a mild ID may respond adequately to simple open-ended questions, but someone with a moderate ID may respond better to closed questions. A surprising amount of information can be obtained by allowing people to tell their own story using open questioning. However, this may be difficult for some, as such questions require a high level of cognitive and communication skills (Sigelman 1982, cited in Prosser & Bromley 2012).

A nurse may advise officers, or enable better understanding for the person with ID, when officers are questioning a suspect or victim with ID. These are the main points to remember when conducting such an interview:

- Closed questions increase the risk of acquiescence so the validity of the answer should be tested using cross-questioning and extra probing.
- Multiple-choice questions pose their own difficulties, especially in remembering the choice of replies, and may lead to the individual merely echoing the last choice given.
- Either/or questions are considered better than multiple choice and yes/no questions (Emmerson et al. 1999), as they offer a choice of only two responses and further clarification may be sought (Sigelman et al. 1981, cited in Prosser & Bromley 2012). Suggestive and leading questions should be avoided with people with ID, as there could be a distortion of the interviewee's own story in order to fit preconceptions.

● Abstract questions may confuse the interviewee because they make greater demands on language abilities, as do sophisticated vocabulary and jargon.

# In court

Being in court usually provokes anxiety, as people are often in awe of legal jargon and traditions. People with ID may be particularly affected by the use of complex language and questioning styles. O'Kelly *et al.* (2003) found that judges did not intervene in such situations to modify this process and ensure a fair trial.

In law *actus rea* is a behaviour or its consequences and *mens rea* refers to the person's state of mind at the time of the alleged offence. Both behaviour and state of mind need to be considered when major offences have taken place. It is often believed that people with ID do not have the capability to know what is right and what is wrong. The Mental Capacity Act (2005) went some way to changing this view. Since this legislation, for the first time since the 1800s, people with ID are presumed to have capacity. Their incapacity must now be proven – and not the reverse. The issue of capacity is further complicated, as people's capacity may fluctuate because of physical or mental health issues and anxiety.

The court sometimes takes intellectual disability into account during the trial and sentencing but some strict criteria are used. For example, the criterion for having an ID is considered to be an IQ of 70 or below. The judge is required to ask for expert evidence if they suspect that the person may have ID. Obviously, this may not always be recognised and such expertise will not always be sought (Grant *et al.* 2005).

Recent research (Prison Reform Trust 2007a) found that:

● Over a fifth of prisoners said they did not comprehend court procedures or what was happening to them.

● Some prisoners did not understand why they were in court or what they had done wrong.

● A fifth of prisoners said more useful and personal support in court would have helped.

● Over a third of prisoners said that they would have been assisted by the use of simple language in court and having things explained to them.

However, it is possible for vulnerable defendants to have certain changes made to the courtroom, and the lawyer can request these changes on their behalf. For example, a witness may be less anxious if the public gallery is cleared. In addition, screens can be used to ensure that the witness cannot see the public. Other helpful measures may include the removal of wigs in the court and the use of communication aids, video-recorded evidence or live TV links that allow the witness to give evidence from outside the court (The National Autistic Society 2006).

# In prison

The vulnerability continues when people with ID are held in custody. The *No One Knows Report* (Prison Reform Trust 2007a) surveyed a sample of the prison population and estimated that there are almost 6,000 men, women and children with ID in British prisons. A further quarter of the prison population has a borderline ID. However, the majority of these remain unidentified, as the prison service has no routine screening for ID and prison staff are not trained to identify people with ID in their care.

Research in three prisons and young offender institutions (Mottram 2007) found that the average IQ in each was well below 90 (people with IQ scores of 90 can be considered as having a borderline ID and be treated in specialist services, if they have other specific needs). Mottram also found that many prisoners had difficulties with literacy and communication whilst in prison. Over two-thirds of prisoners had problems with reading prison information and filling in prison forms, as well as difficulties with verbal comprehension. Over half of prisoners said they found it difficult to make themselves understood in prison. It is more than likely that similar difficulties are experienced at the police station and in court.

Their vulnerability means that they are more likely to suffer bullying and abuse than other prisoners, despite being entitled to protection through legislation (Home Office 1984). *The Reed Review of Services for Mentally Disordered Offenders* (Reed 1992) stated that offenders with mental disorders should be diverted from prison to healthcare because of this vulnerability.

The *No One Knows Report* (Prison Reform Trust 2007a, p.1) contained the following testimony:

> **Being in prison is frightening. People shout a lot. It's noisy. You don't know what's happening to you. They do things to you and take over. People who work in prison need to know how to support people with learning difficulties and disabilities.**

The Prison Reform Trust report (2007a) concludes that the prison regime should include education, health and social care and rehabilitation. There is a lack of rehabilitative courses available for people with ID in prisons (McCardle 2010). According to both *The Bradley Report* (Bradley 2009) and the Prison Reform Trust report (2007a), people with intellectual disabilities already have difficulty accessing training and therapeutic programmes in prison. In 2005, an amendment to the Disability Discrimination Act (DDA) (Great Britain 1995) placed statutory duties on public bodies to prevent discrimination towards, and harassment of, disabled people through the development of disability equality schemes. In 2010, the new Equalities Act (Great Britain 2010) replaced much of the DDA, but retained the Disability Equality Duty set out for public bodies such as the courts, prisons, police, probation, health and social services.

All this implies that there is greater potential for miscarriages of justice for people with intellectual disabilities than for those without. These shortcomings also constitute potential non-compliance with ECHR rights, the Disability Discrimination Act and, specifically, the Disability Equality Duty.

In 1999, the United Kingdom Central Council for Nursing, Midwifery and Health Visiting (UKCC and the University of Central Lancashire 1999) commissioned one of the first large projects to provide an overview of nursing in secure environments. The points listed below demonstrate how things may, and may not, have changed (compared with the findings of the Prison Reform Trust 2007b):

- In 1999, 50 per cent of people with an ID were identified by prison staff but this rarely led to support. In 2007, 47 per cent of prison staff thought it likely that all prisoners with ID would be identified, but over a third stated that the information received was unreliable. In 2007, over a third of prison officers reported that the prison had a Learning Disability Nurse available.

- In 1999, 50 per cent of people with an ID were scared and bullied. In 2007, 60 per cent of prison officers reported that prisoners with ID were more likely to be victimised by other prisoners.

- In 1999, people with an ID were reported to be least likely to have a job, know their parole or release date, be in touch with their family or friends, ask for help, know what to do when they were unwell or how to make a complaint. In 2007, 16 per cent of prison officers suggested that the prison had support from mental health and/or intellectual disability services and a quarter had support for prisoners with ID; yet a quarter also reported that they were aware of activities that excluded prisoners with ID and this hindered their progress through the system.

- In 1999, people with an ID were reportedly most likely to spend time alone, and be subject to control and restraint. In 2007, 13 per cent of prison officers reported that their prison had advocacy arrangements for prisoners with ID, and fewer than 19 per cent said that they believed prisoners with ID spent more time in their cells than other prisoners.

- In 1999, people with an ID were more than three times as likely as the comparison group to have spent time in segregation. In 2007, three-quarters of prison staff reported that the quality of support for prisoners with ID was still 'low' or 'fairly low'.

- In 1999, prisoners with an ID were reportedly almost three times as likely to have clinically significant depression and anxiety. In 2007, the Prison Reform Trust reported that 72 per cent of male and 70 per cent of female sentenced prisoners suffered from two or more mental health disorders; in Scotland 70 per cent of prisoners were known to have mental health problems, and as many as 7 per cent may have had psychotic illness – a rate seven times higher than in the general population (Prison Reform Trust 2007b).

Therefore, since 1999, we have made some progress in identifying and treating people with an ID in the prison service. Mental health and protective needs are being met more effectively, but there is still some way to go in protecting prisoners with an ID from bullying and offering them vital advocacy and learning opportunities.

According to the *Bromley Briefings* (Prison Reform Trust 2008), over 80 per cent of prison staff say that information accompanying people into prison is unlikely to show the presence of intellectual disabilities or difficulties prior to their arrival. Yet, despite these worrying statistics, the Learning Disability Screening Questionnaire (LDSQ) that was piloted across prisons until March 2010 has still not been made routinely available across the prison estates.

Not surprisingly then, people do not stand out in a population where most offenders are young males, and from deprived and dysfunctional backgrounds, many with literacy problems, substance abuse, symptoms of mental disorder, and long-standing behavioural problems. The prevalence of these symptoms appears to be increasing (Hayes 2002). Furthermore, the long-stay hospitals for people with mental illness and ID traditionally dealt with offending behaviour without recourse to criminal justice. In recent years, de-institutionalisation, and lack of forensic/specialised community services, have led to inadequate options for diversion from the criminal justice system. This has in turn led to higher conviction rates. Coupled with higher recidivism rates (especially in sexual offences), the result is higher numbers of people with ID being in either the CJS or forensic healthcare (O'Brien 2009).

## Current policy in practice

The Mental Health Act (MHA) states that 'a learning disability is, in general, regarded as a mental disorder because it is a disability of the mind' (DH 2008, 1.13, p.19). The Act's appropriateness is still called into question for people with ID because, unlike the rest of the population, they may still be detained without symptoms of mental illness if they are considered to exhibit 'abnormally aggressive or seriously irresponsible conduct' (DH 2008, 1.14, p.19). Further, a person with ID cannot be detained 'solely on the basis of a learning disability' without such aggressive or irresponsible conduct. However, they remain the only group who can be detained under the Act without evidence of mental illness (DH 2008, 1.15, p. 20).

Some policies overlap and send conflicting messages. It is clear that forensic services for people with ID should be developed with this specific population in mind, but there are compelling arguments against the subsumption of people with ID within mental health legislation (DH 1999). Meanwhile, *Valuing People* (DH 2001) recommends the use of generic mental health services for people with ID.

## The end of the criminal justice system journey

Following sentencing from the magistrate's court, many people are released because the time that they have spent on remand covers the sentence. These individuals are invariably lost to any follow-up. In fact, the majority of people released from prison are not subject to supervision by the Probation Service; only those sentenced to a year or more, or who are under the age of 21, receive supervision. Offenders serve custodial sentences partly in prison and partly in the community on licence. The licence will have standard conditions such as 'staying out of trouble' and 'staying in touch with probation services', plus some possible additional elements such as residency or curfew requirements. Breach of licence can result in a return to custody.

Where people have been accessing treatment in prison, it is important to ensure that their healthcare engagement continues once they leave prison. Some services are provided to this group via voluntary or third sector organisations, but they are inconsistently commissioned and remain isolated examples of good practice that do not meet the needs of all offenders (Bradley 2009). It is important to ensure that responsibility for care is passed on to the relevant services, and that they are engaged well in advance of discharge. This helps people to continue with their treatment in the community.

Primary responsibility for the resettlement process, in particular the completion of the resettlement plan, falls on the Prison Service and the National Probation Service, although a prisoner's responsible local authority can and should be involved. Local authorities have a statutory duty to assess an individual's need for services identified in the resettlement plan. If there is a need for these services, there is a duty to provide them. For adults, this assessment is also the gateway to assessment by other agencies. If, during the assessment process, it appears that there may be a need for the provision of health or housing services, the local authority has a responsibility to notify the relevant primary care trust or housing department and require it to carry out the necessary assessment.

It is in the interests of a local authority with a prison in its catchment area to identify vulnerable prisoners proactively, well in advance of their release, and to identify their responsible local authority. The authority where the prison is located can then ensure that the 'home' local authority takes responsibility for the prisoner before their release, rather than 'picking up the pieces' after the prisoner has been released and has presented themselves as homeless to the nearest housing office.

At the time of release, prisoners may find themselves in a different part of the country to that in which they were resident at the time of sentence or arrest. Different rules for establishing responsibility for different services mean that prisoners may have a responsible local authority in one area and a responsible Clinical Commissioning Group (CCG) in another. This can lead to disputes between agencies as to who is responsible for assessing a prisoner and providing them with health, housing and community care services. Resolution of these disputes can take a lengthy period, hence the need for early identification of those who may be 'in need' and who is responsible for them.

Funding responsibility for healthcare in England falls to the CCG for the area in which a person is registered with a GP or, if they are not registered, the area in which the person is 'usually resident'. This is important in terms of ensuring continuity of care and access to services, as prisoners are not always released into their home CCG.

Primary healthcare is often a gateway to other services, so failure to register or engage with a GP can have wide-ranging consequences. Lord Darzi's review (Darzi 2008), and subsequent development of primary care services, has provided a significant opportunity for offenders with mental health problems or ID, thanks to its emphasis on addressing health inequalities and improving access to primary care. This builds on the excellent examples of work already under way in individual localities and GP practices.

As liaison and diversion services often hold valuable information concerning an offender's mental health problems or ID, they are well placed to identify those who will require resettlement support at a very early stage. These services should be responsible for ensuring that arrangements for resettlement for vulnerable prisoners are in place prior to their release. In particular, these services need to build up strong working relationships with community mental health teams to ensure that they are alerted to offenders as they are released from prison.

## Improving practice

The issues raised in this chapter suggest a number of developments that could helpfully contribute to safeguarding the vulnerable person as they traverse the criminal justice system. First and foremost, people's vulnerability needs to be recognised at an early stage so that services can be put in place to ensure fairness, equity and justice.

From a policy perspective it would be helpful to provide greater clarification and guidance on:

- Terminology – different language is often used to describe vulnerable people, and information is often presented in a way that they do not understand.
- Special measures – variation in appropriate adult (AA) schemes could be usefully resolved and placed on a statutory footing; systems to identify ID offenders should be introduced at all stages of the CJS pathway; measures to protect the vulnerable offender should be robustly applied; fitness for interview needs to be addressed.
- PACE provisions and legal advice – these need to be simplified and further training is required to ensure that their provisions are consistently applied to vulnerable offenders.
- Criminal responsibility and diversion – the recommendations of the *Bradley Report* (Bradley 2009) need to be consistently implemented and compliance audited throughout the country.
- Cooperative working – local services need to ensure that working practices help to protect the vulnerable offender at each stage of the CJS journey

From a health and social care professional's perspective, the journey of an ID offender should be followed in order to consider:

- What actually happens to a person with ID when they get into trouble with the police in their area?

- How do the police respond?
- How do the police know if somebody has ID or requires an appropriate adult?
- How available are appropriate adults in your own area?
- Is there a criminal justice liaison and diversion scheme? Are people with ID included? Is there expertise in ID?
- How accessible is information for suspects with ID at the police station?
- What support is available for defendants with ID in court? How accessible is court information?
- What options are available locally for attendance at a community intellectual disability service as part of a community order? Are the courts aware of this option?
- What support can community ID services give probation teams?
- What 'in-reach' support can community ID services give prison staff?
- What sort of links exist between the police, probation services, youth offending teams, courts, prisons, community intellectual disability services and adult social services? What are relationships like? How often do they meet? What about shared training?
- What role can ID Partnership Boards play? Is there a coordinating role.

In the past ten years, understanding of the issues concerning vulnerable people in the CJS has developed significantly. However, progress has remained inconsistent and patchy and it is still 'a postcode lottery' regarding the type of service that may be available in a particular area. The above lists suggest that major challenges still lie ahead, and it is noteworthy that in 2013 the Centre for Mental Health announced a year-long review of developments since the publication of the *Bradley Report* recommendations in 2009. Although progress has been slow, it is to be hoped that this will provide a further impetus for developments.

# References

Beail, N. (2002). Interrogative suggestibility, memory and intellectual disability. *Journal of Applied Research in Intellectual Disabilities*. **15**, 129–37.

Beail, N. (2004). 'Chapter 8: Approaches to the evaluation of outcomes' in Lindsay, W.R., Taylor, J.L. & Sturmey, P. (eds). *Offenders with Developmental Disabilities*. Chichester: Wiley.

Bradley, K. (2009). *The Bradley Report*. London: Department of Health, The Stationery Office.

Brown. H., Stein, J. & Turk, V. (1995). The sexual abuse of adults with learning disabilities. *Mental Handicap Research*. **8**, 3–24.

Clare, I.C.H. (2003). 'Psychological vulnerabilities of adults with mild learning disabilities: implications for suspects during police detention and interviewing'. Unpublished PhD thesis. London: Institute of Psychiatry, King's College.

Darzi, A. (2008). *High Quality Care for All: NHS next stage review final report*. London: Department of Health.

Day, K. (1994). Male mentally handicapped sex offenders. *The British Journal of Psychiatry*. **165**, 630–39.

Department of Health (1999). *Report of the Expert Committee: Review of the Mental Health Act 1983*. London: The Stationery Office.

Department of Health (2001). *Valuing People: A New Strategy for Learning Disability for the 21st Century*. London: The Stationery Office.

Department of Health (2008). *Code of Practice Mental Health Act 1983*. London: The Stationery Office.

Department of Health. (2009). *Healthy Children, Safer Communities*. London: The Stationery Office.

*Disability Discrimination Act*. (1995). London: The Stationery Office.

Down's Syndrome Association (2007). *Information for Employers*. Middlesex: The Down's Syndrome Association.

Emmerson, E., Hatton, C., Bromley, J. & Caine, A. (1999). *Clinical Psychology and People with Intellectual Disabilities*. Chichester: Wiley.

*Equality Act*. (2010). London: The Stationery Office.

Fazel, S., Xenitidis, K., & Powel, J. (2008). The prevalence of intellectual disabilities among 12000 prisoners – A systematic review. *International Journal of Law and Psychiatry*. **31**, 369–73.

Gomez de la Cuesta, G. & Mason, J. (2010). *Asperger's Syndrome for Dummies*. Chichester: Wiley.

Grant, G., Gowrad, P., Richardson, M. & Ramcharan, P. (2005). *Learning Disability: A Life Cycle Approach to Valuing People*. London: Open University Press.

Gudjonsson, G.H. (1997). *The Gudjonsson Suggestibility Scales Manual*. Hove, East Sussex: Psychology Press.

Gudjonsson, G.H. & Henry, L.A. (2003). Child and adult witness with intellectual disability: the importance of suggestibility. *Legal and Criminological Psychology*. **8**, 241–52.

Gunn, M. (1994). The meaning of incapacity. *Medical Law Review*. **2**, 8–29.

Hann, P. & Tate, G. (2010). *Interpreting in Police Settings Guidance and Information:*
http://www.northeast-bslenglish-interpreters.co.uk/policesettings.html (Last accessed 8 July 2014).

Harrington, R. & Bailey, S. with Dr P. Chitsabesan, Dr L. Kroll, Dr W. Macdonald, S. Sneider, C. Kenning, G. Taylor, S. Byford & B. Barrett (2005). *Mental Health Needs and Effectiveness of Provision for Young Offenders in Custody and in the Community*. Youth Justice Board for England and Wales.

Hayes, S.C. (2002). Early Intervention or Early Incarceration? Using a screening test for intellectual disability in the criminal justice system. *Journal of Applied Research in Intellectual Disabilities*. **15**, 120–28.

Hodgins, S. (1992). Mental disorder, intellectual deficiency and crime: evidence from a birth cohort. *Archives of General Psychiatry*. **49**, 476–83.

Holland, T., Clare, I.C.H. & Mukhopadhyay, T. (2002). Prevalence of criminal offending by men and women with intellectual disability and characteristics of offenders: Implications for research and service development. *Journal of Intellectual Disability Research*. **46**, 6–20.

Home Office (1984). *Police and Criminal Evidence Act*. London: The Stationery Office.

Inglis, P.A. (2010). Characteristics of nursing staff in medium secure settings. *Journal of Learning Disability and Offending Behaviour*. **1** (2), 30–46.

Inglis, P.A. & Dale, C. (2010). Justifications in detainment – from ideology to practice. *Journal of Learning Disability and Offending Behaviour*. **1** (1), 46–59

Kaufman, A.S. & Lichtenberger, E.O. (1999). *Essentials of WAIS-III Assessment*. Chichester: Wiley.

Kebbell, M.R. & Hatton, C. (1999). People with mental retardation as witnesses in court. *Mental Retardation*. **3**, 179–87.

Lindsay, W.R. & Taylor, J.L. (2005). A selective review of research on offenders with developmental disabilities: Assessment and treatment. *Clinical Psychology and Psychotherapy*. **12**, 201–14.

McBrien, J. (2003). The intellectually disabled offender: Methodological problems in identification. *Journal of Applied Research in Intellectual Disabilities*. **16** (2), 95–105.

McCardle, I. (2010). Learning disabilities and access to offender programmes in prison: A High Court decision. *Journal of Learning Disabilities and Offending Behaviour*. **1** (2), 27–30.

MENCAP (June 2004). *Treat me right!: Campaigning report calling for better healthcare for people with a learning disability.* http://www.mencap.org.uk/node/5880 (Last accessed 8 July 2014).

*Mental Capacity Act* (2005). (c.9) London: The Stationery Office.

Michael, J. (2008). *Healthcare for All. Report of the independent inquiry into access to healthcare for people with learning disabilities.* http://webarchive.nationalarchives.gov.uk/20130107105354/http://www.dh.gov.uk/prod_consum_dh/groups/dh_digitalassets/@dh/@en/documents/digitalasset/dh_106126.pdf (Last accessed 8 July 2014).

Mottram, P.G. (2007). *HMP Liverpool, Styal and Hindley Study Report.* Liverpool: University of Liverpool.

National Autistic Society (2006). http://www.autism.org.uk/ (Last accessed 8 July 2014).

O'Brien, G. (2009). *Findings from National Research Study. The 8th International Conference on the care and treatment of offenders with a learning disability.* Preston: UCLAN.

O'Kelly, C.M.E., Kebbell, M.R., Hatton, C. & Johnson, S.D. (2003). Justice intervention in court cases involving witnesses with and without learning disabilities. *Legal and Criminological Psychology.* **8**, 229–40.

Personnel Today Magazine (2007). http://www.personneltoday.com/Articles/2007/05/29/40782/ learning (Last accessed 8 July 2014).

*Prison Fellowship International* (2013). Accessed at: http://www.pfi.org/cjr/human-rights/vulnerable-populations (Accessed on: 3/3/13)

Prison Reform Trust (2007a). *No One Knows. Offenders with learning difficulties and learning disabilities – review of prevalence and associated needs.* http://www.prisonreformtrust.org.uk/Portals/0/Documents/No%20One%20Knows%20Nancy%20Loucks%20prevalence%20briefing.pdf (Last accessed 8 July 2014).

Prison Reform Trust (2007b). *Identifying and supporting prisoners with learning difficulties and learning disabilities: the views of prison staff.* http://www.prisonreformtrust.org.uk/Portals/0/Documents/No%20One%20Knows%20preliminary%20report.pdf (Last accessed 8 July 2014).

Prison Reform Trust (2008). *Bromley Briefings, Prison Factfile.* Prison Reform Trust: London.

Prosser, H. & Bromley, J. (2012). Interviewing People with Intellectual Disabilities, in *Clinical Psychology and People with Intellectual Disabilities.* (2nd ed.). Chichester: Wiley.

Quarmby, K. & Scott, R. (2008). *Getting Away with Murder: Disabled People's Experiences of Hate Crime in the UK.* Report by Scope, Disability Now and the United Kingdom's Disabled People's Council.

Reed (1992). *Reed Review of Services for Mentally Disordered Offenders and others requiring similar services – People with learning disabilities (mental handicap) or with autism.* (Department of Health and Home Office 1992). London: The Stationery Office.

Riding, T., Swan, C. & Swan, B. (2005). *The Handbook of Forensic Learning Disabilities.* Oxford: Radcliffe Publishing.

Rutherford, M. (2010). *Blurring the Boundaries: the convergence of mental health and criminal justice policy, legislation, systems, and practice.* London: Centre for Mental Health.

Seaward, S. & Rees, C. (2001). Responding to people with a learning disability who offend. *Nursing Standard.* **15** (37), 36–39.

Smith, D.J. (February 2000). The power of mental retardation: Reflections on the value of people with disabilities. *Mental Retardation.* 70–72.

Swain, J. & French, S. (2000). Towards an affirmation model of disability. *Disability and Society.* **15** (4), 569–82.

Talbot, J. (2008). *Prisoners' Voices: Experiences of the criminal justice system by prisoners with learning disabilities and difficulties.* London: Prison Reform Trust.

Taylor, J. (2013). *Care and Treatment of Offenders with a Learning Disability.* Conference presentation. Newcastle.

The Arc (2006). *The Arc's Justice Advocacy Guide: An Advocate's Guide on Assisting Victims and Suspects with Intellectual Disabilities.* Washington, DC, USA: The Arc of the United States. Thomas, P. (2011). 'Mate crime': ridicule, hostility and targeted attacks against disabled people. *Disability and Society.* **26** (1), 107–11.

Thomas, P. (2011). 'Mate crime': ridicule, hostility and targeted attacks against disabled people. *Disability and Society.* **26** (1), 107–11.

UKCC and the University of Central Lancashire (1999). *Nursing In Secure Environments*. London: UKCC.

UKLDCNN (July 2005). *A Vision for Learning Disability Nursing: A Discussion Document*. London: United Kingdom Learning Disability Consultant Nurse Network.

Walker, N. (1991). Dangerous mistakes. *British Journal of Psychiatry.* **158**, 752–57.

White, R. & Willner, P. (2003). *Memory as artefact in the assessment of suggestibility.* Paper presented at the Third Seattle Club Conference. Edinburgh. 11th–12th December 2003.

Wilson, C. & Brewer, N. (1992). The incidence of criminal victimisation of individuals with intellectual disability. *Australian Psychologist.* **27**, 114–17.

Winter, N., Holland, A.J. & Collins, S. (1997). Factors predisposing to suspected offending by adults with self-reported learning disabilities. *Psychological Medicine.* **27** (3), 595–607.

World Health Organisation (1992). *ICD-10: International Classification of Diseases and Related Health Problems.* (10th Revision). Geneva, Switzerland: WHO.

# 10

# Governance and quality in criminal justice health services

Elizabeth Tysoe and Paul Tarbuck

The Association for the Prevention of Torture (APT 2004, p. 189) states that:

> The physical and mental health of detainees is particularly important, as imprisonment deprives them of the possibility to care for their health themselves, and can itself have a negative effect on detainees' physical and mental health. The detaining authorities take on responsibility for ensuring that prisoners have access to satisfactory health, healthy living and working conditions, and appropriate medical care.

In the UK there are several independent regulatory and inspection agencies that are obligated to ensure that detaining authorities exercise their responsibilities in these areas. One such agency is Her Majesty's Inspectorate of Prisons (HMIP); others include Her Majesty's Inspectorate of Constabulary, the Care Quality Commission (England) and the Health Inspectorate Wales.

This chapter describes the work of HMIP in ensuring equitable standards of healthcare in custodial settings. Prisons are generally used throughout this chapter to illustrate how governance and quality are inspected, as the inspection method is largely transferrable to other parts of the criminal justice system where detention occurs. Other places of detention, such as police custody, are referred to specifically when considering particular points.

Similarly, the term 'detainee' is used throughout this chapter to refer to those in custody. In reality, several different terms are used, often depending on the setting. Police custody staff refer to 'detained persons' (DPs), whilst court staff and prison staff refer to 'prisoners'. In immigration removal and detention centres, those held are referred to as 'detainees'.

Detainees and prisoners often require a high level of healthcare. However, this chapter focuses on the primary physical and mental healthcare of prisoners and the essential underpinning clinical governance arrangements.

Clinical governance is a system by which organisations take responsibility for continuously improving the quality of their services and ensuring high standards of care. They do this by creating an environment in which excellence in clinical care will flourish (Scally & Donaldson 1998).

For a comprehensive guide to expected components of healthcare in prisons, see *Health in prisons: a WHO guide to the essentials in prison health* (WHO 2007, p. 2), which states that:

> **Many essential components are required to achieve a health promoting prison, including political leadership, management leadership and leadership by each staff member. Healthcare staff members have a special role to play, but prisoners also have a role, and community support is important.**

The main focus of inspections by HMIP is outcomes for detainees, not the management of places of detention. However, it is recognised that management and leadership have a bearing on outcomes.

Positive outcomes should ensure that convicted detainees are less likely to offend after release and, in health terms, their detention should not contribute to ill health and should in fact promote their health and well-being. Robust clinical governance arrangements are essential in order to deliver and replicate acceptable standards of quality in the treatment of detainees. HMIP seeks to ensure that:

> **...Prisoners are cared for by a health service that assesses and meets their health needs while in prison and which promotes continuity of health and social care on release. The standard of health service provided is equivalent to that which prisoners could expect to receive elsewhere in the community. (HMIP 2012)**

## Her Majesty's Inspectorate of Prisons (HMIP)

HMIP was created in its current role in 1982, under the 1982 Criminal Justice Act, which amended the Prison Act 1952. It is independent of the government and has a statutory duty to scrutinise and report on conditions for, and treatment of, those in prisons, young offender institutions and immigration detention facilities. Its purpose is to ensure independent inspection of places of detention, report on conditions and treatment, and promote required outcomes both for those who are detained and for the public. HMIP places high values on:

- Independence, impartiality and integrity
- The experience of detainees, which is at the heart of inspection
- Respect for human rights, which should underpin the treatment of human beings
- Diversity, which is to be embraced, ensuring that equality of outcomes for all should be pursued
- Individuals and organisations having capacity to change and improve
- Playing a part in initiating and encouraging change (Criminal Justice Joint Inspection 2013).

Together with Her Majesty's Inspectorate of Constabulary, HMIP inspects police and court custody in England and Wales. It inspects other places of detention by invitation, including military detention facilities in the UK.

The Prisons Inspectorate of Scotland is clear as to the reasons why independent inspection is important (PIS 2006, p. 6):

> Prisons are by nature closed institutions, often far from the public eye, where one group of people has considerable power over another group. However well prisons are run, the potential for abuse is always present. The strong possibility that abuses will eventually be uncovered is also a protection for prison staff who want to resist a culture of ill-treatment and inhumanity but who may be under pressure from other staff. The publication of inspectors' reports keeps prisons and prison conditions in the public and political eye.

# The national preventive mechanism

The Inspectorate's work constitutes an important part of the UK's obligations under the Optional Protocol to the Convention against Torture and other Cruel, Inhuman or Degrading Treatment or Punishment (OPCAT). OPCAT is an international human rights treaty that establishes an international inspection system for places of detention, designed to strengthen protection for people deprived of their liberty. It was adopted by the United Nations General Assembly in 2002. It recognises that such people are particularly vulnerable and aims to prevent them being ill-treated by establishing a system of visits or inspections to all places of detention. OPCAT requires that states designate a 'national preventive mechanism' (NPM) to carry out visits to places of detention, to monitor the treatment of and conditions for detainees and to make recommendations regarding the prevention of ill-treatment.

The UK ratified OPCAT in December 2003 and designated its NPM in March 2009, through a written ministerial statement. The UK's NPM is currently made up of 20 visiting or inspecting bodies who visit over 200 places of detention such as prisons, police custody settings, immigration detention centres, children's secure accommodation and mental health institutions.

In England and Wales, these bodies or agencies are: Her Majesty's Inspectorate of Prisons (HMIP), Independent Monitoring Boards (IMB), the Independent Custody Visiting Association (ICVA), Her Majesty's Inspectorate of Constabulary (HMIC), the Care Quality Commission (CQC), the Healthcare Inspectorate of Wales (HIW), the Children's Commissioner for England (CCE), the Care and Social Services Inspectorate Wales (CSSIW), the Office for Standards in Education (OFSTED), and lay observers (LOs).

In Scotland, they are: Her Majesty's Inspectorate of Prisons for Scotland (HMIPS), Her Majesty's Inspectorate of Constabulary for Scotland (HMICS), the Scottish Human Rights Commission (SHRC), the Mental Welfare Commission for Scotland (MWCS), the Care Inspectorate (CI), and the Independent Custody Visiting Association Scotland (ICVAS).

The relevant agencies in Northern Ireland are: the Independent Monitoring Boards (IMB), Criminal Justice Inspection Northern Ireland (CJINI), the Regulation and Quality Improvement Authority (RQIA), and the Northern Ireland Policing Board Independent Custody Visiting Scheme (NIPBICVS).

HMIP has the broadest remit of all the designated bodies. As well as providing the coordinating function for the NPM, it must respect the role and jurisdiction of its partner bodies, and map the powers, functions and any differences of role between NPM members. As coordinator of the NPM, HMIP also has to share information on carrying out preventive work, assess the need for consistency and inform society of the NPM's activities. In practice this is by the publication of annual reports (UKNPM 2013). HMIP liaises with the other international human rights bodies, and health and social care inspection and regulatory agencies in the UK, which form part of the NPM. Each member of the NPM has a right of unrestricted access, including the power to make unannounced visits to their respective custodial settings.

## The role of the health inspector

The Association for the Prevention of Torture (APT) asserts that healthcare professionals (HCPs) must be members of the teams that undertake NPM preventative visits (APT 2008, p.10). The HCP role is to:

- Analyse all conditions of detention with a 'health' component
- Identify and document cases of torture and ill-treatment
- Evaluate general healthcare services
- Check standards of ethical practice in places of detention.

A medical perspective is vital in all reflections on preventing torture and improving the system and conditions of detention, including observations on legislative aspects, and in discussing medical issues with relevant national health authorities (APT 2008, p. 9).

Due to the complexity of inspection, a team of inspectors is required to ensure that a comprehensive 'healthy prison' assessment is made. Within each prison team there will be core inspectors, associates from other NPMs (such as the CQC or HIW and OFSTED) as well as representatives of other statutory inspectorates such as Her Majesty's Inspectorate of Probation. Health inspectors include health practitioners and pharmacy and substance misuse specialists. Others, such as dental specialists or psychological trauma specialists, are made available as required. Inspections of police custody are carried out jointly with HMIC, who provide expertise in that specific area. Particular guidance is available for inspectors undertaking this type of work (APT 2013). The Council of Europe is encouraging member states to develop their NPMs; in several member states there are, as yet, few inspectors and they tend to be drawn from the medical, legal or paralegal professions.

## Frequency of inspections

Each criminal justice sector has an agreed schedule of inspections over a specified period of time. The frequency of inspections varies in each part of the criminal justice system. As a minimum, prisons are visited by HMIP every five years, and on average every two to three years, although those holding children and young people are visited annually. Immigration centres are inspected at least once every three years too. Police and court custody centres are visited at least once every six years, with some return visits if the initial visit found particularly poor practice.

Inspectors are on the ground for up to two weeks, and the majority of inspections are unannounced. The cycle of inspections may be changed following receipt of intelligence that gives rise to concern. Intelligence about prisons may be received from the government prison department or via the Independent Monitoring Board (IMB) statutory annual reports. Early inspection triggers may include an unexplained increase in untoward events at a prison, or some factor causing concern to the public. For example, if the Prison and Probation Ombudsman (PPO) detects an inexplicable rise in deaths in custody in a particular prison, this would suggest that early scrutiny is needed. Health inspectors have established communications with colleagues from government health authorities who may have particular concerns about healthcare at an establishment. Occasionally, the concerns are acute and a change of inspection programme is implemented to allow an immediate visit to the place in question. Worrying findings from an inspection may lead to an early repeat inspection.

Prisoners frequently write to the Chief Inspector of Prisons about their individual concerns, or family, legal and other representatives write on their behalf. The Chief Inspector does not have authority to investigate the circumstances of individual detainees. There are other agencies empowered to do this, such as the Prison and Probation Ombudsman (PPO) or local Patient Advice Liaison Services (PALS) for healthcare-related concerns. Enquirers are directed from the Inspectorate to these sources of help. However, the accumulation of comments, criticisms and complaints helps to form an impression of a place of detention, and helps determine the sequence and frequency of inspections. The communication and social media – including the written press, local radio, television and Twitter feeds – may also provide insights into prison life. Data from these sources is sifted for accuracy and treated cautiously, as it may be ill-informed or lacking in balance.

# Healthy prisons

The concept of a healthy prison is one that was first set out by the World Health Organisation (WHO 1995). HMIP promotes the concept of 'healthy prisons'. Healthy prisons are those in which staff members work effectively to support prisoners and detainees to reduce reoffending and achieve other agreed outcomes. This definition is now widely accepted as what ought to be provided in any custodial environment. It rests upon four key tests:

● Safety: prisoners, particularly the most vulnerable, are held safely

● Respect: prisoners are treated with respect for their human dignity

● Purposeful activity: prisoners are able, and expected, to engage in activity that is likely to benefit them

● Resettlement: prisoners are prepared for release into the community, and helped to reduce the likelihood of reoffending.

HMIP makes judgements about the performance of a prison against the four key tests. Judgements range from there being no evidence that outcomes for prisoners are being adversely affected in any significant areas (a healthy prison) through to evidence that the outcomes for prisoners are seriously affected by current practice (an unhealthy prison). The bulk of healthcare considerations sit within the respect key test.

There are well established and shared healthcare ethics that are expected of all HCPs working in places of imprisonment. They are encapsulated in the Oath of Athens (ICPMS 1979, p.1):

> We, the health professionals who are working in prison settings, meeting in Athens on September 10, 1979, hereby pledge, in keeping with the spirit of the Oath of Hippocrates, that we shall endeavour to provide the best possible healthcare for those who are incarcerated in prisons for whatever reasons, without prejudice and within our respective professional ethics. We recognize the right of the incarcerated individuals to receive the best possible healthcare. We undertake:
>
> 1. To abstain from authorizing or approving any physical punishment.
>
> 2. To abstain from participating in any form of torture.
>
> 3. Not to engage in any form of human experimentation amongst incarcerated individuals without their informed consent.
>
> 4. To respect the confidentiality of any information obtained in the course of our professional relationships with incarcerated patients.
>
> 5. That our medical judgments be based on the needs of our patients and take priority over any non-medical matter.

In the UK there are a variety of practice codes, conventions and protocols based on Hippocratic ethics such as *The Code* for nurses and midwives (Nursing and Midwifery Council 2008) and nationally agreed clinical guidelines from sources such as the National Institute for Health and Care Excellence or the United Kingdom Resuscitation Council (2010). With these various imperatives in mind, it is usually clear to inspectors (who are from a healthcare professional discipline) whether or not healthcare services are premised on acceptable ethics and standards and are 'healthy' or 'unhealthy', meaning that outcomes for prisoners are safe and good or unsafe and poor.

## Health expectations for prisons

The outcomes against which judgements are made are set out in *Expectations* (HMIP 2012). The first edition of *Expectations* was published in 2001, and the fourth in 2012. *Expectations* sets out the basis on which HMIP will fulfil its statutory and NPM obligations by reporting to the relevant Secretary of State on 'the treatment of prisoners and conditions in prisons' (Section 5A of the Prison Act 1952, as inserted by section 57 of the Criminal Justice Act 1982).

There are 107 expectations associated with adult prisons and each has related indicators that would be expected if the expectation outcome is achieved (although the establishment may demonstrate that the outcome is achieved in other ways). There are 22 expectations specifically for police custody. The prison expectations are used as a guide to examine the experience of prisoners; 17 expectations directly concern health services, with 104 indicators of outcomes for prisoners.

An example of a health expectation is shown in Table 10.1 (below). The expectation contains a standard statement, followed by indicators that may demonstrate achievement. This expectation directs the health inspector to coordinate this area of scrutiny with 'core' inspectors examining general complaints. Finally, there is a reference section that outlines authorities and sources underpinning the expectation. Sources include international and UK law, authoritative human rights precedents and treaty agreements.

HMIP expectations reflect the complexity of custodial life. The complexity is such that healthcare, whilst having its own expectations, also forms part of the indicators in other areas of expectation. For example, health inspectors in prisons must cross-reference their findings with those of other inspectors who are looking at safety, self-harm/suicide, vulnerability, safeguarding and risk. Public health indicators are also to be found in other areas of expectation, such as access to fresh air and clean water, nutrition, sanitation, activity and rest.

Expectations are constantly under review, to reflect the ever-changing world of custody. For example, the current (2012) edition of *Expectations* for adult prisons is being reviewed to ensure that the United Nations (UN) standards for the treatment of women prisoners and non-custodial measures for women offenders, known as the 'Bangkok Rules', are adequately reflected and referenced in the document (United Nations General Assembly 2010). In reviewing *Expectations*, care is taken to preserve principles arising from historical sources of good practice, such as the focus on child welfare in the 'Beijing Rules' (United Nations General Assembly 1985) concerning the administration of juvenile justice.

## Table 10.1: Sample HMIP health expectation

| |
|---|
| **Expectations:** Governance arrangements |
| **Prisoners are aware of the prison health services available and how to access them.** |
| Indicators<br>• Prisoners are given information about prison health services, in a format and language they can understand, which explains how to access services.<br>• Prisoners know how to comment/complain about their care and treatment and are supported to do so when necessary.<br>• Prisoners who make complaints against staff and/or other prisoners are not discriminated against and are protected from possible recrimination.<br>• Responses to complaints are timely, easy to understand, are dealt with by a health professional and deal directly with the prisoner's concerns. |
| **Cross-reference with:** complaints. |

## Sources of evidence and methodology

The following section refers to a typical inspection of an adult prison, but the general principles are the same whatever setting is being inspected. There will however, be some references to other custodial settings, where necessary to make a specific point.

In making judgements about the health of prisons, certain key sources of evidence are scrutinised: inspector's observations; prisoner surveys; discussions with prisoners (individually and in groups); discussions with staff and relevant third parties; and documentation, such as policies, minutes of meetings, reports and clinical records.

Observational approaches will include the use of all the senses but the most important of these are watching and listening. Meeting prisoners on the wings to listen to their perceptions of healthcare is crucial; and inspectors need to be cognisant of age, gender, ethnic origin and disability issues when engaging with prisoners and checking on equity of access and the availability of services.

In addition, health inspectors need to adapt their working methods to suit the circumstances of a particular inspection, as no two prisons are the same. For example, health services with primary care working hours (often found in category C and D prisons) will require inspection when sessional primary care clinicians are in the prison. In category A and B prisons, there are usually extended health centre hours and some secondary services on a sessional basis. These will require scheduled appointments and evening visits to observe medicine rounds; or to check that custody officers coming onto night duty are familiar with healthcare and support requirements for particular prisoners. It is always useful to sit with patients in the waiting rooms to see what they see. It may also be necessary to observe clinical consultations and treatments, subject to consent. Where key clinicians are unavailable, telephone or email contact may be needed.

HMIP researchers use surveys to provide quantitative data representing the views of a random sample of prisoners. Results show the collective response (in percentages) from prisoners in the establishment being inspected, compared with the collective response (in percentages) from respondents in all establishments. For example, a category B prison is compared to all other category B prisons. Health-related data is provided for a number of categories in the survey, including general information; reception, first night and induction; safety; health services; drugs and alcohol; and preparation for release.

Prisoners are invited to make free text comments to supplement their survey responses, and survey data from inspections is published with the final report. Statistically significant differences between the prison and the comparator are referenced in the report and will usually invite comment. For example, in a prison where there is significantly higher dissatisfaction with food or visiting arrangements than in comparator prisons, inspectors will pay particular attention to these crucial factors in the life of prisoners. It is possible to compare the contemporary prison survey with previous surveys so that movement over time can be considered. Differences may indicate areas for additional scrutiny or areas where improvements have occurred. Survey data may also be analysed to produce information on prisoners with particular characteristics such as age, disability, ethnic origin, gender or religion.

HMIP researchers may interview a sample of prisoners on a confidential basis during inspections, to produce qualitative data. The data is tabulated and used by inspection teams to guide enquiries. Sometimes prisoners prefer their comments to be unattributed and this wish is respected.

## Sequence of events during an inspection

An inspection week begins with survey groups. Randomly selected prisoners are invited to attend these groups, which are often based on themes such as age, gender or ethnicity. Prison staff are not present in the groups. A semi-structured approach is used to generate comment that can be used to supplement other data arising from service users. Perceptions of, and satisfaction with, health services are a topic within survey groups.

Comments from these groups may give rise to particular areas of scrutiny, as they represent the shared experience of prisoners. For example, where prisoners on one wing do not appear to have the same access to the General Practitioner as prisoners on other wings, this will require investigation. In police custody, inspectors try to speak to as many individual detainees as possible to hear their views; and they also speak to legal representatives about their clients' experiences.

During an inspection, it is necessary to understand the context of care as well as scrutinising the service. Health inspectors will try to speak to health service commissioners, provider representatives and interested third parties such as governors, gymnasium staff, visiting specialists and, occasionally, patients' relatives.

The health inspector will also review a great deal of service documentation related to each expectation. Documentary information will give an impression of the 'health' of the service. Inspectors look for records of external scrutiny of custodial health services; compliance with standards; actions taken to rectify deficits and improve services; learning from detainees' comments, complaints and untoward events; and engagement with other prison departments as appropriate. Table 10.2 (below) indicates the minimum information requirements associated with the governance arrangements expectations.

## Table 10.2: Minimal information requirements

| **Expectations:** Governance arrangements |
| --- |
| ● Health needs assessment and associated action plan |
| ● Contact details of local service commissioners |
| ● Contact details of all service providers |
| ● CQC/HIW registration details |
| ● Prison/Health Partnership Board minutes for last six months |
| ● Prison health promotion action plan |
| ● Clinical governance meeting minutes for last six months |
| ● Serious and untoward incidents reports for 12 months, including summary |
| ● Complaints reports for last six months |
| ● PHPQI self-assessment and associated action plan |
| ● Patient forum minutes for last six months |
| ● Staffing structure and organisation chart |

- All staff professional registration details and additional qualifications
- Staff training needs analysis
- Staff training records for previous 12 months
- Clinical supervision policy
- Staff clinical supervision records
- Clinical audits undertaken in previous 12 months
- Communicable disease policy
- Multi-agency information-sharing protocol
- Infection control policy
- Infection control audit (last) and associated action plan
- Cleaning schedule
- All resuscitation equipment checking lists
- Record of training of custody staff in resuscitation skills, including staff locations
- Prisoner consent/capacity form
- General Practitioner rota and special interests
- Safeguarding of vulnerable adults policy
- Child protection policy
- Health information for prisoners (reception, induction, wings)
- PALS (Patient Advice and Liaison Service) contact information

Health inspectors will look at clinical records, waiting lists and relevant protocols; and they will also follow up issues raised by them. For example, if prisoners tell inspectors that they have to wait several days to see a doctor, the inspector will investigate their claims to see if the issue is because of a lack of consultation time, problems with the management of the waiting list or delays in the application system.

## Deliberations and judgements

During inspections a mixed-method approach to data gathering, applying both qualitative and quantitative methodologies, is used. All findings and judgements are triangulated, which increases the validity of the data gathered. Triangulation, in this respect, means that one evidence source is corroborated by at least two other sources (although sometimes an incident/perception may be so important as to stand alone).

It is important to have a balance of both quantitative and qualitative evidence sources. Inspectors need to seek supporting evidence from alternative, but relevant sources (HMIP 2008). The most reliable data is acquired from objective sources and official records. However, due to the nature of the work, a lot of data is subjective, and therefore open to distortion by memory, perception and personal interpretation.

For example, in a situation where a detainee has been subjected to a planned removal in which restraint has been used, an inspector would expect to see video footage of the event, speak to the detainee and staff involved, and see written records of the event. The inspector would also expect that a member of health staff would be present and that there would be a written entry in the detainee's clinical record, detailing any traumatic aspects of the removal, healthcare interventions and, if necessary, a pictorial record of any injuries sustained such as reddening of the skin or abrasions.

Multi-disciplinary and multi-agency teams of inspectors meet each day during an inspection. At these meetings, uni-disciplinary perceptions are subject to challenge from others in order to arrive at a consensus judgement. For example, the perceptions of HMIP core and health inspectors are shared with CQC and OFSTED colleagues to consider whether health promotion and well-being strategy and practice is effective in offering prisoners opportunities to access nutritious food and physical exercise.

Judgements on the outcomes for detainees result in: recommendations for actions to bring about compliance with expectations; or housekeeping points, which are suggestions for immediately achievable quick changes to reduce risks/improve outcomes; or citations of good practices. In total, 99 per cent of HMIP health recommendations are accepted by places of detention. The ratio of good practice citations to recommendations has increased in the last few years. It was 1 to 25 in 2010, and 1 to 19 in 2012. This may suggest that outcomes for detainees have improved in that period of time.

## Governance of prison healthcare

Clinical governance is particularly important in the hidden world of criminal justice settings. It provides a framework to ensure that those detained receive care from appropriately trained staff, using evidence-based practices. Where clinical governance is well embedded, detainees and the public can be assured that health services available to detainees are of a similar standard to those in the National Health Service (NHS). Moreover, governance (in custodial health services provided by the NHS) ensures levels of transparency and scrutiny by external health authorities that enable compliance actions to be instigated in cases where standards have fallen to unacceptable levels. Governance expectations are listed in Table 10.3 (below).

# Table 10.3: Governance expectations

- Prisoners are cared for by a health service that accurately assesses and meets their health needs while they are in prison and promotes continuity of health and social care on their release.
- Prisoners benefit from health services that are safe and accessible, and maintain their decency, privacy and dignity and promote their well-being.
- Patients are treated with respect in a professional and caring manner, which is sensitive to their diverse needs, by appropriately trained staff.
- Prisoners are aware of the prison health services that are available and how to access them.
- All prisoners receive information about health promotion and the control of communicable diseases.

Outcomes of healthcare for prisoners have improved consistently since the introduction of NHS commissioning of services in prisons and the implicit clinical governance and performance scrutiny. For example, the Prison Health and Performance Quality Indicators (PHPQI) (DH 2008) provide a self-reporting mechanism that informs commissioners about trends in developments and management information for the prison-health strategic group; and provides a framework for peer review. The PHPQI also enable services to identify where effort and investment is required to maintain and drive up standards. It is hoped that NHS commissioning of healthcare services in police custody, anticipated from 2014 (NHS England 2013), will similarly improve outcomes for detainees.

Assessment of need is a vital part of the governance process. Only by identifying the health needs of a particular population can a health provider ensure that the services provided are appropriate. For example, an establishment holding juveniles needs access to the services of a children's and young persons' psychiatrist, nursing staff with experience of working with young people, and appropriate resuscitation equipment, to give just a few examples.

Where clinical governance processes are weak, there is the potential for care to be compromised and outcomes for those detained to be poor.

# Delivery of physical healthcare in prisons

Physical health expectations are that:

- Prisoners' immediate health and social care needs are recognised on reception and responded to promptly and effectively.
- Prisoners' individual healthcare needs throughout their time at the prison are addressed through a range of care services.

Coyle (2009) reviewed international instruments on the requirements for healthcare in prisons and concluded that, as a minimum, there should be: initial medical screening on admission; regular out-patient consultations; emergency treatment; suitably equipped premises for consultation/treatment; an adequate supply of medications from a qualified pharmacist; facilities for physiotherapy and rehabilitation; and any special diets thought to be medically necessary.

How care is delivered and received, and the experience of those detained, are at the heart of inspection of all places of detention. Whilst clinical governance (with policies, protocols and evidence-based care plans), provides a framework within which care can be delivered, it is of no use to detainees in police custody if they have to wait for hours to see a health professional or cannot receive medication that they have previously been prescribed in the community. Delivery of care and patients' perceptions of health services start from the moment they enter a custodial setting.

In prison settings, the time a prisoner spends in reception with health services staff offers a good opportunity to screen for vulnerabilities and take action to ensure the prisoner's safety on their first night. However, this is not the best time to undertake a full health assessment, asking about vaccination history, childhood illnesses, doctor's name and address and the like. Such information is much easier to elicit once the prisoner has had a good night's sleep and made phone calls to relatives. Inspectors will also scrutinise the care of those with lifelong conditions to ensure that they are being cared for in line with national service frameworks and evidence-based best practice.

In police custody, detainees should be asked whether they wish to see a health professional, and the custody sergeants can ask for a healthcare professional to see a detainee at any point during their stay. The care provided by the HCP, who is independent of the police and the custody process, can have a profound effect on the detainee. If they are treated with respect, given time to explain their fears, and they are given the medications they were prescribed in the community, their anxieties about being in custody are likely to be reduced.

# Vulnerable groups

## Women (ante-natal and post-natal)

All women in prison have specific needs, but those who are pregnant or who have recently given birth have particular issues. Inspectors expect women to have access to ante-natal services just as they would in the community. Such services should include offering women choices about their pregnancy, being sensitive to their needs, and providing support for any decisions they make. If they choose to continue with the pregnancy, they should receive the same level of ante-natal care that they would receive in the community, relevant to their vulnerabilities.

In 2013 there were seven mother and baby units in women's prisons in England and Wales. *Prison Service Instruction 54/2011* (HMPS 2011) states:

> **To reflect society's normal assumption that the best place for a young child is with his or her parent, the English and Welsh prison service has allowed mothers to care for their babies in prison. To allow this to happen, a Mother and Baby Unit is designated living accommodation within a women's prison, which enables mothers, where appropriate, to have their children with them whilst in prison.**

The environment in these units has to be 'child centred', staff are recruited specifically to work with the mothers, and everything possible should be done to mitigate the fact that the baby/young child is living within the walls of a prison. Prospective mothers have to apply to reside in one of these units. Requests are considered in terms of the child's welfare, the mother's sentence plan, and the health and safety of other mothers and babies on the unit at the time. There should be support for the women whatever decision is made.

Women can only keep their children until the child is 18 months old. There must be a 'separation plan' in place from the moment the baby enters the unit, which again should include support for the mother. The children should be subject to the same health and child development checks as they would be in the community. Their care should be provided by a community GP, not the prison health services. Women in the units should have access to the same range of purposeful activity as those without children. The children should attend nursery – within the centre and the nursery should be inspected by the Office for Standards in Education (OFSTED).

## Children and young offenders

The number of children in custody in the UK is reducing significantly as community sentencing is preferred and parts of the children's estate have been decommissioned. However, this has had an unfortunate consequence in that children who are in custody are now being held further from home than before. In March 2011, 30 per cent of children were held over 50 miles from home, and 10 per cent over 100 miles away (Murray 2012). This inhibits the ability to sustain strong family ties, which has a big impact on maintaining mental resilience and well-being. This may lead to separation anxiety and behaviours that are driven by emotional distress. Inspectors are keen to observe interactions between children and young persons in custody and those who care for them – these relationships are crucial in ensuring that emotional issues do not spiral into pathology or acting out. It is vital to have systems in place to safeguard vulnerable young people.

A further consequence of the shrinking estate is that children left in custody are likely to be those who have the most complex needs and they will be concentrated in fewer areas. In such environments, there are increased risks of untoward events leading to stress and potential physical injury both for staff and children. Indeed, empirically, inspectors are seeing increased levels of violence, and violence of a more serious nature, in young offender institutions – especially where gang cultures have been imported from the community. Surveys regularly indicate that a third of boys feel unsafe in their establishments at some point whilst being detained (Murray 2012).

In health services for young people, the expectation is that assessment and treatment should be appropriate to the stage of development and age. For example, we expect to see screening for illnesses such as Chlamydia (as is available in the community), and the availability of immunisation and vaccination programmes such as meningitis C, and for epidemic infections such as measles. We also expect to see good working relationships with the prison gymnasium to promote healthy approaches to fitness training and to ensure that sports injuries are treated correctly.

## Older prisoners

Research shows that people age quicker biologically while they are in prison, sometimes by up to 10 years more than their chronological ages (Wahidin & Cain 2006). In inspecting health services for older prisoners, the care of prisoners aged 50 years and above is examined. As of 30 September 2012, there were 9,913 prisoners aged 50 or over in England and Wales. This number included 3,333 aged 60 and over. Prisoners aged over 50 make up 11 per cent of the prison population, and this has risen from 7 per cent in 2002 (Ministry of Justice 2012). As older prisoners are a largely compliant population, their specific needs may be overlooked in a system geared towards managing the much larger proportion of younger people. Older prisoners are more likely to have health problems than the rest of the population; they may have restricted mobility and they may be isolated from friends and family.

At the time of writing, there is significant variation across the prison estate in England and Wales in terms of service provision and standards for older prisoners. Service provision to address the health and social care requirements of older adults has been defined in the *National Service Framework for Older People* (DH 2001). However, the extent to which the framework has been adopted differs between prisons.

In some prisons, safeguarding arrangements are not used to ensure the care of elderly prisoners who are frail or experiencing aspects of dementia. Around 2 in 5 older prisoners reported that they felt unsafe in prison at some time; 15 per cent stated they felt unsafe at the time of the inspection; and 1 in 5 older prisoners said they had been victimised by other prisoners (HMIP 2011–12). Some prisons have formal systems of using prisoners acting as carers for older prisoners who have difficulty in caring for themselves. Provided that these carers are properly trained and supervised, this is welcomed.

The majority of prisons have special clinics for older prisoners but the services provided vary significantly in terms of quality, the age of prisoners targeted, the assessment tools used, and the support services available. There are few discrete services for older prisoners with complex needs who require greater supervision and support. This problem is compounded by restrictions placed on prisoners with mobility issues because of unsuitable prison environments and reduced numbers of in-patient beds in prisons._

Older prisoners are disadvantaged by limited access to community screening programmes, including bowel and abdominal aortic aneurysm (AAA) screening. This is despite the fact that AAA is more likely to be found in males over the age of 65, and bowel screening in the community is specifically offered to those people over the age of 60. Targeted immunisation and vaccination programmes are expected (for annual pandemic influenza, for instance), and these do tend to be available to the majority of physically vulnerable adult prisoners.

In our original thematic report on older prisoners (HMIP 2004), only one prison was reported as having developed a system that flagged up when women were due to be recalled for health screening procedures such as mammography. Of the women in the overall sample group, only 8 (15 per cent) had undergone mammography and only 20 (37 per cent) had had a cervical smear within the previous five years. Many had been identified as requiring mammography or cervical screening – or had requested these themselves – when they were at a previous prison. Moving from prison to prison, often at short notice, meant that they missed screening appointments and it took months to reach the top of the waiting list at the next prison. One female prisoner said that she had been told she needed breast screening but was still waiting for an appointment three months later.

Since the 2004 thematic report on older prisoners (HMIP 2004), palliative care has generally improved, though it needs to be consolidated, as there remain significant barriers to good care. Turner et al. (2010) found that many prison staff had little experience of caring for prisoners with palliative needs, and many specialist community staff have little experience of prisons.

Some commentators have suggested that there has been some success in bringing about change as a result of the HMIP approach (Hayes & Shaw 2011, p. 44):

> This suggested that prison establishments were acting on the Inspectorate's criticisms and recommendations. This was interesting, given there was no formal necessity to make changes to the environment or regime for older prisoners, and suggests HMIP are a powerful agency in effecting change within the prison system.

## Allegations of ill treatment

Allegations of ill treatment by detainees are always taken seriously by inspectors, and especially so when they are part of a cluster of complaints. Health inspectors support core inspectors in this regard, by discussing situations with healthcare practitioners and examining contemporaneous health records of alleged incidents which, subject to medical confidentiality, may then guide further enquiry. In prisons,

HCPs complete specific sections of untoward event forms, which are scrutinised for information on injuries that detainees may have received, such as friction burns to the wrists as a result of restraint. This type of information helps to establish the facts regarding an alleged incident. Occasionally, there are comments in clinical records in which healthcare practitioners have placed on record an explicit refusal to assent to a chosen course of action by prison officers.

It is rare, but not unknown in English and Welsh places of detention, to find acts of commission that amount to inhumane or degrading treatment. However acts of *omission*, whilst still not typical, more commonly lead to such circumstances. For example, detainees may be left without active treatment for withdrawal from substances and this amounts to inhumane treatment. Likewise, it is inhumane to put a physically disabled prisoner in a cell on an upper landing when it is known that the prisoner finds it painful to ascend stairs. Each situation has to be assessed on its merits. In some cases, what constitutes inhumane and degrading treatment eventually comes down to a value judgement.

## Delivery of mental healthcare in prisons

Mental health expectations are that:

- Prisoners with common mental health problems are recognised and supported by health staff and specialist services at the prison, and have unhindered access to help in pursuing recovery.
- Prisoners' severe and enduring mental health needs are recognised and supported by health staff and specialist services at the prison, and they have unhindered access to help.

An enduring concern of OPCAT is that detainees who are vulnerable because of mental health problems receive appropriate care and treatment, and that psychiatric interventions and psycho-active substances are not sanctioned by the state for inappropriate non-therapeutic uses. UK mental health law allows for treatment to be administered against a patient's wishes in defined circumstances but the law is not applicable in prisons.

Pre-detention morbidity may be made worse by incarceration. Detainees are often imprisoned alone in cells or with other detainees – not of their choice – for extended periods of time. Some cells, such as those in police and court custody, are impersonal and stark. The regime in some places may be too busy to allow time for communal support. And some detainees may be facing circumstances, or are in a place, which for them holds no hope – such as immigration remand centres, from which they are likely to be deported.

In prisons and young offender institutions, the vulnerable or the less mentally robust may be more susceptible to adverse activity related to gang culture, criminal affiliations or exploitation. For example, adult prisoners are sometimes bullied for tobacco and prescribed medications that others will sell for profit, and some young offenders may resort to self-harming in response to being bullied because they behave in different ways. Occasionally, prisoners in segregation areas will deliberately behave in an anti-social way in order to be placed in segregation, thereby ensuring that they are protected from conflict with members of other gangs. These and other factors may increase feelings of depersonalisation, alienation and isolation, which may be triggers for psychiatric morbidity.

Where detainees experience longer sentences, inspectors will ascertain if there are protective factors within the setting that are available to support vulnerable detainees. Protective factors may include access to buddy schemes, listeners or health trainers, counsellors, the chaplaincy, education and the gymnasium. Critical in maintaining the safety of a vulnerable detainee is an effective personal officer scheme that involves liaison with healthcare services. The most effective and supportive places of detention will have a regular multi-departmental forum to which all departments bring concerns about individuals. For instance, there may concerns about detainees who have received bad news from home; those with self-harming tendencies who are facing considerable stresses; or detainees with mental health problems who are declining health interventions.

Mental healthcare pathways should be explicit in a custodial setting (DH 2005). Minimal components include primary and secondary mental health levels of care. More mature services will embrace the principles of recovery working and engage detainees on that basis. This is a potential area of tension between healthcare and other departments, as it is difficult to advocate that individuals be allowed to manage their own mental health problems on over-populated wings and within inflexible regimes. A detainee may be able to manage their anxiety related to compulsions in private at home, but this may not be possible where they have to share a cell or wash in the same facilities as others. Some behaviour related to traumatic re-enactment may be more disturbing without the detainee realising it (Rogers & Law 2010). Whatever the pathology, a detainee's behaviours may appear antagonistic to others and lead to friction.

Inspectors need to check that screening for mental health problems begins at reception and occurs in depth during the first week of detention. In addition to assessing for common mental health problems such as anxiety and depression, and psychotic illnesses, more advanced services will assess for factors associated with learning disabilities. More detailed levels of assessment should be available thereafter, such as those related to acquired brain injuries, dementia-related problems and personality disorders. Ideally, there should be a dual diagnosis specialist available to work with detainees who have enduring, complex mental health and addiction problems. Liaison with other prison departments is crucial in setting up observation schedules to monitor behaviours and to determine joint care plans. In a good service, detainees with mental health problems will be supported to manage their own care, with written or computerised self-help materials, books on prescription, training in relaxation or other forms of tension reduction, and solution-focused, brief supportive psychotherapy. Detainees with more complex problems will have access to visiting psychiatric specialists such as a psychiatrist, community mental health nurse, clinical psychologist or speech and language therapist. It is expected that there will be regular multi-disciplinary meetings to discuss and allocate referrals – ideally there should be an open system of referral that is subject to triage at primary level.

The prescribing of psycho-active medicines for anxiety, depression or psychosis should be in accordance with national guidelines such as CG113, regarding generalised anxiety disorder in adults (NICE 2011). Where medications are used atypically, there should be evidence that this has been discussed by the multi-disciplinary team. For example, a common problem in detention is inability to sleep; and hormonal sleeping aids licensed for short-term use with older adults are sometimes prescribed for young people over protracted periods, which is not in accord with NICE guidance ESUOM2, regarding sleep disorders in children and young people with attention deficit hyperactivity disorder (NICE 2013). This should be justified, preferably by a documented discussion with a pharmacist or lead doctor, as should novel practices designed to avoid the diversion and trading of medication, such as ensuring that patients eat a dry cracker after taking liquid medications to reduce the likelihood of regurgitation.

Prisoners with personality disorders or intractable interpersonal problems should have access to referral to a psychologically led service such as a therapeutic community within a prison, or a psychologically informed planned environment (PIPE). Some aspects of their stay in these detention communities may depend on them participating in other programmes related to sentence planning and so inspectors should check availability of these programmes (successful participation may also be a requirement of the Parole Board).

Some detainees may require assessment and treatment by a hospital mental health service. Where this is being considered, inspectors will need to check that the process involved complies with the hospital transfer guidelines (DH 2011) and, in particular, that transfer is expedited promptly. The use of accommodation such as segregation to minimise friction with other detainees whilst waiting for transfer may, potentially, exacerbate suffering and is unacceptable. Where this situation is occurring, inspectors expect to see evidence of the detainee's case being raised with service commissioners for action.

## HMIP reports and quality control

An inspection visit concludes with a 'hot' feedback session to the governor or director of the place of custody and their invitees. A written summary of initial findings is left with the governor for prompt consideration. A full written report is published approximately 16 weeks after the hot debrief. Reports are directed at the relevant Secretary of State, Members of Parliament and other interested parties. Findings are communicated to other agencies, such as the Prisons and Probation Ombudsman, to ensure that the work of inspectoral agencies is coordinated.

As part of the process, a draft report is sent to the place that has been inspected. This provides an opportunity to correct any factual inaccuracies or misperceptions. There are a number of internal quality control mechanisms built into the report production process. These include several stages – review, peer review and independent professional editing – to ensure that the report is written in plain English.

Health inspectors are also subject to testing of inter-rater reliability. The Chief Inspector or Deputy Chief Inspector visits during inspections to check perceptions with inspectors and potential judgements. There are also group development activities, in which table top situations are analysed. There is an annual programme of formal peer review, in which inspectors interrogate and comment upon each other's reports. In addition, informal peer review occurs via discussion of technical issues at team meetings and inspector-to-inspector sharing of findings and concerns inviting comment from colleagues to check their perceptions and judgements.

Following an inspection visit, places of detention are asked for their views on the inspection process. This data is used to improve the inspection process and, occasionally, to give individual performance feedback to inspectors.

## Conclusion

In conclusion, robust clinical governance arrangements must be in place to check the quality of the care provided. These arrangements cover the structures, processes and culture of healthcare organisations, including those providing services to some of the most vulnerable groups in society. Inspection provides an independent 'critical eye' to assess such structures and how they affect outcomes for patients.

## References

Association for the Prevention of Torture (2004). *Monitoring of places of detention: a practical guide*. Geneva: APT.

Association for the Prevention of Torture (2008). *Visiting places of detention: What role for physicians and other health professionals?* Geneva: APT.

Association for the Prevention of Torture (2013). *Monitoring police custody – a practical guide*. Geneva: APT.

Coyle, A. (2009). *A Human Rights Approach to Prison Management: Handbook for Prison Staff*. (2nd ed.) London: International Centre for Prison Studies.

Criminal Justice Joint Inspection (2013). About Her Majesty's Inspectorate of Prisons. www.hmcpsi.gov.uk/cjji/about-cjji/about-the-cj-inspectorates/hmip/ (Last accessed 12 July 2014).

Department of Health (2001). *National Service Framework for Older People*. London: DH.

Department of Health (2005). *Offender Mental Healthcare Pathway*. London: DH.

Department of Health (2008). *Guidance notes: Prison health and performance quality indicators*. London: DH.

Department of Health (2011). *Good Practice Procedure Guide: the transfer and remission of adult prisoners under s47 and s48 of the Mental Health Act*. London: DH.

Hayes, A., & Shaw, J. (2011). Practice into policy: The needs of elderly prisoners in England and Wales. *Prison Service Journal*. **194**, 38–44.

Her Majesty's Inspectorate of Prisons (2004). *A thematic review of older people in prisons in England and Wales.* London: HMIP.

Her Majesty's Inspectorate of Prisons (2008). *Inspection Manual.* London: HMIP.

Her Majesty's Inspectorate of Prisons (2011–12). *Aggregated older prisoner survey data; all inspections 2011–12.* London: HMIP. Unpublished in aggregated form.

Her Majesty's Inspectorate of Prisons (2012). *Expectations v: Section 2: Respect – preamble to Expectations* 32–44. London: HMIP.

HM Prison Service (2011). *Prison Service Instructions 2011–54.* http://www.justice.gov.uk/offenders/psis (Last accessed 12 July 2014).

International Council of Prison Medical Services (1979). *The Oath of Athens.* Athens: ICPMS. http://www.medekspert.az/en/chapter1/resources/The%20Oath%20of%20Athens.pdf (Last accessed 12 July 2014).

Ministry of Justice (2012). *Offender Management Statistics Quarterly Bulletin, April to June 2012: Table A1.8.* London: The Stationery Office.

Murray, M. (2012). *Children and Young People in Custody, 2011–2012.* London: The Stationery Office.

National Health Service, England (2013). *Securing Excellence in Commissioning for Offender Health.* London: Department of Health, NHS Commissioning Board.

NICE (2011). http://publications.nice.org.uk/generalised-anxiety-disorder-and-panic-disorder-with-or-without-agoraphobia-in-adults-cg113 (Last accessed 12 July 2014).

NICE (2013). http://www.nice.org.uk/Advice/ESUOM2 (Last accessed 9 July 2014).

Nursing and Midwifery Council (2008). *The Code: Standards of conduct, performance and ethics for nurses and midwives.* London: NMC.

Prison Inspectorate of Scotland (2006). *Standards Used in the Inspection of Prisons in Scotland.* Edinburgh: PIS.

Resuscitation Council (UK) (2010). *Resuscitation Guidelines.* London: Resuscitation Council.

Rogers, A. & Law, H. (2010). 'Working with Trauma in a Prison Setting' in Harvey, J. & Smedley, K. (eds) *Psychological Therapy in Prison and Other Settings.* London: Willan.

Scally, J.G. & Donaldson, L.J. (4 July 1998). Clinical governance and the drive for quality improvement in the new NHS in England. *British Medical Journal* **317** (7150), 61–65.

Turner, M., Payne, S., Kidd, H. & Barbarachild, Z. (2010). *Dying behind bars: an evaluation of end of life care in prisons in Cumbria and Lancashire.* http://www.lancs.ac.uk/shm/research/ioelc/groups/media/mturner_150410.pdf (Last accessed 12 July 2014).

UKNPM (2013). *Monitoring places of detention: third annual report.* London: The Stationery Office.

United Nations General Assembly (1985). 96th plenary meeting (29 November 1985). *United Nations Standard Minimum Rules for the Administration of Juvenile Justice (The Beijing Rules).* New York: UN.

United Nations General Assembly (2010). 65th session: Third Committee: Agenda item 105 (05th October, 2010). *United Nations Rules for the Treatment of Women Prisoners and Non-custodial Measures for Women Offenders (The Bangkok Rules).* New York: UN.

Wahidin, A. & Cain, M. (eds) (2006). *Ageing, Crime and Society.* Devon: Willan Publishing.

World Health Organisation (1995). *Health in Prisons Programme.* Copenhagen: WHO.

World Health Organisation (2007). *Health in Prisons: a WHO guide to the essentials in prison health.* Copenhagen: WHO.

# 11

# Learning opportunities from inquests

Jane Littlewood

This chapter highlights some common issues and challenges faced by healthcare professionals providing effective healthcare in custody. The text is written from the perspective of a healthcare solicitor representing the interests of doctors and nurses at coroners' inquests and supporting them through the process. The aim is to raise awareness and promote good practice through discussion and consideration of key points at specific stages throughout the chapter. As this chapter discusses issues relating to both police custody and prison settings, the terms 'detainee' and 'prisoner' are both used to denote the person in custody. At the time of writing, long-awaited reform of the coronial system brought by the Coroners and Justice Act 2009, Coroners (investigations) Regulations 2013 and the Coroners (Inquests) Rules 2013 was implemented on 25 July 2013, and the practical impact of this reform is still being worked though. The aim is to improve the inquest experience for all involved.

## A death in custody

When a death occurs in police custody or prison, investigations by the Independent Police Complaints Commission (IPCC) if in police custody, or the Prisons and Probation Ombudsman (PPO) if in prison, precede the inquest and provide valuable information for future risk avoidance. There will usually also be a clinical review and subsequent report of the medical care provided, which is made available during the coroner's inquiry.

   The coroner's role is to register and investigate the circumstances of a death. Inquests are held in public. When a death occurs in custody, the coroner may sit with a jury, whose role is to determine the facts relating to the cause of death and arrive at a conclusion, with the coroner's direction as to the law. Very often the conclusion (previously known as a verdict) will take the form of a narrative description of events leading to the death.

   The purpose of an inquest is not to apportion blame. Rather, it is a fact-finding investigation to ascertain when, where and how the deceased came to die. At an inquest, most of the time is spent looking at 'how' death occurred. At custody inquests, coroners and juries have a wide remit to look into the broad circumstances surrounding the cause of death.

The coroner will ensure that the bereaved family is at the centre of the process and has an opportunity to play an active part. Article 2 of the European Convention on Human Rights, incorporated into UK law by Section 6 of the Human Rights Act 1998, provides that everyone's right to life shall be protected by law. The coroner will consider the state's systems put in place to safeguard life and any lessons to be learned (for example, see the case of R (on the application of Lewis) v HM Coroner for the Mid and North Division of the County of Shropshire). After hearing the inquest evidence, a coroner may write a report recommending that action be taken to prevent other future deaths.

Individual doctors and nurses may be legally represented at an inquest if the coroner considers them to have a proper interest in the proceedings. It is sometimes necessary for individuals to have their own representation, separate from that of their employer, if there is a risk of conflicting interests either between employees or between an individual employee and the employing organisation. There may have been a disciplinary investigation, ending in the staff member being dismissed or suspended pending the inquest outcome. Evidence at an inquest can have an impact on related proceedings, such as an investigation by a regulatory body or even the police. The family of the deceased may pursue a civil claim for negligence, for instance. Individuals may contact their medical defence organisation for advice regarding representation.

The healthcare needs of people in custody are frequently complicated by drug and alcohol abuse, poor physical and mental health, violence, behavioural problems and security considerations. For healthcare practitioners, working in secure settings can be extremely challenging but also very rewarding.

The death of any patient is, of course, distressing but the added strain of an inquest can take its toll on the mental and physical well-being of the healthcare practitioners involved. If all goes well, the coroner's inquiry should leave everyone involved with a sense of closure and the feeling that at least something positive has been achieved by learning lessons from a tragic loss.

## Communication problems

There are many detainees in police custody and prison suffering from poor mental health. Inquests may conclude that the deceased died, in part, because the risk of them taking their own life or harming themselves was not recognised and appropriate precautions were therefore not taken. In such cases, the coroner might refer to 'missed opportunities'. Coroners often focus on the quality of the initial risk assessment because this may trigger a 'domino effect' of missed opportunities. However, the initial assessment is only part of an ongoing duty to carry out risk assessments, and communication is key to their effectiveness.

It is essential that all information relating to risk travels with the detainee on their journey through the criminal justice pathway. The Person Escort Record (PER) is a document used by the criminal justice services to communicate information about the detainee's risk and vulnerabilities whilst being escorted and/or transferred. The PER flags up any alcohol and drug problems as well as self-harm and suicide risk. The PER is sometimes accompanied by copy risk assessments and medical notes, although it may be safer to assume that the additional documentation is not attached, and ensure that crucial information is recorded prominently on the form itself.

For example, an inquest jury may need to consider whether the PER was adequately completed, whether risk assessments and/or medical reports were attached, and whether the police verbally conveyed information to transport staff. Likewise, they will need to consider whether transport staff failed to act on information in accordance with their own procedures or themselves failed to request information from the police. Later on, when the individual arrived at prison, the jury will need to know whether prison officers attributed appropriate weight to the information, and whether healthcare staff obtained and read the medical records and PER when carrying out the first reception health screen.

In healthcare in-patient settings, which are found in some (but not all) prisons, all important information and any changes in the situation should be recorded in the case notes and care plans within the healthcare record, and be reviewed at each new assessment. A thorough recorded assessment allows others to see potential areas of concern, flags up risk and the plan for further management, and is particularly important at shift changes, for new staff and for visiting prison doctors in order to facilitate fully informed decisions.

The failure to record a change in situation is often criticised at inquests. If there is no record of an assessment, it may be suggested that the assessment did not take place. For example, it could be suggested a prison officer did not check the cell at the time they say they did, if there is no written record.

The difficulty for healthcare staff is that they are usually extremely busy. Security measures can slow down the provision of care. For example, there may be times when the prison is in 'lock down' and movement across the prison is restricted; however, even at these times, it is important that record keeping is maintained. It may be suggested that there was a duty to pass on information, to act on information received, and to seek out information. The Nursing and Midwifery Council (NMC) provides guidance regarding record keeping (NMC 2009).

## Risks while in police custody

On arrival at the police station, many detainees are under the influence of alcohol and/or drugs. Initially they may be extremely agitated and violent but later calm down, having been left in a cell to sober up. Healthcare practitioners may instruct that the person should be observed and roused at specified intervals to check that they are responsive.

Communication between the healthcare practitioner and custody staff is important, particularly when it comes to the type and frequency of checks that should be made and observations that should be recorded. The making of records contemporaneously, or as close as possible in time, ensures that instructions and important information will be seen by new staff coming on duty.

It can be difficult to distinguish real risk from perceived attention-seeking behaviour and/or the influence of alcohol and drugs. Detainees potentially facing a long sentence, or having no prior experience of being in custody, may be at increased risk. In such cases, it may be necessary to place the detainee in a camera cell for constant observation or transfer them to hospital. Certain items of clothing that could be potentially tied around the neck may be removed. The key points are listed below.

It is important:

- When assessing risk of self-harm, to highlight the specific factors that make self-harm more likely and less likely
- To consider a detainee's previous experience of being in custody and the length of the sentence they may face
- When relying on a detainee's account of the relevant history, to ensure that the entry in the record makes it clear that this is what the person indicated – for example, by using phrases like 'told' or 'according to' in order to alert others to the fact that this may not be the complete story
- To ask about the circumstances of any previous episodes of self-harm
- To consider whether the detainee has been medically assessed as having suicidal ideation
- To consider the level of observations required
- If the detainee is too unwell to be in a cell, to consider the need for transfer to hospital
- To ensure that adequate information is included in the PER completed by the custody officer for onward travel with the detained person, particularly regarding issues involving drugs, alcohol, self-harm and suicide risk.

# Risks while in prison

## On arrival at prison

Reception healthcare screening is usually the first point of contact with prison healthcare staff for the new prisoner. Lack of accurate information is a common problem for healthcare staff at this stage, as they often have to rely on what they are told.

A registered nurse will identify any significant health issues via a reception screening and assessment process. However, it is risky to rely on the prisoner's own account of their substance misuse and treatment history. Prisoners may exaggerate or be unclear as to the type and frequency of their drug use. Staff will question the prisoner to elicit their drug history, and they need to document any additional information that is forthcoming.

All staff need to be up to date in respect of policies and procedures. They must acknowledge receipt and understanding of such documentation and be given the opportunity to discuss policies and procedures at team meetings. Agency staff will need access to the email system within the prison to ensure that they receive all relevant information. Key points are listed below.

It is important to:

- Have access to medical records as soon as possible on the individual's arrival at prison
- Prioritise those prisoners who need to see a doctor quickly on arrival
- Ensure that there are no missed opportunities to identify risk in the reception process
- Develop effective systems of information handling and sharing to ensure that receiving facilities have full and timely access to health-related information.

## Physical health risks in prison

Staff may suspect that a prisoner is pretending to have a fit to obtain more medication but seizure is a real risk during detoxification. Referral to hospital may be indicated in order to investigate an underlying medical problem.

A prisoner's aggression may hinder or delay clinical intervention. Staff may feel at risk themselves and unable to come close enough to safely observe or carry out tests.

Staff may be accustomed to seeing prisoners lose weight and vomit, due to detoxification from drugs. The effects of dehydration on the body should not be underestimated, as death from dehydration can occur suddenly. It is particularly important to monitor fluid intake/output. Observations should be recorded, and a care plan put in place. Recorded observations ensure continuity on a change of shift. Healthcare staff may need to consider whether a prisoner can be cared for adequately at the prison, or if transfer to hospital is required.

The coroner will examine any missed opportunities for medical intervention. Observation and communication are of crucial importance when there is a risk of the prisoner's health deteriorating further. Detoxification is a serious condition, from which patients take time to recover. However, this should not rule out consideration of other possible causes of ill health, with appropriate precautions being taken to ensure that staff are able to recognise and act promptly in response to a serious deterioration. Staff cannot always foresee such events but reasonable precautions should be taken. The key points are listed below.

It is important to:

- Escalate any concerns regarding the ability of the nursing staff to carry out adequate observations
- Have sufficient numbers of regular staff available who are familiar with procedures and patients, rather than relying too much on agency staff

- Review whether handover arrangements are adequate, particularly in terms of allowing staff enough time to review records
- Seek informed consent before undertaking any examination or investigation or providing treatment, in order to protect an individual's personal autonomy and dignity.

## Control and restraint procedures

Staff recognising behavioural precursors to violence and aggression may try to defuse a situation by using de-escalation techniques, but sometimes it is necessary to use hands-on control and restraint procedures. The role of healthcare staff in an episode of control and restraint is usually centred on monitoring the prisoner (i.e. checking that the prisoner is breathing and conscious throughout the procedure) and providing guidance for colleagues after the incident regarding observations and relocating the prisoner. Nursing staff are trained to oversee the process, to ensure that it is carried out safely and to know when to intervene clinically. In unplanned incidents of restraint, staff may need to move the prisoner away from others to seclusion.

Having been through the physical exertion of restraint, the person is assessed before being left and then observed. When giving evidence at an inquest, doctors and nurses may need to describe the circumstances of a restraint. It may be suggested that the restraint contributed to death, due to unreasonable force, unnecessarily prolonged restraint and/or an inappropriate technique having been used.

## Looking to the future

The last decade has seen the transfer of responsibility for healthcare in public prisons from HM Prison Service to wider NHS and private providers. There is currently some concern about the number of people entering the criminal justice system in police custody with significant health problems. In view of this, the possibility of also transferring custody suites to NHS and private providers is being discussed.

With an ageing prison population, caring for people with mental health problems and/or learning disabilities in custodial settings seems likely to remain just as challenging in the future. In 2009, Lord Bradley's review, commissioned by the Secretary of State for Justice, recommended improvements across the criminal justice system (Bradley 2009). Work is currently underway to promote the aims of diversion and liaison, which are the continued focus of government attention.

When considering diversion of those with mental health problems away from custody, the abilities of the wider community mental health system are taken into account. Inquests can help highlight the need for closer communication between organisations and the need for additional training – for example, in relation to the power to detain people under mental health legislation for assessment by approved mental health professionals.

## Conclusion

The Ministry of Justice publishes summaries of coroners' reports to prevent future deaths, from which the most recent emerging trends can be seen. In the author's experience of prison inquests, common themes can include the importance of:

- Good record keeping and communication of information/risk
- Suicide risk awareness
- Thorough first reception health screening and availability of support services
- Cell sharing risk assessments (also considering mental state)
- Training in documentation
- Access to and review of medical records at handover and when key decisions are made
- Awareness of policies regarding psychiatric or hospital referrals
- Training in mental health
- Supervision regarding medication.

In response to lessons learned through inquests, managers responsible for healthcare systems need to consider appropriate risk management steps. However, it is also important that individual doctors and nurses remember their own responsibility to keep their skills up to date and to familiarise themselves with all policies and protocols in their place of employment.

## References

Bradley, K. (2009). *The Bradley Report.* London: Department of Health, The Stationery Office.

Coroners and Justice Act (2009). http://www.legislation.gov.uk/ukpga/2009/25/contents (Last accessed: 12 August 2014).

Coroners (investigations) Regulations (2013). http://www.legislation.gov.uk/uksi/2013/1629/part/7/made (Last accessed: 12 August 2014).

Coroners (inquests) Rules (2013). http://www.legislation.gov.uk/uksi/2013/1616/contents/made (Last accessed: 12 August 2014).

Human Rights Act (1998). http://www.legislation.gov.uk/ukpga/1998/42/contents (Last accessed: 12 August 2014).

Nursing and Midwifery Council (2009). *Guidance for Nurses and Midwives.* London: NMC.

# 12

# Professional attitudes and behaviours

Steve Dilworth and Warren Stewart

This chapter explores what it means to be a professional nurse and how nursing attitudes and behaviour influence the whole field of care in secure settings. It also explores how care is in turn influenced by organisational systems, multi-disciplinary colleagues and environments of care, as well as the resilience needed to enable staff working in secure care settings to maintain standards.

We consider the underpinning Nursing and Midwifery Council (NMC) *Code* (NMC 2010), and professional and public perceptions of offenders. We consider the needs of vulnerable and marginalised people and how nursing responds to them. The chapter incorporates a mixture of discussion, case studies and discussion points.

For the purposes of this chapter, the term 'secure care workers' refers to health and social care staff working in custodial environments. There is a current progressive and positive blurring of role boundaries between traditional carer and custodian roles that places 'care' at the heart of all work carried out in custody.

By 'secure environments' we mean prisons, immigration holding centres and police custody suites. We do not include secure hospitals within this term.

We use the term 'detainees' to mean prisoners (whether sentenced or remand), adult (male/female), young offenders, people held in police facilities, those detained in immigration centres and secure special hospitals.

We define 'poor practice' as not doing what one knows to be right.

Whilst the main purpose of this chapter is to explore ideas around professional standards, we also want to signpost best practice. Our deeper hope is that reading these words will help to promote debate about achieving higher standards. This in turn implies that standards of care are not always high enough. It can be difficult for hard-working staff to read the phrase 'must do better' but we trust that there is general agreement that, as professionals, we know that our practice and that of our colleagues is always open to improvement.

This chapter was inspired by the authors' practical experience of working in secure environments. Latterly, this has included delivery of a workshop that placed the need to do the right thing in the context of current professional, legal and ethical standards. Two questions that might enable readers to rapidly assess their own standards are:

● Would I say or do this in front of my manager?

● Would I tell my manager or colleague what I have done or said? If not, why not?

We could say that 'doing right' depends on acting on the right values and attitudes. If this is true, correct and pre-existing manner and personality are basic entry requirements for staff, on top of which education, training and mentorship are added as extras. Recent reports, such as *Crossing the Boundaries* (Baguley et al. 2006), *The Francis Report* (Francis 2013) and the NHS Employers website (www.nhsemployers.org) confirm this assertion.

## Reasons for poor practice

Where practice is poor, we believe it is important to look first for possible underlying reasons and manage these. If practitioners are 'ignorant', ill-prepared, or just do not understand the implications of their actions then help and guidance is clearly indicated. Strict sanctions should be reserved for when a practitioner knowingly acts inappropriately or does the wrong thing.

Where staff are unaware of the right things to do, then gaps in knowledge need to be addressed through education, management and mentoring. Although sometimes difficult, in exceptional cases an honest approach to disciplinary procedures must be followed to ensure longer-term benefits and safe care provision for all stakeholders.

Whatever the reasons for poor care, duty of care remains paramount in all but the most exceptional cases. The NMC (2010) emphasises a duty of care at all times, to all individuals, to ensure that they do not suffer harm or loss. This principle applies to all of those working in custodial settings.

We suggest that the causes of most cases of poor practice lie somewhere between the extremes of ignorance and malice. We encourage sympathetic yet rigorous attention in the light of the difficulties of providing care in custody. The general approach we suggest is to focus on ways to *support* staff to:

● Reject poor or average care: Most staff know the relevant guidelines, in spirit if not word-for-word; they are aware of 'the right thing to do'.

● Build resilience to go beyond merely 'doing enough': Empathy can be reduced and standards of care compromised by inability to maintain resilience in the face of the particular challenges of the environment (Ewers et al. 2002).

One particular aspect of providing care in custody is that security is a competing priority. The need to provide care while also maintaining security can lead to staff feeling professionally compromised in their attempts to uphold the correct standards. This issue needs constant vigilance if it is not to lead to, or excuse, poor practice.

## Case study: Dissonance and resilience in care

Anna is a newly qualified Registered Nurse with an interest in health inequalities and public health issues. She is young and keen to learn, though anxious about her first post – in a large, inner-city local prison.

Anna is assigned to a treatment room on a busy remand wing. She is to work with Diane, who has been qualified for 25 years and has worked in the prison for 17 years.

Anna notices many differences between how she has been trained and nursing practices on the wing. She asks 'naive' questions of Diane on a number of issues and slowly friction develops between the two. Diane sees how Anna deals with the detainees and comments, 'You have a lot to learn young lady.' She later adds, 'They will walk all over you if you carry on like that.' These comments add to Anna's anxiety about dealing with detainees; she also becomes nervous about approaching Diana, fearing her hostility.

One morning a prisoner appears at the treatment hatch and asks for her medication. Anna goes to collect the tablet but Diane abruptly says that treatment time has finished, and she cannot have her medication until lunchtime at the earliest. She goes on to tell the prisoner that she should get out of bed earlier. The prisoner complains bitterly, trying to explain that the tablets make her tired and cause her to oversleep. The situation becomes fraught and Anna tries to defuse it by offering the prisoner her tablet. At this point Diane reacts angrily, loudly threatening to put the prisoner on report if she does not go away.

Anna feels uneasy and concludes that she has not been helpful to either party. She would have issued the medication, even though she realises that this might set a precedent that might be difficult to maintain. She wants to build rapport with prisoners on the wing but feels that the roles and rules prevent this. She wonders if the pressures of the environment will cause her to react like Diane in future. Anna feels very uncomfortable and is unsure how to manage her feelings.

- Is there a right or wrong course of action in this scenario?
- How could Anna increase her resilience?

# About standards

There are many standards to guide practice. Relevant guidance can be found in: *The Code: Standards of Conduct, Performance and Ethics for Nurses and Midwives* (NMC 2010); publications from the Department of Health and National Health Service (NHS), The Royal College of Nursing, and the Nursing in Criminal Justice Services Forum (RCN); HM Prison Service orders and instructions; and local operational policies.

Walsh *et al.* (2013) write extensively about the negative impact of rigid roles within secure care and we suggest that standards are intended to be soft and flexible, rather than hard and rigid. We think of rules as boundaries, not barriers. To illustrate, in certain sports the pitch is clearly marked, and the rules are explicit and agreed. Yet within these rules, creativity can be abundant – within the further limitations of the skills of the players, the imagination of managers and the eyesight of referees.

When providing care, attitudes and behaviours should be consistent with standards, yet flexible enough to include common sense and professional judgement. We must seek creative ways to manage dilemmas without compromising the clear boundaries that exist for sound reasons. For example, with regard to confidentiality, we know that collaboration between custody staff is vital and we must consequently find ways to share information across the custody team.

# Emotional labour, dissonance and resilience

If rules are clear and staff are informed and well-meaning, why do problems occur? In order to gain some understanding of this we turn to three key concepts – emotional labour, dissonance and resilience.

Custodial roles can involve stressful interpersonal encounters (emotional labour); sometimes the work can conflict with our way of thinking (dissonance); and this can influence standards of care. We need to deal with these situations by using personal and organisational strategies to cope with and manage any difficulties that arise (resilience).

Care can be influenced, both positively and negatively, by the way staff manage their emotional responses. The term 'emotional labour' refers to how people try to display emotions that will fit with the purpose, culture, expectations, customs and practice of the organisation that employs them. This effort may contrast with what the person actually feels (Theodosius 2008, Walsh 2009).

Secure care workers often meet situations that clash with their own personal or professional ideals, resulting in uncomfortable thoughts and feelings and a gap between how someone feels they should act and the actions they actually want to take. This is known as dissonance – it affects the way people think and feel. In the following example, a social worker recalled meeting an offender for the first time (Guthrie 2013):

I have a vivid memory of walking down the staircase. I remember my knees were wobbling, thinking how I was going to cope, sitting in a small room with no windows with the man who had done these awful, awful things … I read his file and, as anyone would be, was horrified by the details of the crimes. I kind of pulled myself together, went to the waiting room and called his name … we sat down in the office … I introduced myself and I asked him to tell me what he thought I needed to know about him. He looked me in the eye and said, 'I've done some really dreadful things and the first thing I think about in the morning and the last thing I think about at night is the harm I have caused … and now I'm trying to rebuild my life.'

I felt very challenged because on one level I was struggling with the feelings that any human being would have on meeting someone who has committed dreadful, dreadful acts of sexual abuse that have caused such harm to the boys and their families, and on the other hand I met a human being who was sitting across the table asking for help.

**Do I respond as a human being, emotionally, and treat him with disgust, or do I respond as a professional and do what I could to assist him to rebuild a life?**

Walsh (2009) notes that dissonance is more pronounced for secure carers than for other custody staff, as the overriding philosophy of 'health and care' for nurses competes with the importance of 'security' carried by other prison staff. As the key principle of care takes root in offender settings, along with an increased emphasis on rehabilitation and reduction of re-offending rates, this apparent gap in priorities is likely to narrow. Walsh (2009) acknowledges that nurses who work in secure environments engage in emotional labour to manage their dissonance when dealing with dilemmas and difficult patient behaviours. This skilled work provides an outlet for strong feelings being experienced and expressed by detainees.

Secure care staff engage in emotional labour through *surface* or *deep* acting. The former is relatively benign, a sometimes helpful ability to deceive others about how we are really feeling without deceiving ourselves (Theodosius 2009), as in the example above.

Deep acting is where we deceive ourselves about our true emotions as much as we deceive others (Hochschild 1983). This type of acting can contribute greatly to the psychological and physical well-being of the patient (Mann & Cowburn 2005). However, while it is helpful to the detainee, it can be exhausting for the nurse.

Resilience can be defined as, 'the general capacity for flexible and resourceful adaptation to external and internal stressors' (Klohen 1996, p. 1068). Increasing awareness of emotional labour is a good first step towards developing the emotional intelligence needed to increase resilience and well-being, thus offering some protection from the effects of occupational stress and burnout (Grant & Kinman 2011).

# Burn-out and freeze-out

A consequence of failing to balance emotional labour and the emergence of dissonance in the secure care worker is a drift towards burn-out or, perhaps more typically, freeze-out. Burn-out can be defined as a psychological state characterised by a cluster of symptoms including emotional exhaustion, depersonalisation and decreased sense of personal accomplishment (Maslach et al. 1996). Secure care staff can experience tiredness, reduced resilience and limited job satisfaction. There may be frustration in the face of custodial impediments to providing care, relatively low degree of engagement by detainees and the slow progress of recovery.

Workers in secure settings are vulnerable to burn-out (Stewart & Terry 2014). There is evidence in the wider literature to suggest higher than average rates of burn-out (Dickinson & Wright 2008, Mason 2002), especially for those dealing with patients suffering from serious mental illness (Savicki & Cooley 1987). This is particularly significant, as a correlation exists between nurses identified as experiencing burn-out and 'reports of fair to poor quality of care on their units, decreased job satisfaction, and increased risk of failure to recognise patient distress' (Aitken et al. 2002, p.1987).

At times, toxic emotional labour can lead to care workers becoming cold and cynical. We suggest the term 'freeze-out' to capture the way this contributes to reduced empathy, avoiding patients and evaluating clients more negatively (Ewers et al. 2002).

The net result of all the above is adverse effects on both the health of staff and the standard of care they deliver (Ewers et al. 2002). There are also financial (Wright 2005) and 'quality of care' (Coffey 1999) implications. Given 'higher expectations from public services in the context of cuts in funding' (Storey 2011), it is important to address the poor practice and inefficiency resulting from burn-out and freeze-out. There is some evidence to suggest that engaging in the supportive, reflective mechanism of clinical supervision, and maintaining learning via continuing personal and professional development are helpful resilience-boosting strategies for qualified nurses working in secure environments (Stewart & Terry 2014). Engaging in reflective dialogue with a trusted colleague in relation to practice issues has also been shown to be helpful when processing emotional elements of secure care work (Walsh 2009); and learning about engagement strategies and other patient factors helps to increase practitioner knowledge and understanding, thereby reducing the risk of burn-out (Ewers 2002, Doyle 2007, Redhead et al. 2010).

# Boundary violation

By 'boundary' we mean an agreed or imposed rule, a limit to the extent of a relationship. A counsellor may offer a client undivided attention and unconditional positive regard but if that client calls at 2am then these conditions would not apply. In this situation, a boundary has been broken. In custody settings, professional relationship boundaries are complicated by the custody context (Schafer & Peternelj-Taylor 2003, p. 606):

> The ability to establish therapeutic relationships and maintain boundaries is among the most important competencies required … although well-functioning boundaries tend to go unnoticed, most individuals recognise when someone has crossed the line…

## Case study: Emotional labour and boundary violation

Jermaine is detained in an inner-city police station after a violent argument with an older male who he describes as his partner. He is 19 years old and has a history of homelessness and drug misuse.

Following a medical screen, during which he said little, Jermaine asks for a quiet chat with the nurse, Jenny. He recognises something caring in Jenny's nature and tentatively discloses a history of sexual abuse from early childhood into his teens. He believes this has caused a variety of problems, including unstable relationships and destructive behaviour. He warns Jenny that he self-harms by lacerating his genitals and explains how this emulates the abuse he experienced. He expresses anxiety and vulnerability and says that he has self-harmed in the past at similar times of high emotion.

Jenny listens attentively and is privately troubled by the graphic disclosure. She masks her true feelings by re-creating the verbal and non-verbal expressions that she has used in other caring situations. Although she has encountered self-harm before, this method of self-harm leaves her confused and somewhat disgusted. She feels powerless to intervene.

Nevertheless Jenny decides to try to support Jermaine and creates a behavioural contract with him to help the custody suite officers manage his behaviour. Jermaine is grateful and seems pleased with the idea; he promises to follow the programme.

When Jenny returns to work the following day, the case is discussed in handover and she learns that Jermaine used a plastic knife to inflict several wounds around his groin. The officers felt he was high suicide risk, limited his personal belongings and placed him in basic conditions. When Jenny finds him he is looking preoccupied but does not appear regretful, saying he could not help himself. He asks her to try to get his belongings back. Jenny notices a rising sense of anger towards him, which she tries to suppress. She feels betrayed and wants to berate him for not sticking to the agreed plan. She feels she has wasted time and effort listening to him. In the notes she records that he is not genuinely mentally unwell and that he has abused the care offered to him.

She later reflects on her feelings and actions, judging them unprofessional, as Jermaine does have needs.

- Consider how this case study relates to the concepts of emotional labour, dissonance and boundaries discussed earlier.
- What might have helped Jenny deal with this situation?

## Exercising judgement and making judgements

We offer the following thinking tool for practitioners grappling with finding a balance between exercising judgements and being judgemental:

## Table 12.1: A thinking tool for practitioners

| Exercising judgement | Being judgemental |
|---|---|
| ● Basing decisions and observations on a situation using codes of practice, explicit assumptions and evidence | ● Basing decisions and observations on a person or people using personal beliefs and implicit assumptions |
| ● Using language like: | ● Using language like: |
| – There is no right or wrong… | – Right and wrong |
| – The facts are… | – You/they are… |
| – The evidence is… | – You/they always… |
| – The assumptions are… | – I can't because you/they… |
| – The pros and cons are… | – I am at fault |
| – The principles are… | – You/they are at fault |
| – The values are… | – I am great |
| – The impact is… | – You/they are |
| – My experience is… | **ARROGANCE AND FEAR** |
| **ASSERTION AND HUMILITY** | |

*Personal communication: created by Anna Coen (AC Integration 2013), reprinted by kind permission of Anna Coen.*

# Factors influencing care in custodial settings

Ensuring that detainees with health and social needs can access professional, dignified care is a complex aim that needs the skilled cooperation of many professional groups and the willing involvement of the recipients of the care. Crucially, achieving this aim must include significant attention to many factors, including the physical environment.

The model below represents the dynamic relationship between four key elements that influence care:

1. The secure care worker
2. The detainee
3. The wider multi-disciplinary team (MDT)
4. The prison environment.

*Figure 12.1: Factors influencing care*

We outline some of the themes arising from this dynamic combination of factors without claiming to provide a fully comprehensive picture. We trust that the examples we use will encourage the reader to seriously consider the influencing factors that may be at play in their own workplaces.

## 1: Secure care workers

This term includes nurses, care assistants, social workers, psychologists and therapists from many disciplines, working in a variety of settings. This umbrella term can be extended to include prison officers (Tait 2008), court staff and police custody officers, many of whom provide some degree of care in first night centres, older prisoners' residential units and other areas involving health and social care.

The particular example of registered nurses provides a stepping stone to considering all secure care workers, as nursing practice is bound by guidelines that are applicable across caring roles. Nurses have a key responsibility to teach what is right and wrong, keep their skills and knowledge up to date, and treat patients with dignity and respect. 'Nursing may not be easy to define but patients know when they get good nursing and when they do not' (Richie & Hall 2009, p. 9).

The Nursing and Midwifery Council's *Code* lists the key points (NMC 2010): Nurses must:

- Treat people as individuals
- Respect people's confidentiality
- Collaborate with those in your care
- Ensure you gain consent
- Maintain clear professional boundaries
- Share information with your colleagues
- Delegate effectively
- Manage risk
- Use the best available evidence
- Keep your skills and knowledge up to date
- Keep clear and accurate records
- Act with integrity
- Deal with problems
- Be impartial.

The need for compassion in nursing is self-evident but, as we write this chapter, it is a topic of much public, political and professional debate (DH 2012, p.12):

> There is also a growing recognition, at all levels of the health, care and support systems, that we have to change our culture if we are to change our care. The reports on Winterbourne View and Mid Staffordshire will be a call to action for everyone.

We return to the theme of culture later in this chapter but at this point we note that the Department of Health, through the Chief Nursing Officer Jane Cummings, goes on to emphasise the values that must be embedded in all nursing practice. These values, generally referred to as 'the 6 Cs', are: compassion, caring, competency, communication, courage and commitment.

## Case study: The code of conduct and professional dilemmas

A young female detainee returns to the healthcare centre from the visits area, escorted by a healthcare assistant (HCA) and a custody officer. The detainee was disruptive during an appointment with immigration officials. She was observed shouting and kicking furniture and was eventually restrained after becoming aggressive towards staff as they intervened. She settled after speaking to a residential manager, and agreed to walk back to her room under escort. However, she continued to use threatening gestures and verbally abuse the staff accompanying her. Her escorts were losing patience as the situation escalated once more amid heated verbal exchanges. The team leader was on hand to receive the group and guide the detainee to her room.

As the detainee reluctantly re-entered her room, she spat in the face of the HCA and pulled the door behind her, catching the HCA's forearm in the process. The HCA recoiled at first but infuriated, and in the heat of the moment, she was seen to spit back. The reaction was spontaneous and no saliva left her mouth but the extent of the behaviour was obvious. The door was quickly closed by other staff, to great relief. All those present had seen this event but no words were exchanged for a few moments until the HCA tried to justify her behaviour, saying that she disliked spitting more than anything; this appeared to confirm her intentions.

The residential manager challenged the team leader in private, stating that he 'couldn't believe what he was seeing' and asking angrily why the HCA had not been immediately questioned or even suspended following her behaviour. He gave little opportunity for a response and left, saying it just wasn't good enough and that he would report the whole matter to the director immediately. The team leader tried earnestly to explain how the incident was out of keeping with his colleague's usual behaviour, and that the HCA had struggled to return to her role after being assaulted at work some months earlier.

The team leader knew that the HCA had breached professional standards and that disciplinary action would follow. He wondered if he should have been more direct, and whether his lack of action would be interpreted as weakness or complicity. But the situation was complicated, as they had worked together under difficult circumstances and supported one another for several years.

- Has the code of conduct been breached by the team leader and/or the HCA?
- Can lack of action be justified in any way?

## 2: The multi-disciplinary team

Beyond the secure care workers specifically, the wider multi-disciplinary team includes many whose role does not traditionally prioritise the provision of care. Collaborative working within this wider group, especially in relation to 'difficult' clients, allows us to see and therefore use multiple perspectives to our advantage. This in turn makes it more likely that correct standards will be maintained.

Tait (2008, p. 7) describes several prison officer 'types' and asserts that care is now 'everyone's business'. She uses the phrases 'turn-key' and 'care-bear' to describe types of officer at the extremes of a spectrum before identifying five distinct approaches to the matter of caring:

> ...true carer, limited carer, old school, conflicted and 'damaged'. Officers with each caring style shared a particular view of prisoners as a group, and varied in their adherence to traditional prison officer cultural norms. Length of experience and gender were related to caring approach, as were work environment and experience of trauma...

Professor Alison Liebling provided an interesting perspective in her evidence to the Justice Committee (House of Commons Justice Committee 2008/09, p. 5), saying that:

> ...there is a better alignment between the aims of the prison and the inclinations of prison officers, so I think officers have become quite comfortable with the public protection framework, and in that sense there is less role conflict in the prison officer, they have found a way to combine their two security and care roles.

Consider whether you have ever seen other staff members intimidating, labelling, avoiding or ignoring detainees, or 'seeing the crime rather than the person'.

- Have you ever behaved in any of these ways yourself?
- Why do you think staff sometimes slip into such behaviours?

## 3: Detainees

Detainees are a challenging group to care for, as their health and social needs are an extensive, diverse and complex mix of mental health issues, social problems, learning disabilities and physical health problems. Sex offenders need special accommodation and require special skills to treat, and there are logistical challenges when detainees need to access secondary care services.

Detainees often have a heightened sense of frustration, fear, isolation and anger. They tend to be very aware of whether their needs are heard, and whether staff attitudes are caring or uncaring. The incidence of anger towards authority and complaints from healthy detainees is much higher than in the general population.

Research has consistently found high rates of mental disorder among offender populations. For example, 72 per cent of male and 70 per cent of female sentenced prisoners suffer from two or more mental health disorders; additionally, 62 per cent of male and 57 per cent of female sentenced prisoners have a personality disorder (Prison Reform Trust 2010).

In considering the available literature, the stand-out issue is the controversial diagnosis of personality disorder. Few healthcare professionals like taking care of people with personality disorders and they often lack knowledge, experience and skill in this area. Consequently, difficult encounters are the norm. A key threat to the nurse–patient relationship comes from the boundary-pushing behaviour of personality disorder patients who are said to 'differ in the way that they think, feel, relate to others, and contain (or fail to contain) their impulses (Bowers 2002, p. 4). Their behaviour can be difficult, obnoxious, threatening and they are hard to manage in institutional settings', (Bowers 2002, p. 22, p. 4).

Citing Coid (1992), Bowers (2002) underlines the difficulty, saying that 'a proportion of prisoners in the UK are clinically indistinguishable from the personality disorder population of the High Secure Hospitals'.

Nevertheless, we are faced with a dilemma in relation to the term 'personality disorder'. The tendency to typecast people, on the grounds of a diagnostic label, can be a questionable practice in this area of work. After all, can any of us say that we are 'personality ordered'? The fact is that we all display multiple personalities. Thus, what 'I' say that 'I' believe at one moment can be (and often is) completely contradicted by what I say and do in another moment.

We therefore urge wariness when labelling others, especially when the label is used in a pejorative way, leading to dismissal, exclusion and contempt rather than acceptance, inclusion and understanding. As Terry Pratchett put it in his novel *Jingo* (1988, p. 199):

> It was so much easier to blame it on Them. It was bleakly depressing to think that They were Us. If it was Them, then nothing was anyone's fault. If it was Us, what did that make Me? After all, I'm one of Us. I must be. I've certainly never thought of myself as one of Them. No one ever thinks of themselves as one of Them. We're always one of Us. It's Them that do the bad things.

Having said this, if we expect staff to care for people who are seen as the most difficult in society, and in the most difficult circumstances, then they need help and support rather than criticism and censure. Youngson (2011) highlighted the need to overcome:

> the tension between our models of impersonal, institutionalised care and the desire for healing that brings people into the health professions. This healing is needed as much by the practitioner as those receiving care.

## 4: Custodial environments

Understanding emotional labour in secure environments depends on understanding its cultural norms. In this section we therefore focus on the culture of care in custody settings. We believe that the nature of the environment (physical and relational), noise, regimes, systems and processes can all work against the intention to provide care.

Culture is above all 'the way we do things round here'. We have covered the range of standards that are supposed to (and do) underpin practice but culture goes beyond such guidance. There is a great difference between the clarity of the written rules and the mystery of the unwritten rules. The latter are often unspoken and yet conveyed through a kind of tacit, sign language: 'an elaborate and secret code that is written nowhere, known by none, and understood by all' (Sapir 1927, p. 556).

To illustrate, consider the power differences between those who work in prisons and those who are 'guests'. At an obvious level, the uniform worn shows who holds the keys. Beneath the surface, there are rules and regulations. The regime is enforced or relaxed according to the knowledge, experience or even whim of those 'in charge'. Less obvious but equally important are the psychological and emotional power dynamics, which are explored later in this chapter.

Overall, we can say that secure settings are not designed as nurturing places (Ginn 2012, p. 1): 'Prison is a difficult place in which to provide health services, and concerns about the health of prisoners and the quality of healthcare available to them are long standing.'

## Cultural competency

Tangential to the notion of culture is the concept and skill of cultural competency (Wilson *et al.* 2003, p. 8): 'Responsible, competent nurses choose to examine effective and culturally relevant methods of applying the nursing process with persons from diverse cultures.'

Although the Equalities Act 2010 covers traditional categories of protected characteristics, such as age, race, gender, religion, disability, marital status, pregnancy and sexual orientation, we also need to consider attitudes to people from different cultural groups.

The proportion of foreign nationals in UK prisons, youth offending centres and immigration holding centres had risen from 8 per cent to 13 per cent of the total population in 2011 but has since decreased marginally in the period up to 2013 (Ministry of Justice 2013). This was demonstrably higher than the UK community average, of approximately 9 per cent, according to the 2011 Census. In terms of religious denomination of detainees, 12.5 per cent stated they were Muslims and a further 5 per cent were made up of smaller groups of Buddhists, Sikhs, Jewish and 'others' (Bergman 2011). Significantly in relation to cultural and spiritual practice, of the British nationals in custody, 20 per cent stated they were from minority ethnic groups.

This contrasts with much lower staff ethnicity rates which have remained relatively stable over the past four years – with only 5.6 per cent of police and 5.7 per cent of prison staff coming from minority ethnic backgrounds (Ministry of Justice 2010). These figures should be set in the context of reduced staffing levels and treated with caution as there has been a mild increase in the numbers of staff declining to state their ethnicity or indicating their ethnicity as 'not known' (Ministry of Justice 2013). Despite equalities training, it can be difficult for staff to know and understand the customs and traditions of all major faiths and cultures. We suggest adopting an open-minded approach and spending some time and effort finding out about the needs of detainees. Evidence suggests that people from minority backgrounds want to be asked about their preferences, and are happy to talk about their needs without feeling uncomfortable.

## Case study: Cultural competency

Ali is a young man from Afghanistan; he has been admitted to an in-patient unit from the remand wing of a busy young offender institution, on the recommendation of a mental health worker who felt he wasn't coping.

The mental health worker was unsure of the authenticity of his story but Ali described seeing his father and eldest brother killed by local militia men when he was 13; he then lived with the threat that he or other family members could meet the same fate. At the age of 16, he fled to Pakistan and then onto relatives in the UK. However, he struggled to adjust, failing to gain employment and feeling that he was a burden to his extended family. His mental state deteriorated and he was eventually picked up by the police for breaking a shop window. He was found at the scene and had not resisted arrest; he was described as 'vacant'.

Since admission, although quite isolated, he has begun to mix with other Muslim residents and is gradually becoming more approachable, sharing pleasantries with a few trusted staff. He appears sociable but finds it difficult to sustain conversations. Staff are unsure if this is because of his mental state or because English is not his first language. The general opinion of residential staff is that he is odd and marginalised on the unit.

Ali regularly declines medication, saying he takes strength from reading the Qur'an, which he appears to be doing on an increasing basis. He has been observed washing rigorously several times a day and sometimes will not respond to staff. At times he appears to be talking to himself.

When the prison made a small change to a routine, i.e. issuing breakfast packs with the evening meal, Ali was observed only carrying what he could hold in his right hand and continually dropped items as a result. Each day the servery staff shouted at him to pick up his food, he quietly ignored them and struggled on. A nurse observed this situation and interpreted it as evidence of obsessive compulsive behaviour and reported it in his nursing notes and to the duty doctor.

- How do you view the behaviour of the servery and nurse staff?
- Do the staff understand detainee's needs and communicate effectively about these? Are they being abusive or racist?
- Are care staff swayed by others' opinions?

## Practical ways forward

Around 15 years ago, the United Kingdom Central Council examined the practice of nurses working in secure environments (UKCC 1999). Several reports and inquiries around that time advocated significant changes in both educational and clinical practice (Fallon 1999, RCN 2009, Bradley 2009). Significantly, the reports highlighted a lack of induction, clinical supervision, mentoring and continuing professional development, which were said to exacerbate the sense of isolation felt by secure care workers.

## Continuing personal and professional development (CPPD), clinical supervision and reflective practice

In 2008, Dickinson and Wright conducted a literature review on the causes of burn-out in nurses working in secure settings; their review recommended clinical supervision, psycho-social interventions training and stress management training to alleviate the problem. Three further studies regarding implementation of psycho-social intervention skills training among forensic in-patient staff provided evidence for reduced burn-out (Ewers 2002, Redhead et al. 2010, Doyle 2007).

In terms of evidence to support clinical supervision, Butterworth et al. (1997) used a range of standardised measures to demonstrate that clinical supervision can stabilise, and in some cases reduce, measurable stress levels in nurses. Research by Burnard et al. (2000), and later Brunero and Stein-Parbury (2008), also suggests 'a positive correlation between clinical supervision and a reduction in burnout'. Hingley et al. (1986) highlight the efficiency savings to organisations through reduced sick leave and reduced staff attrition within the nursing workforce.

Other work by Walsh (2009) and Walsh and Freshwater (2009) discusses the benefits of clinical supervision. Clinical supervision, and reflective practice more generally, can be used to support staff in a number of ways, including seeking feedback and analysing difficult clinical encounters. Further to this, Walsh asserts that clinical supervision can help to develop emotional intelligence, which can in turn help individual staff members to process emotional labour. These ideas appear well supported in other arenas of care by authors such as Jackson et al. (2007) and Grant and Kinman (2011), who relate these processes to the development of personal protective strategies to boost resilience.

In essence, reflective practice means taking the time to think about what one does at work. In our opinion, it is best done in company, with one or more other people who agree with and know about the spirit and purpose of reflective practice. Reflective dialogue and group discussions help to make creative solutions more likely. However, we should stay alert to the risks of 'mutual misery' – a tendency to go round in circles of negativity. We see reflective practice as pivotal in its own right – a forum in which to celebrate success and gain job satisfaction and a bridge to educational interventions. It also provides a framework for a confidential professional relationship: practice deficits can be safely revealed where they occur, and a process of remedial work can be developed.

'Reflective practice' is admittedly an imperfect label, which is open to multiple definitions and interpretations, but we have gradually come to favour it over 'clinical supervision'. This shift of language has been prompted by our experience of the way in which the term 'clinical supervision' can provoke difficulties. For clinicians, the word 'supervision' continues to carry a sense that one will be overseen by another; it implies hierarchy instead of inviting an emphasis on 'super' vision – seeing more or more clearly. For other staff in custody settings, prison or police officers, the word 'clinical' is exclusive, apparently only referring to those who have clinical responsibility in their roles.

## Case study: Group reflective dialogue

Jemma, an experienced local community psychiatric nurse, facilitates a monthly reflective practice group for three junior team leaders in a busy inner-city prison. The group is composed of: Denise, a band six team leader in primary care; Jimmy, a senior healthcare officer with various operational responsibilities; and Wendy, a team leader from in-patient services.

One discussion spotlighted a 27-year-old West Indian male who was dividing opinion among staff. He was admitted to the health wing for observation following unusual behaviour in the prison. Since admission he had been good-natured, if a little demanding. He kept busy with minor tasks and Wendy took him on as an informal cleaner. This led to problems with other prisoner-cleaners but he had responded well to the responsibility and Wendy felt she was helping to manage his behaviour.

Jemma helped the group to talk about the impact he was having on the team and other detainees.

*Jemma*: What do we know about him?

*Jimmy*: The lads in reception said he had been picked up in the locality by the police when his car was pulled over. Their searches found that he had broken bail.

Wendy: Not a great deal. He sometimes seems a bit odd but there is little sign of severe mental disorder. Generally he comes across as quite simple. He described working as a refuse worker in a recycling plant and claimed he'd never tried to evade capture but was just minding his own business.

Denise: I interviewed him for his initial reception health screen; he was in good shape physically but said he was known to Belle View Psychiatric Hospital in Jamaica, if it exists.

Jemma: How do staff respond to him?

Wendy: Most of the staff find him amusing, he's not afraid to speak his mind and appears to be trying hard... He wants to help.

Denise: I want to like him but something makes me suspicious. For example, when I've spoken to him as duty nurse in the evening he's presented differently – more pushy, hostile.

Jimmy: I really don't know, I've seen him on the exercise yard, he makes me and the lads feel uneasy. He's quite isolated, he just does his push-ups on his own. It's like he's either preparing himself for a fight or challenging folks. There certainly seems to be tension when he is around.

Denise: I tend to agree. If he is not mentally unwell, should he be on the healthcare wing?

Wendy: He needs to be assessed before we can do anything.

Jemma: Can we find more information on him? Could we get his old hospital records?

Wendy: It would be almost impossible to get anything from Belle View, but I can try.

Jimmy: I can get security to go back to the police to see if there is any other information on him.

Denise: I could talk to the wing staff to see how he was before admission.

Jemma: Do you think we need to do anything in the short term?

Jimmy: He shouldn't be out of his cell in my view and he hasn't applied for employment yet. While I agree he appears to be doing well on it, the other prisoners see it as unfair. Also, he hasn't been risk assessed for the job.

Denise: I tend to agree. Let's get him assessed by the psychiatrist and see what other information we can find.

Wendy: OK, I agree with your comments but it leaves me in a difficult position. I feel partially responsible, as it was me who encouraged him. On the other hand, I think he looks to me for support. I know I have bypassed a couple of regulations, allowing him out of his cell to clean. I guess it solved a problem for us when we were short-handed the other day.

*Jemma*: OK Wendy, don't blame yourself. That kind of dependence can make people want to help.

The detainee reacted badly to being told he couldn't come out of his cell to help with the cleaning; he destroyed some belongings, threw the remnants into the corridor and deliberately flooded the area. The effort it took to get through to his previous hospital was justified when Wendy found out that he was well known to the Jamaican authorities. He had been detained on the grounds of his behaviour and risk to the public. He had also been charged several times with accounts of assaults and rape.

- What are the main issues in this scenario?
- What might have been the consequences of not engaging in honest reflective discussion?
- What positive outcomes came from the supervision?

Taking time to stop and think about practice is gradually emerging as a natural addition to professional care work. There is a general consensus that this is 'a good thing' even though robust evaluative literature is sparse (Mann, Gordon & MacLeod 2009).

In terms of increasing individual resilience, the wider evidence appears to suggest two things:

1. CPPD can reduce burn-out in nurses by increasing empathy and knowledge of patient factors.

2. Clinical supervision/reflective practice can help to develop emotional intelligence, which can boost resilience and support well-being among custodial nurses.

We therefore encourage secure care workers and their managers to provide the resources for staff to engage in these activities and for researchers to continue to evaluate such activities.

For those interested in closing this gap, we propose the use of a four-stage model to evaluate reflective practice, using the following questions:

1. Does reflective practice happen?

2. Do we know how to do it?

3. Does it make a difference to (and according to) practitioners?

4. Does it make a difference to recipients of care?

Each level demands a new and deeper level of evaluative research.

# Conclusion

Throughout this chapter, we have offered a broad range of discussion points and some case studies to assist reflection. Our general aim has been to stimulate some thought on professional practice issues, and to encourage secure care workers to proactively engage in internal (and external) dialogue, to be guided by this and to do the right thing (rather than the easiest thing).

We have asserted that when individual and organisational resources are low, a dynamic combination of factors can affect secure care workers' attitudes, the quality of their relationships and ultimately the standard of care. We have drawn on evidence from the field, and from related areas of care, to show that engaging in CPPD and supportive professional relationships can support practitioners' well-being, help to maintain therapeutic optimism and in turn maintain professional standards.

We are often told that 'what is good for us is good for our patients'. This implies that we should value ourselves and our contribution, and look out for our colleagues and support them when we provide less than proper practice. It tells us that taking time to reflect should not be regarded as a luxury – it should be viewed as an essential aspect of developing ourselves and good practice. Our aim is to inspire secure care workers to stay fresh in the face of inter-personal and organisational pressures, to take pride in the smallest of achievements, and to listen and respond to their own instincts and intuition within the context of practice guidelines.

# References

2011 Census. *Key Statistics for Local Authorities in England and Wales. Ethnicity and National Identity in England and Wales.* London: Office for National Statistics.

Aitken, L., Clarke, S., Douglas, M., Sloane, D., Sochalski, J., Jeffery, H. & Silber, M. (2002). Hospital nurse staffing and patient mortality, nurse burnout, and job dissatisfaction. *Journal of the American Medical Association.* **288** (16), 1987–93.

Baguley, I., Gallon, I., Alexander, J., & McGonagle, I. (2006). *Crossing the Boundaries: Multidisciplinary Health and Social Care Provision in Prison Healthcare.* CCAWI. Centre for Clinical and Workforce Innovation and Excellence, University of Lincoln.

Bergman, G. (2011). House of Commons Library Standard Note: SN/SG/4334. *Prison Population Statistics.* London: Ministry of Justice, National Offender Management System and HM Prison Service.

Bowers, L. (2002). *Dangerous and Severe Personality Disorder: Response and role of the Psychiatric Team.* London: Routledge.

Bradley, K. (2009). *The Bradley Report.* London: Department of Health, The Stationery Office.

Brunero, S. & Stein-Parbury, J. (2008). The effectiveness of clinical supervision in nursing: an evidenced based literature review. *Australian Journal of Advanced Nursing.* **25** (3), 86–94.

Burnard, P., Edwards, D., Hannigan, B., Fothergill, A., Cooper, L., Jugessur, T. & Adams, J. (2000). *The Effectiveness of Clinical Supervision on Burnout in Community Mental Health Nurses in Wales.* Cardiff: University of Cardiff.

Butterworth, T,, Carson, J., White, E., Jeacock, J., Clements, A. & Bishop V. (1997). *It's Good to Talk: Clinical Supervision and Mentorship, An evaluation study in England and Scotland.* Manchester: University of Manchester.

Coffey, M. (1999). Stress and burnout in forensic community mental health nurses: an investigation of its causes and effects. *Journal of Psychiatric and Mental Health Nursing.* **6** (6), 433–43.

Coid, J. (1992). DSM III diagnosis in criminal psychopaths: a way forward. *Criminal Behaviour and Mental Health.* **2**, 78–79.

Department of Health (2012). *Compassion in Practice. Nursing, Midwifery and Care Staff: Our Vision and Strategy.* London: The Stationery Office.

Dickinson, T. & Wright, K. (2008). Stress and burnout in forensic mental health nursing: A literature review. *British Journal of Nursing.* **17** (2), 82.

Doyle, M. (2007). Burnout: the impact of psycho-social interventions training. *Mental Health Practice.* **10** (7), 19.

Ewers, P., Bradshaw, T., McGovern, J. & Ewers, B. (2002). Does training in psycho-social interventions reduce burnout rates in forensic nurses? *Journal of Advanced Nursing.* **37** (5), 470–76.

Fallon, P. (1999). *Report of the Committee of Inquiry into the Personality Disorder Unit, Ashworth Special Hospital.* London: The Stationery Office.

Francis, R. (2013). *Report of the Mid Staffordshire NHS Foundation Trust Public Inquiry.* London: The Stationery Office.

Ginn, S. (17 September 2012). Healthcare in prison: Prison environment and health. *British Medical Journal.* **345**, e5921.

Grant, L. & Kinman, G. (2011). Exploring stress resilience in trainee social workers: The role of emotional and social competencies. *British Journal of Social Work.* **41**, 261–75.

Guthrie, L. (2013). *Working with sex offenders.* BBC Radio 4 programme iPM, broadcast 18 May 2013.

Hingley, P., Cooper, C. & Harris, P. (1986). *Stress in Nursing Managers.* London: Kings' Fund.

Hochschild, A (1983). *The Managed Heart.* Berkeley, CA: University of California Press.

House of Commons Justice Committee (2008/09). *Role of the Prison Officer.* Twelfth Report of Session.

Jackson, D., Flirtko, A,. & Edenborough, M. (2007). Personal resilience as a strategy for surviving and thriving in the face of workplace adversity: a literature review. *Journal of Advanced Nursing.* **60** (1), 1–8.

Klohen, E. (1996). Conceptual analysis and measurement of the construct of ego resiliency. *Journal of Personality and Social Psychology.* **70** (5), 1067–79.

Mann, K., Gordon, J. & MacLeod, A. (2009). Reflection and reflective practice in health professions education: a systematic review. *Advances in Health Science Education.* **14**, 595–621.

Mann, S. & Cowburn, J. (2005). Emotional labour and stress within mental health nursing. *Journal of Psychiatric and Mental Health Nursing.* **12**, 154–62

Maslach, C., Jackson, S. & Leitter, M. (1996). *Maslach Burnout Inventory Manual.* Palo Alto, CA: Consulting Psychologists Press.

Mason, T. (2002). Forensic psychiatric nursing: a literature review and thematic analysis of role tensions. *Journal of Psychiatric and Mental Health Nursing.* **9** (5), 511–20.

Ministry of Justice. National Statistics. (2013). Statistics on Race and the Criminal Justice System, 2012. A Ministry of Justice Publication Under Section 95 of the Criminal Justice Act, 1991.

NHS Employers (2014). http://www.nhsemployers.org/RecruitmentAndRetention/Employment-checks/Employment-Check-Standards/Pages/Employment-Check-Standards.aspx (Last accessed: 12 August 2014).

Nursing and Midwifery Council (2010). *The Code: Standards of Conduct Performance and Ethics for Nurses and Midwives.* London: NMC.

Pratchett, T. (1998). *Jingo.* London: Corgi Books.

Prison Reform Trust (2010). *Bromley Briefings Prison Factfile.* London: Prison Reform Trust.

Redhead, K., Bradshaw, T., Branyion, P. & Doyle, M. (2010). An evaluation of the outcomes of psycho-social intervention training for qualified and unqualified nursing staff working in a low-secure mental health unit. *Journal of Psychiatric and Mental Health Nursing.* 2011, **18**.

Richie, D. & Hall, C. (2009). *What is nursing? Exploring theory and practice.* Transforming Nursing Series. Learning Matters Series. Poole: Sage.

Royal College of Nursing (2009). *Health and Nursing Care in the Criminal Justice Service.* London: RCN.

Sapir, E. (1927) in Mandelbaum, G.B. (ed) (1949). *Selected Writings of Edward Sapir in Language, Culture and Personality*. Berkely, CA: University of California Press.

Savicki, V. & Cooley, E. (1987). The relationship of the work environment and client contact to burnout in mental health professionals. *Journal of Counselling Developments*. **65**, 249–52.

Schafer, P. & Peternelj-Taylor, C. (2003). Therapeutic relationships and boundary maintenance: the perspective of forensic patients enrolled in a treatment program for violent offenders. *Issues in Mental Health Nursing*. **24**, 605–25.

Statistics on Race and the Criminal Justice System (2010). A Ministry of Justice Publication Under Section 95 of the Criminal Justice Act, 1991.

Stewart, W. & Terry, L. (2014). Reducing burnout in nurses and care workers in secure settings. *Nursing Standard*. **28** (34), 37–45.

Storey, J. (2011). 'Chapter 1: Changing theories of leadership and leadership development' in *Leadership in Organizations, current issues and trends*. London: Routledge.

Tait, S. (2008). Care and the prison officer beyond 'turnkeys' and 'care bears'. *Prison Service Journal*. **180**, 3–11.

Theodosius, C. (2008). *Emotional Labour in Healthcare: The unmanaged heart of nursing*. London: Routledge.

United Kingdom Central Council for Nursing, Midwifery and Health Visiting and University of Central Lancashire (1999). *Nursing in Secure Environments*. London: UKCC.

Walsh, E. (2009). The emotional labor of nurses working in her Majesty's (HM) prison service. *Journal of Forensic Nursing*. **5**, 143–52.

Walsh, E., Freshwater, D. & Fisher, P. (2013). Caring for prisoners: Towards mindful practice. *Journal of Research in Nursing*. **1892**, 158–68.

Walsh, E. & Freshwater, D. (2009). The mental well-being of prison nurses in England and Wales. *Journal of Research in Nursing*. **14** (6), 553–64.

Wilson, A.H., Sanner, S.J. & McAllister, S.E. (2003). *Diversity Resource Paper*. Sigma Theta Tau International http://www.nursingsociety.org/aboutus/PositionPapers/Documents/Diversity_paper.pdf (Last accessed 13 July 2014).

Wright, S. (2005). Burnout: A spiritual crisis. *Nursing Standard*. **19** (46), 1–24.

Youngson, R. (2011). 'Compassion in healthcare – the missing dimension in healthcare reform?' in I. Renzenbrink (ed.) (2011). *Caregiver Stress and Staff Support in Illness, Dying, and Bereavement*. Oxford: Oxford University Press.

# 13

# On reflection

Elizabeth Walsh and Ann Norman

In this book, we have gathered a wide range of experts to describe the journey through criminal justice health services for both patients and nurses, and explore the wider impact of nursing people in this environment. We have provided an understanding of the various settings within which nurses care, discussed the challenges of caring, and spent time exploring governance, professional development and legal issues. One key principle that underpins nursing care in this field is equivalence with community healthcare, and this is demonstrated throughout.

In Chapter 2, we met Mr Walker who reflected on his experiences of being cared for in criminal justice settings. He identified a nurse working in court who, it would seem, changed his life. Nurses have that ability and it is something that we underestimate, particularly in criminal justice services. This type of nursing is about being *with*, caring *for* and caring about both patients and ourselves. Within nursing, there is often an 'underselling' of expert skills, qualities and attributes; innovative practice is often mistaken for 'just what we do'. We have captured a number of these innovations from a range of skilled and experienced contributors who have highlighted great practice examples for readers to ponder and share.

What has been brought into focus for us during the writing of this book is the importance of the nursing assessment in all areas of criminal justice nursing. The nursing assessment is clearly necessary to anticipate care needs, to prevent health deteriorating and to treat immediate physical or mental health problems. These assessment skills are at the heart of the nurse's role every day, along the whole of the criminal justice pathway. They are valued very highly by our non-healthcare colleagues, and this is particularly evident in police custody settings and sexual assault services.

Nursing in criminal justice services also tends to involve working as part of a multi-disciplinary team, in which the nurse's colleagues are not allied to health but come from completely different disciplines and philosophical positions. Police officers, prison officers, solicitors, magistrates, the judiciary and probation officers all contribute to the care and management of people in contact with criminal justice services and work closely with nurses.

We note the very real potential for nurses to identify with non-healthcare professionals, thus moving from a nursing focus to a security/disciplinary focus. To counteract this, we suggest that nursing staff working closely alongside other non-healthcare professionals should always ask themselves:

- Is this appropriate?
- Is this acceptable?
- Is it safe?
- Is it professional care that I am giving?

This book challenges some frequently held beliefs and attitudes towards the people who are cared for in criminal justice settings, where competing priorities are the norm. In all professional services there is a need to reflect on our practice. We do this to remind ourselves that we are human: we all make personal judgements that will inevitably affect the care we give. This should be noticed and managed appropriately through clinical supervision and other supportive frameworks in order to maintain high-quality care for a vulnerable group of people.

We have seen throughout this book that the need for information sharing is essential in health and justice nursing practice, but does not always rest comfortably with some staff. This is no reason to withhold all clinical information, professional knowledge or intelligence under the banner of 'data protection'. Reflections on deaths in custody, and inquests following serious incidents, have often demonstrated all too clearly that some information that might have been in someone's best interest to share has been made available too late – with devastating consequences.

We have never implied that nursing in health and justice is an easy professional pathway. Indeed, the loss of someone's liberty means that it is particularly important that nursing is seen as an opportunity to provide safe, compassionate care for vulnerable and often frightened people that puts patient needs at the centre. Nursing provides an opportunity to assert professional values whilst supporting individuals as they are 'processed through a system' that is often dehumanising. Providing an effective nursing service can reduce the impact of this system, which can lead to despair, low self-worth and even self-destruction.

The future of nursing along the criminal justice pathway is evolving. Over the last decade, we have seen nursing move out of prison and into police stations, courts and probation services. However, we believe that there are further, as yet unseen, opportunities for nursing to lead further innovation and development in the care of offenders.

As the value of nursing in criminal justice settings is given more recognition, and practice is developed, the need to develop the knowledge base through research and innovation will become more urgent. Criminal justice nurse experts will offer more to pre- and post-registration nurse education, lead more justice health nursing research and subsequently have a significant impact on policy. Whilst there is a clear role for practitioners in criminal justice settings, we suggest that there is also a growing need to work at the front end of potential offending behaviour by supporting the homeless, engaging in street triage and working with troubled families. Nursing in criminal justice settings will become more visible and effective as mainstream health services and nursing colleagues come into contact with offenders and their families, and recognise the impact they can have.

# Index